T0385111

A BITTERSWEET HERITAGE

VICTORIA PERRY

A Bittersweet Heritage

Slavery, Architecture and the British Landscape

HURST & COMPANY, LONDON

First published in the United Kingdom in 2022 by
C. Hurst & Co. (Publishers) Ltd.,
New Wing, Somerset House, Strand, London, WC2R 1LA
Copyright © Victoria Perry, 2022
All rights reserved.

Printed in Great Britain by Bell and Bain Ltd, Glasgow

The right of Victoria Perry to be identified as the author of
this publication is asserted by her in accordance with the
Copyright, Designs and Patents Act, 1988.

Distributed in the United States, Canada and Latin America by
Oxford University Press, 198 Madison Avenue, New York, NY 10016,
United States of America.

A Cataloguing-in-Publication data record for this book
is available from the British Library.

ISBN: 9781787386969

This book is printed using paper from registered sustainable
and managed sources.

www.hurstpublishers.com

For J, A and O

CONTENTS

A New Mapp of the West Indies or of the Island of America, Richard Morden, 1740

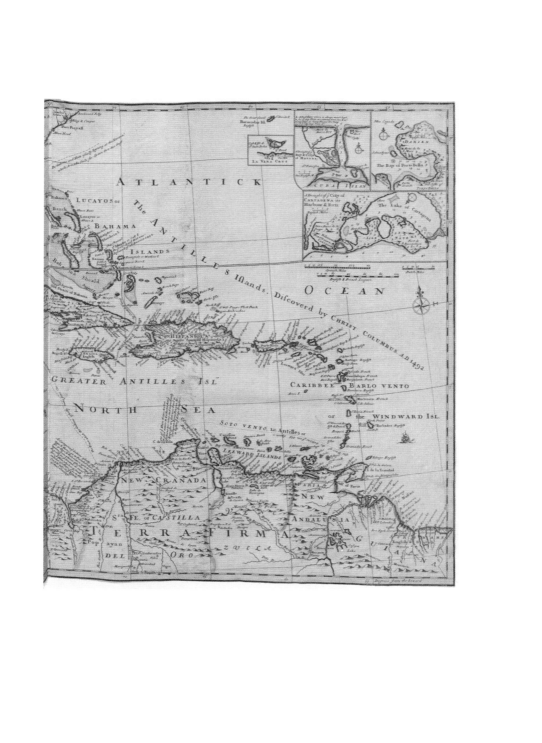

LIST OF ILLUSTRATIONS

PREFACE

A Bittersweet Heritage began as a part-time PhD at The Bartlett School of Architecture, University College London (UCL), where I had originally studied architecture and its histories. I started my doctoral research way back in 2002, not long after my family and I had moved to Hackney. Working and looking after small children in an inner-city area was sometimes challenging; the crowded, culturally diverse London borough was very different from my own rural upbringing on the Welsh borders. But it was also inspirational. Indeed, it was the discovery of historic connections between my childhood home and the Caribbean that piqued my interest in what was then described as 'Black History'. I owe a huge debt of gratitude to Colvestone Primary School and the now sadly defunct bookshop/café Centreprise, both in Dalston, for giving me a different outlook on British history.

My PhD provided space, away from the demands of commercial architectural practice, to read and think more broadly about buildings, landscapes and their histories. I want to thank Professors Adrian Forty and Barbara Penner at The Bartlett, and Miles Ogborn, Professor of Geography at Queen Mary University of London, for their sage advice during my return to academia. My thanks also go to Professor Catherine Hall of the Department of History at UCL, one of the instigators of the 'Legacies of British Slave-ownership' project, for her encouragement.

I travelled a lot during my research, not only visiting buildings, landscapes and archives in Britain, but also sites in the Caribbean and West Africa. The Royal Institute of British Architects (RIBA) and UCL both gave grants, which helped towards the costs. In the West Indies, I was able to present at a conference entitled 'The Colonial Landscapes of the Caribbean,' under the aegis of the University of Southampton and the Institute of Post-Medieval

Archaeology. The conference tours, organised with the help of local history societies, were an illuminating introduction to the complex issues of 'built heritage' in the Caribbean.

My doctoral work, *Slavery, Sugar and the Sublime*, was completed at the end of 2009 and won the RIBA President's Award for Outstanding PhD Thesis in 2010. I would like to thank the academic referees who commented on the manuscript for my subsequent book project. But, with funding spent, the demands of a job and a growing family left no spare time for my goal of transforming the PhD into a book. While I gave a few talks, attended the odd conference and wrote several articles, I reluctantly decided that the book itself would have to be a retirement project. The battered print-out of my thesis and the memory stick containing my work were stuffed into a drawer, awaiting that day.

During this time, Madge Dresser, Honorary Professor at the University of Bristol, and a pioneer in exploring the historic links between slavery and that city (and beyond), kept me up to date with scholarship in the field. And in 2013, I was able to contribute a chapter to a book she co-edited, *Slavery and the British Country House*, published by English Heritage. That same year, the Committee of the Association for Studies in the Conservation of Historic Buildings (ASCHB) allowed me to set up a symposium, 'Conservation & Post-Colonialism', to explore some of the issues my PhD had raised. But, as some attendees made clear, interest in the global histories of Britain's buildings and landscapes was then 'niche'.

But seven years later, in 2020, following the killing of an African American man, George Floyd, by a Minneapolis police officer, Black Lives Matter protests spread across the Atlantic. The toppling of the bronze statue of slave-trader Edward Colston by BLM protesters— which was later hauled dripping out of the Bristol docks into which it had been thrown—was perhaps the most memorable image of a summer of unrest in Britain, paralleling events in the United States. Indeed, it marked a significant shift in the cultural landscape. My thanks go Rachel Reese of The Georgian Group, therefore, who gave me the opportunity to turn a talk I had given on the subject years before into a piece for that winter's newsletter.

No longer just of academic interest, there was clearly a wider public appetite for the subject. So during Covid lockdowns and beyond, I spent evenings, weekends and holidays catching up on new research and wrestling the manuscript into publishable shape. My thanks go to the fantastic team at Hurst Publishers, especially Lara Weisweiller-Wu and Alice Clarke, for their insightful comments and patience. Much appreciation is due to my colleagues at Insalls, too, for their forbearance, as I balanced the demands of the day job with book deadlines, and for the contribution to the costs of image rights. Special thanks are due to Tony Barton and Helen Ensor for their long-term support; to Francis Maude for keeping me abreast of conservation projects in the Caribbean and West Africa; and to Tanvir Hasan, whose edict 'don't sleep, until you've written it' I perhaps took too literally. Thanks also to Ben Clark, Éamonn Ó Ciardha, Clare Creo, Hannah Parham, Isabelle Quet, Robert Thorne, Didier Reck, Andrew Smith and Georges 'Le Slickaphonic' for many conversations over the years.

And, lastly, I of course want to thank my family for their support. Indeed, if it had not been for the forensic fact-checking and editing skills of my husband, Paul Farrelly, a former investigative journalist, the book would never have happened. The arguments in *A Bittersweet Heritage* remain the same today, however, as they were when I wrote my thesis more than a decade ago: that the profits of plantation slavery not only funded great country houses, but transformed some of Britain's most celebrated landscapes, including the Lakes, Snowdonia and the Scottish Highlands, and the way people have viewed the country until this day.

INTRODUCTION

And the wind calls back
blue air across the town; it tears
the thin topographies of dream, it blows me
as by old, familiar maps,
to this affectionate shore, green and crumpling hills,
like paper in the Admiral's fist.
The rain comes down.

Homecoming, by Jamaican poet Dennis Scott,
writing of his return to the Caribbean (1973)[1]

When I was an architectural student in the late 1980s, I spent an idyllic summer working in the grounds of an English country house. I was with a team repairing a derelict garden grotto, part of a wider programme for the restoration of eighteenth-century 'follies', the decorative, often whimsical monuments built to adorn great landscape parks of the time. We camped within the former walled vegetable garden of the estate and, in the long evenings after work, the vista of the sweeping grounds was ours alone. We would picnic in the shelter of a mock neo-classical temple and admire the other 'Gothick' ruins in the grounds. It was a magical experience. The gardens were, as their creators had intended, a landscape of the senses—a grassy version of a mythic Arcadia.

Autumn approached all too fast, and we prepared to return to our studies and the student world of shabby bedsits. During one of the final evenings around the campfire, our project director announced that he was to make a research trip to the Caribbean. We groaned with envy, as he explained how he would spend the next three weeks combing beaches and markets to find conch shells to match the few originals that remained in the grotto.

Then something troubled me. The frivolous folly suddenly became intensely serious. All I knew then of the eighteenth-century West Indies was some school history about the trans-Atlantic slave trade—the triangular link, whereby European manufactured goods were bartered for enslaved West Africans to labour in the tobacco and sugar plantations of Britain's American colonies. But what could possibly be the connection with this English garden grotto, thousands of miles away?

Two years earlier, as a schoolgirl on a church-sponsored exchange trip, I had visited a rundown, Indian Ocean resort in a place called Bagamoyo in Tanzania, east Africa. A little removed from the fraying palm-leaf roofs of the beach bar stood an incongruous, grey stone building that looked a bit like a Scottish church. It was, in fact, the focal point of a nineteenth-century Christian mission. Within the building was a small display, commemorating the Scots explorer David Livingstone and his part in the struggle to abolish the slave trade in east Africa during his expeditions in the late 1800s.[2]

From that exhibition, I discovered that Bagamoyo had once been the centre of the Indian Ocean slave trade: captives were corralled onto the beach, where I had been sunbathing, before being loaded onto waiting boats and shipped to the nearby island of Unguja—known popularly as Zanzibar—and sold on to Arab traders.[3] My Tanzanian colleagues explained that, in Swahili, *Bwaga-Moyo* means 'lay down your heart', and local legends described the elegant merchant houses of Zanzibar's historic Stone Town as being built 'on foundations of African bones'. It was a haunting expression, at once linking fine buildings with the terrible economics that underpinned their construction. Two summers later, when I stumbled across the connection between Caribbean conch shells and the garden folly, those moments in Bagamoyo resonated again: had the English grotto, too, been built on 'foundations of bones'?

As an aspiring young architect, I neither had the time, nor the resources, to find the answers. Some years later, however, while reading a new architectural guide about the borders of South Wales, where I grew up, those thoughts resurfaced. The book mentioned a ruined eighteenth-century country house and estate called Piercefield, near Chepstow. Not only did Piercefield Park command Grade I registered status—a category reserved for just a few of the

English landscapes, parks and gardens nationally recognised to be of 'exceptional interest'[4]—the grounds had been developed in the eighteenth century by Valentine Morris, the Caribbean-born heir to several Antiguan sugar plantations.

Little known these days outside a small, specialist circle of landscape historians, Piercefield had been one of the most popular and influential tourist sites in eighteenth-century Britain. Following the creation of Piercefield's gardens in the early 1750s, hundreds of visitors experienced the 'sublime' views of 'wild' and 'cultivated' nature from the cliffside walks. By the end of the century, a boat tour along the river Wye to visit Piercefield and the nearby ruins of Tintern Abbey had become a fashionable activity for 'genteel' tourists.[5] 'Once again do I behold these steep and lofty cliffs,' wrote William Wordsworth in one of his best-known poems, titled *Lines Composed a Few Miles above Tintern Abbey*.[6] He continues: 'Again I hear these waters, rolling from their mountain springs with a soft inland murmur.' It was an experience that would have been shared by many.

The questions I had asked myself during work on the grotto years before, I realised, were directly relevant to the landscapes of my own childhood. Why had an eighteenth-century Antiguan sugar planter chosen to live in the wooded hills of the Wye Valley? And

Fig. 0.1: *The Abbey and the Upper reaches of the Wye*, William Havell, 1804

what of the other apparent links between the Caribbean and these Welsh border landscapes? Was it just coincidence that an elderly sugar heiress 'Miss Tate' had lived in the big house on the hillside close to my home village? How had a sugar company come to own the forests and pheasant shoots where, as children, my friends and I used to explore? Was it just a rumour that 'Jamaican money' had funded the construction of the large early-nineteenth-century stone house in the valley below? And what were the origins of the curiously named Barbados Woods shown on the Ordnance Survey map above Tintern Abbey, just a few miles downstream?

The historic economics of land ownership were only part of the puzzle. I was struck, too, by the wider issue of British, and indeed American, aesthetic attitudes to 'landscape' and 'nature'. The very cliffs and woods that Wordsworth, and so many others, had closely associated with emotional and physical freedoms—with liberty itself—had, it seemed, also been closely connected with slavery and human bondage. How could this contradiction be explained, and could a closer study of the origins of Piercefield Park yield further clues?

This time I could not let the questions rest. Sadly, the surviving archive records of Piercefield were sparse, but the shell grotto of my student days suggested that there might be other British country houses and landscapes funded with Caribbean wealth that could help put the legacy of Valentine Morris in a wider context. It was at this point, therefore, that I decided to enrol for my PhD. My aim was to find out.

'The wind calls back': legacies of the Atlantic trade

Since I first started my doctoral research back in 2002, there has been a dramatic change in public understanding of the historic relationship between Britain and its former Caribbean colonies. The bi-centenary of the abolition of the British slave trade in 2007, together with lots of project-related government funding, encouraged many museums to hold exhibitions and produce publications about British colonial slavery and its eventual abolition.[7]

Cities like London, Bristol, Liverpool, Lancaster and Glasgow—and smaller towns, such as Whitehaven in Cumbria—publicly acknowledged that plantation-grown products, such as sugar and tobacco, had played a significant role in the development of their eighteenth-century ports.[8] Institutions like the National Trust and English Heritage recognised that the building of some of their eighteenth- and early-nineteenth-century estates was made possible due to wealth created by enslaved Africans.[9]

Generous academic funding since 2009 has also allowed the creation of online databases such as the 'Legacies of British Slave-ownership' project at University College London. The increasing digitisation of archive material over the last decade also means that international Atlantic connections are now more readily researchable.[10] A subject that, when I began my research, had been regarded as belonging to minority courses in 'Black History', has now taken its rightful place in mainstream British history and public discourse.

It was more than a lifetime ago, however, in 1944, that the future prime minister of the independent Caribbean state of Trinidad and Tobago, Eric Williams, wrote a provocative book *Capitalism and Slavery*, one of the first works to argue that Britain's 'Industrial Revolution' was in large part funded by the proceeds of Caribbean sugar plantations and the slave trade. This seminal tract ignited a debate which has occupied academic historians for decades, and research still continues. There is clear documentary evidence that state-funded compensation, paid to plantation owners when British colonial slavery was abolished in 1833, was reinvested into industrial enterprises and railways.[11] But the links between slavery-derived wealth and industrial development prior to abolition have yet to be firmly established.

In his book *Slavery, Atlantic Trade and the British Economy, 1660–1800*, however, maritime historian Kenneth Morgan concludes that, in Britain as a whole, far more money acquired through slavery was spent on the construction of country houses and landed estates than was ever invested into industry.[12] It is an opinion shared by an earlier historian, Richard Pares, who remarked—referring to Fonthill Abbey, a country house built by the Beckford family of planters and merchants—that slavery's profits were spent on 'more Fonthills than factories'.[13] I turn to the extraordinary 'abbey' in the concluding chapter of this book, 'The Mock Turtle's Story'.

But this dichotomy between industry and purely private luxury is perhaps too simplistic. In this book, I show how, from the early eighteenth century, profits from trans-Atlantic slavery not only funded architecture, landscapes and paintings, but were also invested into wider agricultural improvement works and the construction of roads. This wealth, moreover, was instrumental in opening up the 'natural scenery' of Britain's Atlantic West, from the Wye Valley to the mountains of North Wales, the lakes of Cumberland and Westmoreland to the Scottish Highlands. Fashionable landscape touring in remote regions became, therefore, far more accessible and the relationship of Britons to their own country was profoundly transformed as a result.

'It tears the thin topographies of dream': ambition and land

But why should so much slavery-derived plantation wealth have been channelled into the purchase of British land? There are several reasons. Firstly, there were close family links between many colonial settlers in the Caribbean and Britain's eighteenth-century cultural and social elite. Political turmoil—including the English Civil War (1642–51), pitching royalists against supporters of a victorious Parliament, and rebellions after the Glorious Revolution (1688), which re-established a Protestant ascendancy—had left many former members of the gentry dispossessed of their estates. Together with the ruthless English practice of primogeniture (whereby land and its income were inherited solely by the eldest son), this meant that in late-seventeenth- and early-eighteenth-century Britain there were many educated, well-connected young men from elite families who needed a way to earn their own living.[14] And as the richest of Britain's American colonies, the 'sugar isles' of the Caribbean were a compelling option for emigration.

Some of these young adventurers chronicled the exciting opportunities a West Indian expedition offered to acquire wealth and renown. So wrote, for example, the anonymous eighteen-year-old author of *A poetical epistle to a gentleman of the Middle Temple*, describing his sojourn on a Jamaican sugar plantation:

> … ambition was my aim,
> To raise a fortune, or erect a name:
> Midst tropic heats, and sickly climes …[15]

His youth, aspirations and apparent familiarity with the Georgic poetry of the ancient Roman writer Virgil were not unusual among eighteenth-century British emigrants to the Caribbean. But it was not only ambitious teenagers who saw the West Indies as a means to personal advancement. Posts in colonial administration such as customs collectors—or, for the best-connected, a governorship itself—provided generous state salaries and offered lucrative opportunities for investment and speculation. Governors of Jamaica, Britain's largest and wealthiest sugar colony, for example, included the Earl of Carlisle, one of the Caribbean's earliest investors; Sir William Beeston (of Beeston Castle in Cheshire); the Duke of Albemarle; Lord Hamilton; and the Duke of Portland.[16]

Close connections with the British-educated, land-owning elite partly explains why, unlike emigrants to the Spanish, Portuguese and French Caribbean sugar colonies, most successful speculators and colonists in the British Caribbean islands aimed to return to Britain and acquire their own estates, or else expand and improve long-held family lands back home.[17]

The second reason for the strong link between the country estate and Caribbean slavery was the propensity of Britain's international shipping merchants to invest trading profits into agricultural land. Owning large tracts of land was not just a conspicuous display of wealth: it also provided a route to political power: locally, owing to the then restricted voting franchise and therefore the immense election-swaying capacity of wealthy landowners, and thence nationally and internationally, too.[18] And during the eighteenth century, the fastest growing sector of all was the 'Atlantic trade' with Britain's tobacco and sugar colonies in America and the West Indies.

While not all successful sugar planters came from landed backgrounds, and by no means all thriving West India merchants used their profits to purchase British estates,[19] the boasts of one imperialist historian were not without foundation:

> It is not too much to say that there are few, if any noble houses in England without a West Indian strain. Younger sons of the better classes went out to the plantations, and when they had gained fresh strength—physical, material or intellectual—returned home to

7

raise their family higher in the social scale. If not, their daughters married peers or country gentlemen. In this way the Dukes of Fife and Hamilton, the Earls of Rosebery, Radnor, Westmoreland, Lilford, Devon, Caernarvon, Gainsborough, Onslow; Lord Sudely, Yarmouth, Colebrooke, Colchester and scores of others can trace their descent from a West Indian ancestor either in the male or the female line.[20]

Of course, at the time, British colonial business and investment was not just confined to the Caribbean. The tobacco trade with Virginia, in the present-day United States, for example, was for much of the eighteenth century as lucrative as that of sugar. A post in the state-backed East India Company, which allowed unofficial opportunities for 'independent trade', was a popular alternative, too, for ambitious fortune-seekers.[21] Indeed, there were often global links—personal and financial—between colonial adventurers, whichever route they chose.

Investigating the historic relationship between the Caribbean sugar islands and British country estates, however, has been a particularly rewarding task because of the quantity of historic material that remains in British archives. There are several reasons for this, too. The first is the (comparatively) short distance between the British Isles and the Caribbean colonies. In the eighteenth century, it took only six or seven weeks to sail the Atlantic, whereas a voyage to the British trading post of Calcutta, India, for example, lasted seven to eight months.[22] As a result, written trans-Atlantic communication was relatively frequent.[23] Moreover, in the Caribbean, an export-driven plantation economy was well-established by the late seventeenth century. This created a need for accurate records of investments, suppliers, plantation profits and agricultural techniques, so that information could be shared on either side of the Atlantic.

The Caribbean sugar islands, unlike the tidewater tobacco plantation colonies in Virginia, also remained British possessions until the latter half of the twentieth century. It is possible, therefore, to use documentary evidence to examine financial and cultural connections between British estates and Caribbean plantations over a period of centuries. Indeed, in some cases, it is possible to identify by name enslaved individuals, whose labour underpinned investment in houses

Fig. 0.2: The ruins of Piercefield House amid parkland

and landscapes thousands of miles away. It is the carefully compiled accounts, set out in a form recognisable to anyone who has been involved in running a business—the eighteenth-century equivalent of the Excel spreadsheet—that are perhaps the most chilling documents. A 1777 inventory by Piercefield's owner Valentine Morris, for instance, revealed that the 'movable assets' of his Antiguan plantation 'Looby's' included a man given the name Piercefield. He was valued at ten pounds, one shilling and five pence.[24]

'It blows me as by old, familiar maps': tracing the Caribbean connections

Given the cultural importance of the history of transatlantic slavery, the amount of academic research on the topic is, unsurprisingly, vast and constantly increasing. And, though perhaps a less fashionable subject, the catalogue of books and articles examining eighteenth- and early-nineteenth-century British architecture and landscape is also significant. The key, and varied, background works are listed in the accompanying notes and bibliography to this book.

The starting point for my primary archive research was to request a search of the National Register of Archives held by the Royal Commission on Historical Manuscripts at Kew. Long before UCL's online 'Legacies of British Slave-ownership' project, a helpful archivist did a cross-database search of the available material. This revealed more than sixty archives of large British country houses and estates with historic connections to the Caribbean colonies. This list, of course, only comprised places where documentary evidence of their links with West Indian plantations had both survived and was in the public domain. Nick Draper, former director of UCL's study centre, has since observed that by the 1830s, a full five to ten per cent of Britain's country houses were occupied by slave owners, with the percentage being far higher in the regions of major seaports.[25]

But not all country houses connected to the Atlantic trade are in coastal locations. Indeed, there are hints that other notable estates, such as Lady Diana Spencer's family home—the Grade I–listed Althorp, in landlocked Northamptonshire—could also have historic links with the Caribbean colonies. In 1756, John, the first Earl Spencer, stood for election as a Member of Parliament for Bristol, Britain's second West India port. An enslaved African 'owned' by him and his father features in two portraits at Althorp.[26]

Other elite British families certainly did have close ties with the British settlement of the West Indies. Caribbean schoolchildren learn of the seventeenth-century foundation of the island colonies by the 'Lords Proprietors'—the Earls of Pembroke and Carlisle, the Earl of Warwick and Lord Francis Willoughby[27]—and historian Robin Blackburn also notes the particular influence of absentee Barbadian plantation owner Anthony Ashley Cooper, later the Earl of Shaftesbury, on British colonial policy.[28]

However, with these prominent families, following the trail is far more complicated. Historic private papers, if they survive, are not always available for public view, and it was difficult to make a precise connection between wealth created in the Caribbean colonies and expenditure on their estates in Britain itself. The National Register's index search, however—though far from a comprehensive historical record—did provide me with the location of information to delve deeper into the details of this relationship for the estates they identified. My principal sources for archive materials were, as a result, the various County record offices around Britain, supplemented by papers, prints and drawings held in national public archives.[29]

From the sixty or so examples listed in the Register search, I originally chose six estates to examine more closely, so that I could put Valentine Morris's patronage at Piercefield in a wider context. The book looks at three of these in greater detail: Danson Park, in Bexleyheath, near London; Harewood House, near Leeds; and Penrhyn Castle in North Wales. Why these particular choices? I had two main criteria. Firstly, as well as inspecting archival evidence, I wanted to be able to experience a physical object myself: a building, a landscape or at least a painting. Therefore, the places I studied in detail were accessible to the public: Danson is owned by the London Borough of Bexley, Penrhyn by the National Trust and, while Harewood is still in private ownership, the house and park are open to paying visitors.[30]

The three other estates were selected to explore the wider geographic spread of plantation riches within Britain. Although there were particular concentrations of wealth near London, Bristol and Liverpool, the towns and cities of Whitehaven, Lancaster, Glasgow and Edinburgh were also important for the Atlantic trade.[31] But, as I uncovered individual family histories, I discovered a similarity in the way that eighteenth-century absentee planters, Atlantic merchants and Caribbean investors spent their profits. The records of each estate told a similar story. No matter where in Britain their newly purchased or ancestral family estate was located—just a few miles from London, in coastal North Wales, or in the hinterland of smaller Atlantic ports—all were patrons of fashionable architecture and landscape design. Including Valentine Morris, they were also all keen investors in new turnpike roads. This led me, in turn, to read more broadly and reflect on the wider geographic and cultural effects on Britain of the wealth created by Caribbean sugar plantations and the expanding colonial trade. I had stumbled into the rapidly growing academic field of Atlantic history.

One book, in particular, *A Floating Commonwealth* (2008) by Christopher Harvie, helped me formulate my thoughts. He argued that, by the nineteenth century, there were two distinct spheres of influence within Britain: 'a land-based core, centred on the capital, with its establishment parties and elites' and 'the commercial, bour-geois, seaborne chord or arc—now ambiguous and overshad-owed—of "the west".'[32] The political and cultural bonds between port cities such as Bristol, Liverpool and Glasgow, Harvie sug-gested, formed what he labelled a 'consciousness of the western littoral', conveyed by literature, religion, history and the arts.

Harvie's focus was on the late nineteenth and early twentieth centuries, but his concept had a strong affinity with my research. The scope of my investigation, therefore, widened beyond the indi-vidual patronage of British country houses and their designed land-scapes, to the way these landscapes were perceived; represented in paintings, prints and the written word; and directly experienced through the growth of landscape tourism, with its wider effects in Britain and across the Atlantic—both in the Caribbean and the mainland American colonies.

'Like paper in the Admiral's fist': chapter structure

One of the hazards of an investigation into the history of British architecture and landscapes, particularly in the eighteenth century, is the obvious need to focus on elite patronage to understand why buildings and landscapes—and images of them—take the form they do. This can easily lead to a warped historical perspective that con-centrates on the aspirations of the rich and powerful, at the expense of other sections of society. However, while manuscript evidence—such as letters and maps—is naturally concentrated around literate European colonists, buildings and landscapes can provide a means of immediate engagement with the lives of enslaved Africans, who often have few written records of their existence.

I was fortunate to be able to visit the Caribbean and West Africa and see some of these architectural and natural sites for myself. Therefore, in my first scene-setting chapter, 'These Cane Ocean-Isles', I have included depictions of eighteenth-century buildings and landscapes on the former British island colonies and along the Atlantic coast of Africa to give historical context and to provide a counter-point to the studies of elite patronage in Britain which follow.

But this first chapter presented challenges. There is a rich legacy of British colonial-era building in the Caribbean and West Africa, and indeed of architectural scholarship. I did not want this to distract from my ultimate focus on Britain itself, however. I was also aware that I had my own, culturally specific, response to the places that I visited. Touring an old plantation works in the Caribbean, for example, I could certainly empathise with the plight of enslaved workers who had once toiled there and reflect on the irony that the complex was now an expensive hotel. But I could not feel the intensity of the anger visibly experienced by an African American colleague who accompanied me. I thought hard about how to describe these buildings and landscapes. The neutral vocabulary of architecture—merely providing a description of construction materials, window layout or room size—seemed inadequate for such emotionally charged spaces. I decided, therefore, that I would record my own personal response to these sites of slavery, acknowledging that my perspective was that of a white, British female at the beginning of the twenty-first century, and understanding that other readers' interpretations might differ.

From the Caribbean islands, we then cross the Atlantic to a Palladian mansion just outside the nascent imperial capital, before heading to Harewood House in Yorkshire. Both of these estates were transformed by City of London–based Caribbean merchants and financiers. From there, we travel to Bristol and Bath, the Wye Valley, the mountains of North Wales, the port of Liverpool, remote Whitehaven and the Cumbrian Lakes, and to Glasgow and the Scottish Highlands, before returning to the West Indies.

Starting the journey, Chapter Two—'Arts and Elegancies'—examines Danson Park, seat of the Boyd family, plantation owners and slave-traders, who had a flourishing merchanting business based in the heart of the City of London. Set amid an extensive landscape garden on the outskirts of the capital, the Palladian Danson House hints at the might of imperial Rome. The chapter shows how the patronage of this meticulously restored villa was instrumental in transforming a Caribbean-born sugar planter, of French and Irish descent, into an English 'gentleman'.

In Chapter Three, 'Trade and Plumb Cake', we move north to the grand Harewood estate, seat of the Lascelles family, which had also looked to the Caribbean to augment its wealth, and traded from the City of London. With its sweeping Lancelot 'Capability'

Brown–designed parklands and exquisite Robert Adam interiors and elaborate Thomas Chippendale furniture, Harewood is a model example of the glamorous Georgian country house. But, like Danson, it also proclaims its colonial influences, which were very clear to visitors at the time. Indeed, one late-eighteenth-century commentator could not look at 'natural style' landscapes commissioned by patrons such as the Lascelles 'without thoughts of the slavery of the negroes'.[33]

After examining these two estates connected with the port of London, I then turn to the hinterlands of the western Atlantic ports. Chapter Four, 'Refining the World', investigates how the growth of the spa resort of Bath, eighteenth-century Britain's most fashionable town, was bound up with its proximity to Bristol. As economist Adam Smith observed in *The Wealth of Nations* (1776), the expansion of Britain's Atlantic trade had begun to favour western ports over those facing south and east towards mainland Europe.[34] But in this chapter, I suggest that there was not only an economic shift, but a cultural one, too: Bath became the 'cultural capital' of an eighteenth-century Atlantic world.

In Chapter Five, 'Nature's Prospects', I focus on the original inspiration for this book: absentee plantation owner Valentine Morris and his early work pioneering views of the 'sublime' at Piercefield Park on the River Wye. We explore how the popularity of excursions from Bath across the Severn estuary to the cliffside walks at Piercefield was key to the development of picturesque landscape tourism as a cultural activity in Britain—and overseas. The chapter also examines the concepts of the 'sublime' and 'picturesque' in the art and literature of the eighteenth century, and looks at how the two most influential writers about landscape aesthetics, Edmund Burke and William Gilpin, had close personal ties with the trans-Atlantic trade.

Moving north from the Severn estuary, Chapter Six—'Cultivating the Remote'—reveals how wealth from the plantation trade helped to transform perceptions of isolated areas of North Wales, Cumberland and Westmoreland, and the west coast of Scotland. From the 1740s onwards, Atlantic merchants and investors based in Liverpool, Lancaster, Glasgow, Whitehaven and other smaller coastal settlements invested profits from slave-trading and plantations into improving newly purchased country estates and into road construction around them. This injection of capital—coupled with social aspirations to lead the lives of 'cultivated gentlemen'— allowed poor, rain-sodden uplands to be re-imagined as landscape art, as 'scenic' backdrops to new country houses, and saw the transformation of these areas into fashionable tourist destinations: 'Snowdonia', 'The Lakes' and 'The Highlands'.

Chapter Seven, 'Tainted Landscapes', shows how the patronage of prominent planting and trading families such as the Gilpins, Beckfords, Longs and the Jeffersons—including Thomas Jefferson, the third president of the newly independent United States—took the concept of the landscape tour across the Atlantic. Indeed, by the latter part of the eighteenth century, the idea of 'natural scenery'— viewing mountains, rivers and rock formations as art—became a means to celebrate colonial settlement in the British Caribbean and, ultimately, the United States of America.

Finally, in the concluding Chapter Eight, 'The Mock Turtle's Story', I look at the eventual abolition of slavery in the British Empire, and the gradual demise of the plantation economy across the British Caribbean. These developments were symbolically reflected by the collapse of the Beckfords' abbey at Fonthill in Wiltshire, and the 'plight' of absentee Caribbean planters bitingly satirised by Lewis Carroll in his children's book *Alice in Wonderland*. And, amid so-called 'culture wars' in the UK at the time of publication, I also advocate a more open and honest understanding of Britain's globally influential patronage of architecture and landscape in the eighteenth and nineteenth centuries—and of the sources of the wealth which underpinned its enduring legacy.

1

THESE CANE OCEAN-ISLES

These Cane ocean-isles,
Isles which Britain for their all depend ...
What soil the Cane affects; what care demands;
Beneath what signs to plant; what ills await;
How the hot nectar best to christallise;
And, Afric's sable progeny to treat:
A Muse, that long hath wander'd in the groves
Of myrtle-indolence, attempts to sing.

James Grainger, *The Sugar Cane* (1763)

If you are fortunate enough to take a holiday in the Caribbean, some of the most atmospheric places in which to stay are the old plantation inns. One such, on the island of St Kitts, is a former merchant's home filled with antique mahogany furniture and eighteenth-century china. And high up in the hills on the neighbouring island of Nevis, the whitewashed timber boarding and verandas of a former plantation house hotel contrast beautifully with the azure skies and verdant foliage. The owners of other Nevis inns have transformed eighteenth-century sugar works into elegant lounges and dining rooms set in tropical gardens; at one luxury hotel on St Kitts, the walls of the former sugar works form a spectacular frame to the outdoor pool (see Fig. 1.1).

Part of the appeal of these plantation inns is their link with the past. While a stay at an anonymous, multi-national-owned, beach-front hotel may provide all the comforts of home, the inns bring you face to face with the Caribbean's rich, and deeply disturbing, colonial history. Indeed, the owners and managers of many of these busi-

Fig. 1.1: Sugar works to swimming pool, St Kitts

nesses go out of their way to stress the importance of their former colonial connections. The brochure of one inn, for example, describes the building as 'a place of heritage and memories',[1] while another explains how, following 'gentle conversation' in the antique-filled drawing room, 'two rings of the bell' announce the call to dinner, 'as they have done in the West Indies for hundreds of years'.[2] For the European or North American visitor escaping the gloom of dark winter days back home, the combination of brilliant sunshine, sparkling blue seas, lush vegetation and characterful accommodation is truly seductive. As one British journalist exclaimed: 'it was the nearest thing to Eden I have ever experienced'.[3]

But, of course, when these buildings were first constructed, the British viewed Nevis, St Kitts and their other island territories very differently. The mid-eighteenth-century Caribbean was certainly not seen as a tropical paradise. As George Maxwell, a London-based sugar trader and former plantation owner, wrote to one of his Caribbean clients on a cold English day in November 1743 (when Britain was embroiled in a war with the French and Spanish to dominate the region):

GM [George Maxwell] does sometimes reflect upon times past and almost envies you for your warm sunshine in Barbados, but when he considers again the excessive heat of your weather and that the island is grown hotter still since he came away, by parties brewing up again, he repines the less of his lot and submits to the poking his fire in the country house and warming his fingers and feet over it and often wishes that you would get out of that wilderness.[4]

Maxwell's reference to 'wilderness' was not then a term of approval: it would be another generation before Europeans would begin to appreciate the ecological importance of tropical rainforests and Enlightenment philosopher Jean-Jacques Rousseau would publish his celebration of the 'noble savage'.[5] In the 1740s, when Maxwell was writing, Barbados—like other British-controlled islands in the West Indies, which at that time included Antigua, St Kitts and Jamaica—was seen as nothing more than an offshore farm. The colonies' sole purpose was to grow intensive cash crops, predominantly sugar, for consumers in England, Wales, Scotland and Ireland. It was a business whose demands profoundly influenced British colonial policy for over 200 years and which, for several centuries, was reliant on the labour provided by enslaved Africans.

'Gingerbread cottages' or chattel houses?

At the present-day Hermitage Inn on Nevis, guests can sleep in timber 'gingerbread cottages' set among the palms, breadfruit trees and bougainvillea of the hillside gardens. Simple one- or two-roomed timber structures, painted in sun-bleached pastels, they are miniature versions of the adjacent main house (see Fig. 1.2).[6] However, if you leave the hotel to tour the island, it is clear that these so-called cottages are almost identical to the cramped 'chattel houses' still lived in by the poorer families of Nevis (see Fig. 1.3).[7]

These buildings, in turn, are strongly reminiscent of the huts constructed across the Caribbean years ago to house enslaved African plantation workers, as shown by late-eighteenth-century prints of the islands. Such are the subtle distortions of history that owners of old sugar plantations must make to accommodate today's visitors.

In 2005, changes in trade laws abolished the longstanding subsidies given to Caribbean sugar producers.[8] Faced with competition

Fig. 1.2: Guest cottage at the Hermitage Inn, Nevis

Fig. 1.3: Chattel houses in Nevis

from mainland growers in Central and South America, and from European sugar beet production, many sugar planters have abandoned the crop. Throughout Nevis, acres of acacia scrub have grown wild over former cane fields, as plantation owners turned away from sugar and towards tourism for an alternative source of income. When I first visited neighbouring St Kitts in the summer of 2005, the harvest of the last commercial sugar crop on the island had just got underway. The fields of six-foot-high, green, bamboo-like canes whispered in the breeze, heralding the end of more than 300 years of history. Down a path away from the road, an Afro-Caribbean colleague discreetly took a penknife from his pocket and hacked and sawed through the base of a cane, until it snapped in two. He then cut the stem into sections and handed me and my colleagues a piece. It was an action charged with significance: in the harsh world of the eighteenth-century British Caribbean, if his enslaved ancestors had been caught stealing the valuable crop, they would have been punished by flogging or even amputation.[9]

We crouched in the shade, in silence, chewing on the cane's fibrous interior. It was a gentle, perfumed taste, quite unlike the aggressive sweetness of refined white sugar. However, in our eagerness to try the fresh juice, we had not noticed that the cane was covered in tiny, resinous barbs. Picking the sticky prickles out of my palms, I reflected on the profound effects that sugar cultivation had exerted on the Caribbean. Sugar's uncomfortable history could not be ignored.

Windwards and Leewards

St Kitts is just one in a long chain of several hundred islands—known collectively as the West Indies or the Antilles—that sweeps south in an arc over nearly 2,000 miles of sea, from the Florida peninsula of the United States down to Venezuela. The islands vary in size, from Cuba, which is hundreds of miles long with wide variations in climate and terrain, to those that are little more than rocks (see frontispiece map). Several, like Montserrat, are actively volcanic, and—with one exception—the distance between any of these islands is less than thirty miles.

That exception is the gap between Grenada and Tobago at the southern end of the chain, which once formed the main seaway to the Spanish colonies on mainland Central America. The whole arc benefits from the north-easterly trade winds, which blow moisture-laden air—and, in former times, drove sailing ships—across the Atlantic towards them. Such is the regularity of these winds that they gave the islands a permanent windward side, the eastern, where the swell made it too dangerous to land, and a permanent leeward side, the western, where it was possible for ships to ride at anchor in tolerable safety. Most of the islands' major towns and harbours were built, therefore, facing west towards the calmer waters of the Caribbean Sea, rather than towards the Atlantic's rolling waves.

Since independence, economic and infrastructural development in much of the former British West Indies has been relatively low-key. It is therefore not hard to imagine, particularly in the Leewards (the island group that includes Nevis, Antigua and St Kitts), what the places would have looked like 200 years ago. For the first-time British visitor, the familiarity of the style and form of many of the old buildings is striking: the stone churches and court houses would not look out of place in a provincial English market town or village.[10] Of course, as former British colonies, it is hardly surprising that public and ceremonial buildings should resemble those of the ruling imperial power. Bizarrely, though, the landscape itself also feels recognisable, particularly to those who know the upland areas of the west of Britain. Indeed, the hilly landscapes of St Kitts and Nevis, with green cane fields on the lower ground and woodland on the steep slopes, together with the scudding clouds of a maritime climate, prompted a British colleague on my visit to remark that it looked like 'the Lake District in a heatwave'.

British colonists first settled on the islands of the eastern Caribbean—St Kitts, Nevis, Montserrat and Barbados—in the early seventeenth century. The initial aim was to replicate the success of the colony of Virginia in today's USA and grow tobacco for British markets. However, unlike the Spanish colony of Cuba further to the west, climatic conditions proved unsuitable, and the crops were poor. It was not until the importation of sugar cane and plantation techniques in the middle of the seventeenth century that the British Caribbean colonies began to flourish.[11]

Originally from Pacific East Asia and the Australasian islands, sugar cane was first cultivated by Europeans on the island of Cyprus, by Italian planters. Spanish and Portuguese settlers then transported the crop to their Atlantic colonies of Madeira, the Azores and the Canary Islands, and then to the coast of Brazil. The strong sun and frequent rainfall of the eastern Caribbean proved ideal for sugar planting, too.[12] The combination of the prevailing winds and currents—giving good shipping access—and the increasing demand for sugar in Britain from the late seventeenth century, transformed the fortunes of the colonial settlers, first in Barbados, then St Kitts and the other islands. Within half a century, these struggling, small Caribbean colonies became, in the words of one historian, 'the cockpit of the British Empire'.[13]

Richard Ligon's 1657 map *A Topographicall Description and Admeasurement of the Yland of Barbados* shows the colony shortly after the introduction of sugar cane (see Fig. 1.4). It is a poignant representation of Barbados at the beginning of the era of the export-driven, colonial plantation economy. In the south-west corner of the island, the map shows a series of long, narrow strips of cultivated land, reaching down to the sea. These, as Ligon identifies, were 'The tenn thousand Acres of land which Belongeth to the Merchants of London'. Each plot, indeed, is marked with the name of its owner. However, the map also reveals how much of a speculative and individualistic venture this early colonisation was. For example, no harbour is marked, and each plantation owner appears to have had his own coastal access for shipping. Meanwhile, the camels depicted at the top of the map hint at the experiments carried out to find animals which could be imported to work in the tropical heat.

But, while some of the London-based merchant investors were eventually to reap the rewards of sugar cultivation, they did not, of course, do the work themselves. The first plantation workers were indentured labourers from Britain: people fleeing the upheavals of the English Civil War; convicts; and those desperate enough to risk their lives for a new start several thousands of miles away. Most 'sold' themselves to merchants or plantation owners for five or seven years in exchange for the passage out and food and clothing. At the end of this period, if they survived, they could hope to acquire some land—perhaps five acres or so—of their own.

However, British plantation owners soon discovered from the Spanish and Portuguese, from whom they had adopted sugar-plant-

Fig. 1.4: *A Topographicall Description and Admeasurement of the Yland of Barbados*, Richard Ligon, 1657

ing techniques, that there was another readily available and more efficient, if initially more expensive, labour force: enslaved people from West Africa.[14] Not only were they more accustomed to manual work in the searing heat and humidity, Africans also often had resistance to many of the tropical diseases that killed so many Europeans in the colonies. Moreover, unlike indentured labour, this workforce never had the opportunity to become free, and their children would belong to the plantation owner, too. By the start of the eighteenth century, the majority of the inhabitants of Barbados and the other British Caribbean islands were of African descent.

'Were we not to be eaten by those white men with horrible looks?'

The west coast of Africa, from Senegal to Angola, is scattered with the remains of European colonial forts and settlements built during more than three centuries of slave-trading across the Atlantic. Set amid the pastel-coloured houses, cobbled lanes and lush vegetation of the former French island of Gorée (off the coast of Dakar, Senegal), for example, there is a building called La Maison des Esclaves (the House of Slaves). Built in 1786, this pink-red, lime-washed building, with its colonnaded first-floor veranda, was reconstructed and opened as a museum in 1962. It memorialises the immense human suffering of enslaved people and their forced transport from West Africa across the Atlantic. From the gloom of the rough stone interior of the ground floor, there is a poignant view through a small rectangular opening—known as the 'Door of No Return'—to the vivid blue ocean beyond. It is through this doorway that millions of enslaved Africans allegedly left the continent for the last time.

It is an image of such power that it is easy to understand why the building has become a site of pilgrimage for Europeans and Americans with African ancestry. However, historians differ on the extent to which the island actually played a major role in the slave trade.[15] The infamous 'Door of No Return' itself, for example, overlooks dangerous rocks, making it doubtful if any captive Africans were in fact transported across the Atlantic from there. Rather than a centre of trans-shipment, La Maison des Esclaves could, in reality, simply be a former merchant's house, with living quarters on the first floor and storage on the ground.

However, if you follow the main road leading south of Dakar, through a dry, dusty landscape of peanut farms and mud-walled, tin-roofed houses, you reach the tiny former British protectorate of The Gambia, which was certainly a major slaving centre. The very shape of the country—a strip of land between fifteen and thirty miles wide either side of the winding Gambia river—is a painful reminder of why many British ships first came here: the hinterland for the supply of human cargoes could not be more graphically illustrated. The ruined and overgrown Fort James, built on an island in the middle of the river about fifteen miles upstream from the capital Banjul, was once a major slave-collecting point.

The River Gambia was a particularly popular destination for slave-traders from Lancaster who sailed south in small, fast, two-masted vessels known as Snows or Briggs. Ambitious young men of modest means—often the sons of innkeepers, clockmakers and small farmers from the villages on the southern edge of the Lake District—came here to make their fortune in the 'Africa trade'.[16] But unlike Bagamoyo in Tanzania, which I had seen many years earlier, when I visited The Gambia in 2001, its palm-fringed Atlantic beach resorts of Kololi, Kotu, Fajara and Bakau had no memorials to the men, women and children who were shipped to British colonies in the Caribbean or mainland America.[17] As American author Anne Bailey noted in her pioneering book *African Voices of the Atlantic Slave Trade*, there was an apparent feeling in coastal West Africa at that time that the slave trade should remain a part of history best forgotten.[18]

Attitudes in West Africa have, however, begun to change. In 2003, two years after my visit, Fort James was designated a UNESCO World Heritage Site as a 'unique memorial to the Atlantic Slave Trade'.[19] The desolate so-called 'slave forts' along the Atlantic coast of Ghana, as well as historic slave camps further inland, are also now pilgrimage sites for visitors and Ghanaians alike.[20] While in Sierra Leone, the World Monument Fund—following the example of La Maison des Esclaves in Gorée—completed a major repair and restoration of the ruined British slave-trading fort on Bance (or Bunce) Island in the summer of 2020.[21] I return to the story of Bance and its prominent London owners in the next chapter.

But for many Africans who lived along this stretch of the Atlantic coast during the sixteenth to nineteenth centuries, no reminder of the brutal realities of the slave trade would have been needed: its devastating impact was felt all too sharply. Olaudah Equiano—from the West African Kingdom of Benin (now part of southern Nigeria), and a leading figure in the British eighteenth-century anti-slavery movement—described his first encounter with British slave-traders in his testimony *The Interesting Narrative:*

> The first object which saluted my eyes when I arrived on the coast was the sea and a slave ship which was then riding an anchor waiting for its cargo. These filled me with astonishment which was soon converted into terror .... When I was carried on board I was immediately handled and tossed up to see if I were sound by some of the crew ... were we not to be eaten by those white men with horrible looks, red faces and long hair?[22]

Doubts have been cast on the veracity of Equiano's story as autobiography.[23] Nevertheless, his tale was certainly representative of the fate of many thousands of Africans, who were kidnapped by members of other tribes and then sold on to Europeans to labour in the American colonies. Equiano's vivid prose gives the modern reader a painful insight into the appalling conditions faced by enslaved Africans on the six- or seven-week Atlantic crossing, imprisoned in the oaken hold of a small sailing ship. Equiano recalls:

> The closeness of the place, and the heat of the climate, added to the number in the ship, which was so crowded that each scarcely had room to turn himself, almost suffocated us. This produced copious perspirations, so that the air soon became unfit for respiration, from a variety of loathsome smells, and brought on a sickness among the slaves many of which died.[24]

Following this ordeal, Equiano describes what happened when the ship arrived at Bridgetown, the capital of Barbados:

> Many merchants and planters now came on board though it was in the evening. They put us in several parcels [groups to be sold at the market] and examined us attentively ... We thought by this that we should be eaten by these ugly men, as they appeared to us ... [but] they told us that we were not to be eaten, but to work.[25]

Fig. 1.5: *A Liverpool Slave Ship*, William Jackson, c. 1780

Equiano then explains how the captives were kept for several days in the merchants' yard, 'all pent up together like so many sheep in a fold, without regard to sex or age', before being sold once again to the plantation owners.

As well as its distressing first-hand account of the horrors of the eighteenth-century trans-Atlantic slave trade, Equiano's *Narrative* is all the more striking for the fact that it describes the British planta-tion colonies through the eyes of an African. When he arrived in Bridgetown following his crossing, for example, Equiano recalls: 'As every object was new to me, everything I saw filled me with surprise. What struck me first was that the houses were built with bricks, in stories [sic] and in every other respect different from those in Africa'. It is impossible from Equiano's writings to trace precisely where in Bridgetown these buildings or the merchants' yard would have been. It is likely, though, that they were located near the Careenage, the long finger of water that pushes its way into the city centre, where sleek yachts rather than slave ships now berth. On other islands, however, former slave markets are commemorated more openly. In Basseterre, for example, the capital of St Kitts, the former market site—now named Independence Square and occupied by a huge, ornate fountain—is firmly pointed out to European visitors by local people.

One of the most poignant sites in the Caribbean, however, is located on an island relatively unknown to tourists. The tiny Dutch colony of Sint Eustatius (popularly known as Statia) lies an hour or so by motorboat north-west of Basseterre. The capital, and indeed only town, Oranjestad, is now little more than a sleepy village perched on a steep cliffside. It is only the huge roofless ruins of the yellow-brick synagogue and the vast stone church in the town centre that hint at its former importance. Looking down to the seashore, through the dazzling turquoise water you can see the remains of more than 700 submerged warehouses that once lined the harbour front. But further around the bay, almost completely covered by undergrowth, are the few crumbling walls which are all that remain of the former slave market. Until, the mid-eighteenth century, when they began to face competition from English-based slave-trading consortia, the merchants of Statia had been the main suppliers of slaves for all the plantation owners of the eastern Caribbean.[26]

In the eighteenth century, Oranjestad was a Dutch 'freeport', a place 'of vast traffick from every corner of the globe'.[27] From its harbour-front warehouses, Dutch merchants not only supplied slaves for the colonists, but also provided them with European manufactured goods, 'buckets and tools' and luxury items such as 'rich embroideries, painted silks, flowered muslins, all the manufacture of the Indies'.[28] Here, a planter could stock up with agricultural equipment, buy dress fabrics for his wife and daughters and purchase men, women and children to work for him, for no reward, until they died. Perhaps nowhere else in the West Indies was the commodification of human life so potently laid bare as in the sweep of timber and stone buildings which once lined the bay of Oranjestad.[29]

'How the hot nectar best to christallise'

Like the other nearby Dutch Caribbean islands of Saba and St Maarten, the economy of Sint Eustatius was based on trading rather than planting, so there were few sugar estates. However, on neighbouring St Kitts and Nevis, the acacia scrub that now covers the old cane fields is frequently punctuated with the majestic stone ruins of eighteenth- and nineteenth-century sugar mills. The older works have stumpy towers (see Fig. 1.6)—the remains of windmills—while those from the nineteenth century display tall chimneys (see Fig. 1.7): relics of the attempts to improve industry efficiency using steam power and imported British coal. Inside the roofless structures, frequently over-grown with creepers and tropical vegetation, you can often find abandoned, British-made plant and equipment. From iron cogs to brass bowls known as 'neptunes',[30] they still evoke the efforts involved in transforming the canes into an edible, exportable product.

On the nearby island of Antigua, one windmill on the former sugar plantation of Betty's Hope has been restored as a working museum. It demonstrates how the canes were crushed between iron rollers to release the juice, which would then run through stone or wooden channels to the nearby boiling house (see Fig. 1.8). Fuelled by the cane waste, or 'bagasse', the liquid would then be boiled to remove impurities, and transferred between a series of four or five

Fig. 1.6: Abandoned windmill, Nevis

Fig. 1.7: Abandoned coal-fired sugar mill, Nevis

shallow copper bowls to reduce it to syrup. When ready, the sticky mass went to the curing house, where it crystallised, and the excess liquid molasses were drained off. Finally, the damp, dark brown sugar was packed into oak barrels for export.

One of the most comprehensive descriptions of the eighteenth-century British Caribbean sugar industry is found in a poem, *The Sugar Cane*, written by young Scots doctor James Grainger. He had arrived in St Kitts in 1759 as a companion to a wealthy friend and plantation owner, whom he had met at university in Cambridge.[31] His poem was published in England in 1764, the year after the end of the Seven Years' War (1756–63), which ended disastrously in the Caribbean for France and Spain. As we shall see later, the territory they were forced to cede to Britain significantly expanded the latter's colonial holdings in the Caribbean, prompting a new generation of wealthy Britons to make lucrative investments in the 'Sugar Isles'.

Fig. 1.8: The ruins of a former boiling house, St Kitts

Clearly intended as an update of John Dyer's *The Fleece* (1757), a poem about the culture and economics of the English wool trade, *The Sugar Cane* was a practical guide for the novice sugar planter. Grainger's first advice was, not surprisingly, to choose land carefully. Canes should not be planted on level land near the sea, as they would be 'burnt by the torch of day', he cautioned. Mountainsides were a better location, but ran the risks that 'ravening rats destroy, // Or troops of monkeys thy rich harvest steal'. The best place for a plantation, therefore, was 'Nor from hill too far, nor from the shore'. Grainger also advises the prospective planter to pay close attention to the climate before ordering his enslaved workers to prepare the ground by hoeing the soil into deep ridges and furrows. He explains:

> As art transforms the savage face of things,
> And order captivates the harmonious mind;

Let not the Blacks irregularly hoe;
But, aided by the line, consult the site
Of thy demesnes [lands]; and beautify the whole.[32]

Once the land had been hoed, the young cane shoots (known as ratoons, junks or Gemmy tops) could be planted. When the crop was growing well, the gangs of enslaved Africans were put to work at other tasks: weeding, building tracks and walls or planting hedges, 'to secure the Canes from the Goat's baleful tooth; the churning boar; / / From thieves; from fire—casual or designed'.[33]

Grainger's brief reference to arson attacks is one of the few hints in the poem at the tensions rife in the eighteenth-century Caribbean sugar colonies. However, mighty stone fortresses such as Brimstone Hill, high on a volcanic outcrop on the north-west coast of St Kitts, are enduring reminders of how valuable, and vulnerable, the distant Caribbean islands were considered to be (see Fig. 1.9). Designed by British engineers, but built, reinforced and extended by enslaved Africans, the fort could house 800 British Army officers and enlisted men at any one time.[34] Although the soldiers' presence was primarily to protect the island from invasion by other European powers—and, later, from the forces of the newly independent United States—they were also there to deter potential insurrections by the workers who toiled in the sugar plantations below.

Although sugar cultivation was labour-intensive, arduous work—not least during the five months of harvesting and processing—physical conditions in the Caribbean were, arguably, little worse than in many mid-eighteenth-century industries in Britain. Indeed, late in that century, as the abolition movement gained ground, several plantation owners used comparisons with the working conditions of British coal miners to justify the continuation of slavery.[35] Crucially, though, the semi-autonomous colonies were not subject to British laws governing the treatment of servants and indentured workers. Colonists viewed their enslaved workforce as 'stock' or 'moveable assets', and were free to punish them viciously when captive humans inevitably failed to behave like docile cattle. A Jamaican overseer recorded in his diary, for example, that his slave 'Derby [was] catched by Port Royal eating canes. Had him well flogged and pickled [his wounds rubbed with salt], then made Hector shit in his mouth'.[36]

Fig. 1.9: Brimstone Hill fortress, St Kitts

Nor was this an isolated incident. In 1745, former Caribbean planter George Maxwell wrote apologetically to a young man who had recently returned to England from an unhappy sojourn in Barbados:

> I am extremely sorry, dear sir, at the many disappointments you found ... and that things appeared quite different from what you had been used to here [in London] and expected there. The treatment of the Negroes I might have foreseen, had I considered, would ill suit the gentleness of your nature, but that I happened to overlook, after having lived more years in that island than you have done in the world. It was become familiar to me by use.[37]

It is scarcely surprising, therefore, that sugar planters lived in constant fear of violent rebellion. Yet despite the appalling treatment, enslaved Africans managed, somehow, to establish and maintain their own traditions. The Sunday morning market where they sold the produce they raised on their own 'provision grounds'—land unsuitable for sugar cultivation—became a regular feature of life on many of the islands.[38] As one privileged European visitor observed:

> The Negroes are the only market people. Nobody else dreams of selling provisions … Sunday is the grand day, as then they are all at liberty to work for themselves, and people hire workmen at a much easier rate, than on week days from their Masters. The Negroes also keep the poultry and it is them that raise the fruit and vegetables.[39]

While some enslaved Africans lived in chattel houses supplied by the plantation owners, in the more established colonies many built their own homes from local materials in small villages close to the provision grounds. Because of the impermanent nature of the huts' construction, however, little physical evidence survives on any of the islands, apart from holes where wooden posts supporting the walls and roof of such buildings once stood. And while pits in the ground may lack the immediate, haunting visual impact of ruined sugar works, a visit to the isolated site of a former 'slave village' on the wild, wind-blown Atlantic coast of Nevis is still a powerful experience, not just for those of African descent.[40]

'Bilge-water, sugar and rum': the voyage to Britain

Gazing at the vivid blue ocean beyond, you are acutely aware that Nevis is a tiny island, separated by a vast watery desert from both Europe and the west coast of Africa. However, this sense of distant solitude gives a misleading impression of life in the colony during the eighteenth century. For the Atlantic then was not seen as a barrier, but a passage of communication. While enslaved Africans, of course, would have had no contact with their kith and kin on the far side of the ocean, the links between colonial families, friends and colleagues in Britain and the Caribbean islands were exceedingly close. In fact, the Atlantic winds and currents made ocean travel between Britain and the Caribbean almost as easy and regular as between the islands themselves.

The rigs and square sails of eighteenth-century boats meant that 'beating' against the wind (sailing at an angle, to progress in the direction opposite to the wind) was far more difficult than in today's yachts. With the prevailing easterlies, for example, a voyage from

Barbados to nearby Jamaica would take around a week; but the return sailing would take almost the same time as the six-to-eight-week voyage to the British Isles.

The relative ease of communication, as well as family links to Britain's landed elite, encouraged planters to send their children to be educated in England. This was certainly given impetus, too, by the threat of rebellions by the enslaved workforce and of war between the European colonial powers on and over the islands. One planter's son recalled leaving the 'passion flowers, palm trees, and ring-doves' of his Jamaican home—'for a child, an earthly paradise'[41]—to embark, aged nine, on his voyage to Britain in the 'stuffy and sweltering' hold of a 'black-sided sugar ship', where the air was full of 'bilge-water, sugar and rum'.[42] By the mid-eighteenth century, many of the wealthier planters had moved their entire families to Britain, leaving their estates in the hands of attorneys and overseers.[43]

This exodus was to have three major effects: the creation of a prominent group of expatriate 'West Indians' in Britain; the growing demand for young, educated men to run the plantations on site; and the flow of repatriated capital towards Britain.[44]

One young British visitor, Daniel McKinnen, on his first trip to 'our valuable sugar islands' in 1802, was shocked to find that the streets of Bridgetown, Barbados 'were in great measure unpaved'. He noted in dismay 'the decayed and warped exterior of the wooden houses, the dirty and unfinished fronts of the brick dwellings, with smutty timbers and staggering piazzas [balconies]'.[45] At first McKinnen 'excited an idea that the [British] national character was totally vitiated or lost in this torrid climate'. However, he then realised that the reason for this lack of maintenance was that 'most of the principal inhabitants of the towns intend their dwellings merely as places of temporary residence, till they have acquired the means of removing to a more temperate climate, and naturally feel less solicitous to dispose of their money in objects of unprofitable and temporary concern.'[46]

In Jamaica, the largest and wealthiest of the British colonies at the time, McKinnen found even more evidence of the effects of absenteeism on the island. It is 'naturally a matter of some surprise to a stranger who visits the island to find it almost totally deserted by its principal inhabitants', he wrote. 'In one of the richest districts it is said that of eighty proprietors not three are to be found in this time on the spot.'[47]

For contemporary British visitors to the country's former colonies in the Caribbean, it is noticeable how relatively modest the so-called 'Great Houses' tend to be. While a few grand eighteenth-century examples survive—notably the stone-built Rose Hall in the parish of St James in Jamaica—most plantation houses are much smaller. In comparison with the stucco palaces of eighteenth-century colonial Calcutta, the cotton plantation houses of settlers in the United States, or the residences of Spanish sugar growers in nineteenth-century Cuba, the homes of British Caribbean planters certainly seem frugal.

To the extent that money made from sugar was re-invested in the West Indies, it was largely spent on production—the sugar works themselves—rather than domestic colonial luxury.[48] As McKinnen had already noted over 200 years ago, the culture of absenteeism that developed in the eighteenth-century British Caribbean meant that 'the wealth of the soil is transported and consumed in remote countries'.[49] It is in Britain, therefore, rather than the West Indies, that the spectacular proceeds and legacy of the sugar and slave trade are to be found.

2

ARTS AND ELEGANCIES

For the first time in my life here am I in England,
at the fountainhead of pleasure,
in the land of beauty: of arts, of elegancies.
My happy stars have given me a good estate
and the conspiring winds have blown me hither to spend it.

Richard Cumberland, *The West Indian* (1771)

Danson Park is situated near Bexleyheath in south-east London, equidistant between the financial centre, the City, and the mouth of the River Thames. Though a sprawling suburb of 1930s semi-detached houses, shopping parades and superstores now surrounds it, you can still get a sense of how the estate would have looked some 250 years ago, when the current house was built and the land-scape gardens developed. In the historic north Kent landscape of wide skies and gentle contours, the Danson of the late eighteenth century would have had a commanding presence on top of its low hill. Faced with striking honey-coloured limestone in a county of clay bricks, flints and timber weatherboarding, the house certainly would have stood out—and still does (see Fig. 2.1).

In the late 1700s, a sweep of grassland—the 'great lawn'—led down to the south of the house towards a lake and a small mock temple designed by William Chambers, one of the most famous architects of the day. To the north-west, there was a view across another huge meadow and over the London road to Greenwich. To the north, one could catch glimpses of the naval dockyard at Woolwich and the dull grey glint of the Thames beyond; and to

Fig. 2.1: The entrance elevation of Danson House (© Historic England Archive)

the east, rolling fields and copses stretched as far as the eye could see. The splendour of the estate is celebrated in a painting by landscape artist George Barret from the 1760s (see Fig. 2.2). The main house, pictured at the centre of Barret's composition, was the subject of a meticulous and scholarly repair and restoration under the auspices of English Heritage in the late 1990s. The house and its interior are, therefore, much as they would have been when Danson was first occupied.

A great flight of stone steps leads up to the main entrance and to the mahogany front door, which is set with a glazed vision panel—a single sheet of glass almost thirty inches square, the technical limit of eighteenth-century English glassmaking.[1] Inside, on the 'piano nobile' first floor, are the formal reception rooms. The tone is set by the imposing entrance hall: sparsely furnished, unheated, and with a stone-paved floor, creamy-yellow walls, niches and busts, its design evokes hot climates (see Fig. 2.3). Indeed, the house's entranceway was modelled on the halls of the sixteenth-century

Fig. 2.2: Painting of the Boyd family, George Barret Senior, oil on canvas (© Historic England Archive)

Fig. 2.3: The entrance hall at Danson House (© Historic England Archive)

Italian villas of mason-architect Andrea Palladio (1508–80), whose work was highly fashionable in England when Danson was built.

In reality, though, Palladio's designs were far more suited to the sticky summers of the Venetian hinterland than to the cool, damp English countryside. But the hall is only a transitional space: from there, three further elegant mahogany-panelled doors lead to the principal living spaces.

Through the door on the left is the dining room. Here, the calm simplicity of the entrance hall gives way to a feast of decoration, with glittering sconces, gilded mouldings, colourful wall paintings and fine mirrors.[2] To the right of the hall sits the library, its walls painted in a deep, dark green (see Fig. 2.4).

Fig. 2.4: The library at Danson House (© Historic England Archive)

This was an expensive colour to make before the nineteenth-century invention of synthetic pigments, but it is one that sets off the tall, mahogany-faced bookcases to advantage. A magnificent, finely crafted organ completes this sophisticated display of wealth. Just off the library is the octagonal salon, which is hung with vivid blue 'chinoiserie' wallpaper (see Fig. 2.5).[3]

But it is the central door off the hall which reveals the *pièce de résistance*: a magnificent, oval, top-lit staircase (see Fig. 2.6). Its cantilevered stone treads and mahogany handrail spiral up through the house to a coffered, *trompe-l'œil* dome—a homage in miniature to the ancient Pantheon temple in Rome.

From the fashionable 'natural' style landscaping of the garden to the well-planned kitchens and servants' quarters, and from the elegant design of the counter-balanced, sliding box-sash windows and folding shutters to the oil paintings on the walls, the references to the great buildings of imperial Rome and to the Italian renaissance were hard to miss. Everything about Danson proclaimed

Fig. 2.5: The salon at Danson House (© Historic England Archive)

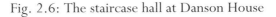

Fig. 2.6: The staircase hall at Danson House

modernity, cosmopolitanism and artistic discernment. Clearly, this was the home of a gentleman of taste and fortune.[4]

From the Caribbean to the capital

Danson's patron, John Boyd, was an absentee West Indian plantation owner, born in 1719 on the Caribbean island of St Kitts, a colony which, at the time, was divided between French and British control. He was the only son of Augustus Boyd, a Scots-Irish émigré who had arrived on the island in 1700, aged twenty, with little to his name.[5] Augustus had first become a plantation manager, then, by 'renting' forty-nine enslaved Africans and some land, began cultivating sugar himself. Eventually, aided by his marriage to a plantation heiress, he became the owner of an estate at Palmetto Point on the western side of St Kitts.[6] However, Augustus's mixed heritage—his mother was a French Huguenot—caused him many frustrations, given the simmering colonial power conflicts between France and Britain at the time. So, in 1735, with the threat of war between the two countries looming, and despite having spent nearly all his adult life in the West Indies, he left the island with his wife and teenage son for a new start in London.

The contrast between St Kitts and the colonial capital could not have been greater. Though nowhere near the size of today's sprawling metropolis, by the 1730s London was still one of the largest cities in the world: home to more than three-quarters of a million people, almost one-tenth of Britain's population, it was already larger than Paris, notwithstanding France's much bigger populace. For, as well as being a centre of political and administrative power, London, unlike the French capital, was also a major seaport. It was the prosperity founded on the salty, silt-encrusted, Thames-side wharves and quays that had attracted migrants from England's provinces. Indeed, almost a quarter of London's population at that time worked in the port and river trades alone.[7]

The later decline of London's shipping trade with the advent of container transportation in the twentieth century, together with the subsequent redevelopment of the City along the banks of the Thames, means that only fragments of the eighteenth-century port survive today. To get a feel for the city which welcomed the Boyd family in the 1730s, therefore, it is necessary to look at old maps, drawings and descriptions written by people of the time. The size of buildings apart, one of the most notable differences between the riverside then and now is the comparative emptiness these days of the Thames itself. Writing in 1723, four years after the publication of his most famous work, *Robinson Crusoe*, Daniel Defoe described the spectacle of the Thames just to the south-east of the Tower of London, a stretch of water known as the Upper Pool:

> [In] that Part of the River Thames, which is properly the Harbour, and where the ships usually deliver or unload their cargoes, I have had the Curiousity [sic] to count the Ships as well as I could, *en passant*; and have found above 2000 Sail of all Sorts, not reckoning Barges, Lighters, or Pleasure-boats and Yachts; but of vessels that really go to sea.[8]

Early eighteenth-century Britain also had a flourishing manufacturing industry—especially woollen textiles and iron goods.

The country's shipping merchants had been assiduous in establishing export markets and the words of one contemporary commentator, Malachy Postlethwayt, give a flavour of the cosmopolitan nature of London's trade during this time:[9]

45

Fig. 2.7: *The Pool of London*, Thomas Luny, c. 1805

The exporter of woolen [sic] *goods*, can as easily export *tin* or *lead or hardware &c* and have his returns by exchange in dollars of *Leghorn*, or ducats of *Venice* as well as dollars *of Spain, or millrees, or moidores of Portugal*. Or, cannot the merchant who sent woolen [sic] goods to *Spain*, or to *Italy* send another species of Woollen goods *to Russia*; and have his returns in *roubles*.[10]

By the mid-eighteenth century, England had already become a modern consumer society and a substantial proportion of the country's population—those regarding themselves as the 'middling sort'—were eager and able to buy imported goods from around the globe. These included fine Turkish carpets; wine and citrus fruits from southern Europe; and, from further afield, easily washable cotton muslins and printed calicoes from India; spices from the East Indies; tea and porcelain from China; tobacco from Virginia; tropical timbers and, of course, sugar from the plantations of the West Indies.[11]

The fastest growing area of overseas trade in the British Isles during this time, and by far the greatest in volume, was with Britain's thirteen mainland American colonies and its thirteen island colonies in the Caribbean. Between the late seventeenth and late eighteenth centuries, the quantity of imports and exports to and from these colonies more than doubled, and by 1771, this Atlantic trade amounted to a third more than that with all European destinations combined.[12] This rapid growth was in no small part due to the succession of Navigation Acts passed through Parliament in the late seventeenth and early eighteenth centuries, including a 1763 bill which required not only that colonial produce be transported solely in British ships,[13] but forbade manufacturing in the American and Caribbean colonies themselves. Everything, therefore, that the settlers might need—tools for the plantations, tables, furniture, crockery, linen, lace and silks, and even basic foodstuffs—was exported from London and Britain's other expanding ports on the Atlantic.

By the time Augustus Boyd and his family arrived in the city, London was eclipsing Amsterdam as Europe's premier port. With his first-hand knowledge of colonists' requirements and his trading contacts in the Leeward islands, Boyd was well-placed to compete with the merchants of Oranjestad to take advantage of the expanding markets of the Caribbean. In 1735, he went into partnership with his brother-in-law James Perchell in a merchandising firm, charging a commission of between half and five per cent on the goods they exported, and a similar amount on the barrels of molasses and damp, raw brown sugar shipped from the West Indies.[14]

The firm was based in Austin Friars, in the closely packed network of streets centred on St Paul's Cathedral, just north of the river. It was a good spot. Almost everything a mercantile partnership required to develop a business of global reach was less than an hour's walk away. In the immediate vicinity were the headquarters of major institutions: the East India Company, the Royal Africa Company and the Bank of England. To the south lay the Thames-side quays and Customs House. The Navy Office and the merchant shipping authority, based in Trinity House, were also close at hand, as were the wholesale produce markets for exports to the colonies: Smithfield for livestock and meat for the plantation owners, and Billingsgate for the barrels of salted fish used to feed the enslaved populations.

Its prime City location to this day means that there are few eighteenth-century buildings left in Austin Friars. Some of the nearby structures, however, such as the duct-shrouded, crane-topped Lloyd's of London insurance building, still house institutions which can trace their origins back to the eighteenth-century shipping industry. Visually, however, the huge scale of many of the new buildings, coupled with road development near the Tower of London, means that the intimately close relationship that the City once had with the Thames is now lost. Indeed, at street level, it is hard to realise you are near the river at all.

In places, though, heritage planning laws have tamed the urban march of global capitalism and its ever-higher towers. Here and there, fragments of the medieval street layout still remain: an intricate network of tiny pedestrianised alleys and courts, which cut through the blocks, giving glimpses into the limestone-and-chrome atria of international banks. It is here that you can find the remains of a far older, but still globally connected, City of London. Just a few minutes' walk from Austin Friars, in St Michael's Alley, is the Jamaica Wine House, quartered in a nineteenth-century building on the site of the original Jamaica House—the first 'coffee house' in London. In the eighteenth century, coffee houses were not just places of refreshment, but important locations for gleaning business gossip and information. Here, news could not only be read in newspapers, but heard straight from the mouths of voyagers freshly disembarked from the trans-Atlantic ships anchored in the Thames.

The names of coffee houses, like those of pubs, often reflected the commodity or area of trade of those merchants to which they catered.[15] The Jamaica would naturally have been the establishment in which to receive news from the West Indies, and Augustus Boyd and his son John may well have been regular customers. Formal business deals and paperwork would, however, be completed in a private office, known as a 'compting house'. The Boyds' own has long since been redeveloped, but if you walk a few minutes northeast to the poorer areas just outside the bounds of the City, such as Spitalfields or Artillery Row, where many eighteenth-century streets survive, it is possible to get an idea of what it may have looked like.

Most urban buildings of the time—whether domestic, commercial or a mixture of the two—were built to standard developers' formats set out in builders' 'pattern books'. They were elegantly proportioned, narrow, terraced buildings, with flat, brick frontages—to prevent the spread of fire—and large windows facing out to the street.[16] Walking south-east from Austin Friars to the now traffic-blighted Minories area of the City, you can still find fragments of 1760s developments built to celebrate the trans-Atlantic trade: America Square, The Circus and, albeit heavily restored and partially rebuilt, The Crescent.

With its sober brick façade, elegant sash windows and iron railings, Number 11, The Crescent looks like a typical Georgian terraced London townhouse. This was, however, the site of the offices of Camden, Calvert and Kent, one of London's largest firms of Africa traders.[17] The residential appearance of The Crescent makes it hard to believe that it once housed the financial centre of a global slave-trading business. But, by today's standards, eighteenth-century merchant shipping companies were very small organisations: often just the owner and several assistant clerks. The post of a clerk in an international compting house was, therefore, a potentially lucrative career opportunity.

So it is at first surprising to discover that after his arrival in Britain, Augustus's son John left London to read theology at Christ Church college, Oxford, rather than becoming a clerk in his father's office. Although the 'livings' paid to eighteenth-century clergymen could well provide a comfortable life, the priesthood seems an odd career choice for the only son of a successful, international merchant. But rather than intending his son to follow a religious vocation, it is likely that Augustus had other motives for his choice of education for John. The colleges of Oxford and Cambridge—along with schools such as Westminster and Eton—were institutions which had for many years provided an education to the sons of Britain's land-owning elite.[18] The academic results of John's theological studies would have been much less important than the assurance that he would be spending two or three years in the company of 'gentlemen'.

Becoming a 'Gentleman'

The concepts of gentility or 'politeness', and the definition of gentlemanly behaviour, were of great importance in eighteenth-century Britain.[19] Shortly before his death in 1729, Daniel Defoe, an acute observer of social mores, had been working on a manuscript entitled *The Compleat Gentleman*,[20] and it is therefore to the author of *Robinson Crusoe* that I turn to clarify what the terms meant at this time.

According to Defoe, the word 'gentleman' was traditionally understood to 'signify men of ancient houses, dignified with hereditary
titles and family honours, old mansion houses … names deriv'd from
the lands and estates they possess, parks and forests made by their
own prescription and usage time out of mind and such like marks of
the antiquity of the race.'[21] Clearly, to be a gentleman, one had to
have money, preferably income from agricultural rents. But by the
1730s, the success of the Navigation Acts and Britain's aggressive
colonial expansion had, as Defoe points out, also provided opportunities in 'Law, trade, war, navigation, improvement of stocks, loans
on public funds' to create, in his words, 'vast and, till of late, unheard
of sums of money amass'd in a short time'. Wealth was no longer the
prerogative solely of those with inherited landed estates.

Though necessary, however, riches alone were not sufficient to
ensure social acceptability. Indeed, according to Defoe and other
contemporaries, a merchant's perceived habit of 'ravening after
money'[22] would debar him from ever becoming a true gentleman.
It was another matter, however, for a merchant's son. If spent correctly, his inherited wealth could open up the possibility of social
advancement. As Defoe argues:

> Call him what you please on account of his blood, and be the race
> modern and mean as you will, yet if he was sent early to school, has
> good parts and has improved them by learning, travel, conversation
> and reading, and, above all, with a modest, courteous gentle-man
> like behaviour; despise him as you will, he will be a gentleman in
> spite of all the distinctions we can make.[23]

As Augustus and John Boyd would have known, being 'sent early
to school' could help the child be rid of the stigma of new, trade-
derived money and secure his entrance into the hallowed halls of
'genteel' society.

And the transformative potential of a 'correct' education for an
aspiring gentleman is recorded in numerous contemporary accounts.
Merchant Robert Maxwell, for example, wrote approvingly in 1744
about a small boy who had been sent to England for his schooling,
exclaiming that 'in short you would not know him again, his speech
is almost quite changed and he will very soon lose the little that he
has left of the Barbados accent and dialect'.[24]

Similarly, absentee planters like the Boyds would have been particularly concerned with developing 'modest, courteous gentle-man like behaviour' to overcome their distant island origins. Caribbean colonists were widely considered to have different social mores to those of polite eighteenth-century British society.[25] In such circles, West Indians were perceived as having coarse manners and were known for their predilection for luxurious—and, in Britain, extraordinarily expensive—tropical foods, such as turtles and pine-apples, and for cooking outdoors over barbecues.[26]

The wealthy but uncultured colonial plantation owner was the subject of many books and stage productions in the second half of the eighteenth century. The flamboyantly brusque, barbecue-loving, Caribbean-born hero of the comedy *The Patron* (1764), by playwright Samuel Foote, for example, is disparagingly described as 'a West Indian of overgrown fortune, he saves me the trouble of a portrait'.[27] And in Richard Cumberland's popular play *The West Indian* (1771), the young man in question apparently has 'enough rum and sugar belonging to him, to make all the water in the Thames into punch'.[28]

Despite the considerable riches many West Indians accumulated, clearly it was not easy to gain the approval of polite society. The supposed failure of Jamaican-born absentee Alderman William Beckford—the patron of a vast Palladian house named Fonthill Splendens in Wiltshire—to adopt the requisite gentlemanly behaviour, for example, meant that even as a powerful City Alderman, Member of Parliament and Lord Mayor of London, he was still not fully accepted by Britain's elite. 'Mr. Beckford wanted the external graces of manners and expression, adorned with those accomplishments, he would have made a first-rate figure', one City commentator snidely wrote.[29]

Beckford became an alderman in 1752 and was first elected Lord Mayor of London ten years later. And like many wealthy planters he liked imported, and expensive, tropical foods. By this time, West Indians were importing huge numbers of turtles from the Caribbean, in barrels of seawater, for their favourite dinner-party delicacy: turtle soup. Indeed, from 1761 (the year before Beckford was appointed Mayor) to 1825, turtle soup was a key feature of the prestigious annual Lord Mayor's Day banquet in London.[30]

Like many affluent West Indians, Beckford had been sent to England to study at Westminster School in London. Clearly, however, having vast resources and receiving an appropriate education were not enough to win social acceptance; as Defoe lays out, other requirements must be met. Among these, was 'travel'. One would imagine that absentees must already have satisfied this criterion, having necessarily made at least one substantial trans-Atlantic voyage. But a journey from Britain's colonies in the cabin of a sugar-laden West Indiaman—as the Atlantic-going merchant ships were known—was not, it appears, the correct form of travel. A true gentleman had to visit Europe.

By the early eighteenth century, making an extended continental visit had become a rite of passage for Britain's male elite. Known as the 'Grand Tour', these lengthy travels would usually culminate in a sojourn in Rome.[31] Here, young men could see for themselves the remains of the civilisations they had spent so much time studying in classics lessons at school. They could walk in the footsteps of the emperors Augustus and Hadrian, contemplate the fertile country-side celebrated in Virgil's epic poem *Georgics*, or—like Danson's architect Robert Taylor—gain first-hand knowledge of ancient Roman architecture.[32]

While it is unclear from the available records if John Boyd made a Grand Tour straight after graduating, he certainly undertook one with his wife and family later in life, visiting the classical remains of Rome and Naples.[33] And, like other wealthy British tourists, he brought back souvenirs in the form of paintings and antique sculptures, which were originally displayed in Danson House.[34] By his mid-twenties, however, having completed his gentlemanly education, he returned to the City and joined his father to form a new partnership, Boyd & Co., which soon received prestigious and highly profitable new commissions to supply the British Army and Navy.[35] Once traders on a far-distant island colony, the Boyds were now at the heart of a new, emerging imperial order. And only three years after founding Boyd & Co., Augustus and John, together with four other London-based West India merchants,[36] became involved in one of eighteenth-century Britain's most lucrative branches of international commerce: the trans-Atlantic slave trade.

In 1748, the Boyds and their new business partners purchased Bance (or Bunce or Bense) Island, an old slave-trading fort in the Sierra Leone River in West Africa, which we encountered briefly in Chapter One (see Fig. 2.8). Like the stone fort on James Island in the River Gambia, the redoubt on Bance had been built by the British-sponsored Royal Africa Company some seventy years before, but abandoned in the face of growing competition by independent merchants trading directly from slaving ships.[37] It is unlikely that the Boyds actually visited Bance before buying, probably gaining their knowledge of this business opportunity instead from conversations with merchants, and from several books on the West African slave trade already published in London, such as *The African Trade* (1745) and *The National and Private Advantages of the African Trade* (1746), both by Malachy Postlethwayt.

Buying the island would undoubtedly have been a risky venture for the recently founded consortium. But the Boyds and their co-purchasers clearly anticipated that the money-making potential would be worth the risks: by banding together to acquire and manage Bance, they hoped to reap the rich rewards of the 'fort trade' it had once conducted. As in the mid-seventeenth century, African traders, supplied with arms by the British slavers, would capture

Fig. 2.8: *Plan and view of Bense Island & Fort. Bunce, Sierra Leone*, William Smith, 1745

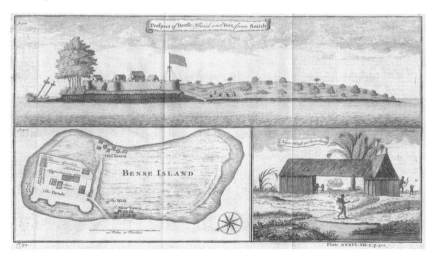

members of other tribal groups, who were then exchanged through barter with the consortium at their garrison on Bance. The captives were then sold on, at a premium, to the slave shippers who could then depart swiftly, with full loads, on their trans-Atlantic voyage.

Bance Island proved to be one of the most financially successful business ventures the Boyds would ever undertake.[38] Between 1750 and 1769, the consortium exported 9,655 men, women and children to be sold to Caribbean planters. Some of the Boyds' slaving profits were invested into East India Company shares (John Boyd later became a director of the company) and some were put into a private bank, while other funds were used to purchase new lands and plantations in Grenada and Tobago. Much of the money, however, was spent on property in Britain itself.[39]

Designing Danson

In July 1753, John Boyd—already the father of three young children with his first wife, Mary—took on a twenty-one-year lease of a 'mansion house' near Bexleyheath, together with forty acres of land, barns, stables, outhouses and gardens, orchards, fishponds and a formal ornamental lake or 'canal': Danson Park.[40] Six years later, he bought the freehold outright.[41] Due to its proximity to both the City and River Thames, this area of north Kent, near Bexley, was particularly popular with successful merchants who wanted to move their families away from the crowded confines of London's financial centre.[42] It was home to at least a dozen prominent Caribbean expatriate families, such as the Mays, the Longs, the Kenyons, the Mannings, the Butlers, the Duponts, the Malcoms, the Adyes and the Willetts.[43] John's father had already leased a house in the nearby village of Lewisham, and their Bance Island colleague John Sargent owned a rambling fifteenth-century manor house, May Place, just a few miles away. Unlike Sargent, however, John Boyd seems to have found the old manor at Danson inadequate and, in 1760, he approached leading architect Robert Taylor to design him a new family home. A man who aimed to be a 'compleat' gentleman required a different sort of residence.

In eighteenth-century Britain, to be considered a gentleman, one needed not only to have riches, education and manners, but also to spend his money in the right way—in short, to have 'taste'.[44] And of all the objects a wealthy individual might acquire during his lifetime, a new, custom-designed house and garden would have been one of the most public—and most expensive—ways of displaying gentility and discernment. Indeed, Danson Park can be seen as a conspicuous exemplar of mid-eighteenth-century British good taste.

Danson's architecture, like most 'polite' new buildings of the time, drew inspiration from villas designed by the Italian mason-architect Andrea Palladio over two centuries before. Palladio amalgamated features of Roman temples and other ancient civic buildings with the vernacular of northern Italy to create aesthetically sophisticated, rural headquarters for the newly acquired agricultural holdings of the elite merchants of the Venetian Republic.[45] Two or three storeys in height, these rough-brick 'farmhouses' were covered with render to imitate stone, and were built to a symmetrical, geometrically organised plan. A careful emphasis on proportions gave Palladio's architecture its simple splendour.

But why would a man who spent his formative years on a small Caribbean island have been interested in designs which alluded to the Roman Empire and its occupation of Britain many centuries before? Was Boyd just blindly following the fashion for Italianate architecture, anxious to prove his taste and status as a gentleman? Or did such classical style have real resonance with the Boyds' own family history and fortunes? Sadly, few records pertaining to the actual construction of Danson survive, so there is no documentary evidence as to why Boyd chose to appoint Robert Taylor as his architect, nor are there any notes from discussions between them. Fortunately, however, Danson's architecture itself reveals a great deal.

As we have already seen earlier in the chapter, Danson incorporates an eclectic mix of advanced eighteenth-century building technology and classical references which hint at the temples of Greece and Rome. And while these classical motifs would certainly have shown Boyd to be a member of the cultured elite, devices that recalled the wealth and might of the Roman Empire would also have had a particular resonance for a West Indian colonialist. The spectacular homage to the Pantheon above Danson's main staircase, for example, was not simply a tribute to an ancient architectural masterpiece. It also alluded to the role that the Boyds were playing—as

Caribbean sugar planters, Atlantic traders and victualling contrac-tors to the Army and Navy—in the creation of a new, British impe-rial order.[46]

Indeed, the evocative classical style of Palladio's villas would have provided an intriguing design prototype for a London-based West Indian merchant.[47] As well as conjuring up images of imperial Rome, Palladio's villas reflected the power and prosperity of fif-teenth-century Venice's maritime merchant elite. In fact, legends of the Venetian Republic were often deployed as an alternative to those of ancient Rome, and held up as historical examples for eigh-teenth-century Britain to follow. This 'Venetian' model found par-ticular favour with City merchants.[48]

However, few eighteenth-century British clients, or their design-ers, would have actually seen one of Palladio's Italian villas in per-son. While many visited Italy's west coast ports such as Livorno (also known as Leghorn) on their way to Rome, the Venetians' Adriatic trading empire had long since declined, and, for the British at least, the Italian region of Veneto in the north-east of the country was now a largely inaccessible backwater. Boyd's architect Robert Taylor, therefore, would likely have gained his knowledge of Palladio's buildings through English translations of his treatise *The Four Books of Architecture* (first published in Italian in 1570, and in English in 1663), and the many publications derived from it.[49]

It is thus worth noting that there are striking differences between Palladio's original sixteenth-century villas and their eighteenth-century British counterparts, like Danson. Some of these can be attributed to variations in available construction methods and mate-rials.[50] Others seem to be more aesthetic choices. For example, rather than a render finish, which could have easily been produced with locally available Kent sands, Danson's brick shell is faced with expensive yellow limestone, whose eye-catching colour would have stood out amid the green hills and brick buildings of Bexleyheath. Fine decorative plasterwork ceilings, polished Caribbean mahogany doors and sophisticated counter-balanced sliding sash windows like-wise do not feature in Palladio's originals.

But the most profound difference between Danson and the villas designed for sixteenth-century Venetian merchants is the way the buildings relate to their surroundings. Notwithstanding their classi-

cal grandeur, most of Palladio's villas were not only the sophisticated headquarters of country estates, but also working farmhouses
surrounded by many acres of productive fields and orchards. Boyd's
neo-Palladian villa, however, was enclosed by vast ornamental
lawns, intended not to produce agricultural income, but to be symbols of status and opulence. With its hill-top location and the composition of the building itself, Danson's main purpose was to visually dominate the surrounding area.

And during the eighteenth century, Danson would have been
even more imposing than today. While the villa itself was not out-
standingly large, two low-curved wings (since demolished, but visible in George Barret's painting in Fig. 2.2, near the start of the
chapter) would have given the building the aspect of a grand palace,
accentuating the impact of the sweeping flight of steps up to the
main entrance and the prominent pediment. This extending effect
was a Palladian device: at Villa Barbaro (also known as the Villa di
Maser) in the Veneto, for example, Palladio had increased the
apparent size of the house by forming symmetrical arcades linking
it to theatrically decorated farm buildings. The wings at Danson,
however, were not designed as barns but as accommodation for
numerous people, twelve horses and three coaches.[51]

While Boyd did not intend the estate to have a primarily agricultural function, he had nonetheless been consistently adding to his
landholdings since the purchase of Danson in 1759. By 1762, he
owned almost 200 acres of land.[52] In eighteenth-century Britain,
land ownership was a mark of social prestige, and conferred distinct
advantages on the largest landowners. Privileges ranged from the
comparatively trivial, such as the right to hunt, to the most important: the ability to act as a justice of the peace and the right to be
elected to Parliament.[53]

An estate plan from around 1762 (see Fig. 2.9) gives us a good
idea of how Boyd intended to use Danson's vast acreage. Once
attributed to Lancelot 'Capability' Brown, the plan has now been
identified as being the work of one of Brown's former assistants,
Nathaniel Richmond.[54] It nonetheless displays all the hallmarks of
the 'natural style' of landscape design associated with Brown.

By the early 1760s, the creation of vast grassy lawns or parks had
become an extremely fashionable activity among British landown-

ers. Indeed, between 1750 and Brown's death in 1783, almost 4,000 landscape parks were created—the majority to designs made by Brown's associates: Richmond, Richard Woods, William Emes, Francis Richardson and Adam Mickle.[55] The so-called 'natural style', of course, owed more to man than nature. For a landowner today—equipped with the hydraulic arms and toothed buckets of earthmoving equipment—gentle earth grading and seeding, with some larger planting, would not be an extravagant form of landscaping. In the eighteenth century, however, it would have been a substantial feat of construction. Earth had to be dug with a spade,

Fig. 2.9: Plan of proposed landscaping at Danson

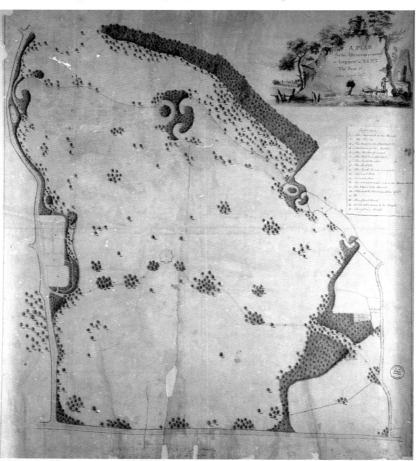

thrown onto a cart or barrow, moved a few feet or more (depending on the desires of the 'improver'), tipped out and compacted ready for the application of topsoil, and for raking and seeding.

Executed in pen, ink and wash, the plan for Danson shows the location of the new house on the highest point of Boyd's landholding (just visible in outline, between two copses, in the centre of the plan). It was all to be surrounded by vast gardens, studded with groups of trees. On the upper half of the image, a seventy-acre 'lawn' leads to an irregularly shaped lake (stretching from the map's legend on the right across to the top left of the plan), bounded by thickets of trees. And at the bottom, below the house, lies another lawn of almost forty acres.[56] The use of the word 'lawn' to describe these vast swathes of grassy land reflected the unease felt by cartographers and landscape designers of the time about calling this land a 'park', a term which had strong historical associations with medieval royal or aristocratic deer parks, found on 'gentleman's land'.[57] Nonetheless, the huge expanse of grass and trees planned at Danson was a conspicuous demonstration that the owner, aristocrat or not, was unquestionably a member of the landowning elite.[58]

The open lawn, proposed to the north of the house (the bottom half of the plan), would have allowed clear views of Danson's pedimented entrance by any traveller on the London to Dover road. Moreover, in the eighteenth century, when the majority of land surrounding the Danson estate would have been enclosed fields rather than houses, it would have been difficult to tell how far Danson's grounds actually extended. So, the 'natural style' of landscaping was remarkably flexible. Boyd was never able to fully realise his plans to create a wide expanse of lawn to the front of the house, as he was unable to purchase all the land he needed. Nevertheless, by building the new sweeping driveway through a thicket of trees (to the lower right of the image), the grounds of the stubborn smallholder who had refused to sell to Boyd were concealed from visitors to Danson.[59] Clearly, therefore, unlike his sixteenth-century Venetian counterparts, Boyd was not attempting to present himself as a sophisticated farmer; even his extensive kitchen gardens and orchards were out of view, at some distance from the house. His desire was for status and spectacle.

But Boyd was in fact a planter and cultivator. Indeed, during the 1760s, as Danson's landscaped gardens took shape, he sold some of his East India Company stock and borrowed extensively to fund the acquisition of new agricultural holdings. But these lands were not next to Danson's lawns, nor even in another part of Kent; they were on the other side of the Atlantic, on the Caribbean island of Grenada. The crop on Boyd's farms was sugar cane—not the oats, barley or wheat typically grown in Britain. Danson was the *capital messuage* (primary holding) of a productive agricultural estate, but one whose farms were located thousands of miles away. Like an international merchant's compting house, Danson, too, was the headquarters of a global enterprise.

Boyd's wife Mary died in 1763, the year in which work began on the construction of Danson House, and he only moved into the mansion in 1768 with his new wife, Catherine. But by the early 1770s, Danson had been completely transformed. Evidently, John Boyd had not been content to use his wealth just to emulate the life of Defoe's traditional landed gentleman. He clearly wanted—and, importantly, had the means—to make another kind of statement, one that used contemporary eighteenth-century design for impact. To an educated audience of the time, Danson's Palladian architecture would have called to mind powerful empires and prosperous international sea trade. While the villa was clearly the residence of a landed gentleman, its design allowed John Boyd to celebrate his colonial merchant roots, too. In the next chapter, I expand on these themes: over 200 miles away from London to the north, we move to magnificent Harewood House in Yorkshire, whose founding family's links to the colonial Caribbean also date to the turn of the eighteenth century.

3

TRADE AND PLUMB CAKE

Even this cake before me, which you so longed for,
is the product of Husbandry and Trade.
Farmer Wilson sowed the Corn, Giles Jenkins reaped it,
Neighbour Jones at the mill ground it, the milk came from Farmer Curtis,
the eggs from John Thomas the Higgler;
that plumb came from Turkey and this from Spain,
the Spices from the East Indies
the sugar we had from Jamaica, the candied sweetmeats from Barbadoes.

John Newbury, 'The History of Mrs Williams Plumb Cake'
The Twelfth Day Gift (1767)

I am at Harewood House on a beautiful afternoon in late spring. Bright sunlight streams through the windows, illuminating pastel-coloured plaster ceilings, white marble overmantels and painted, gilded furniture. Delicately carved white shutters frame the windows, which give views of seemingly endless, emerald-green parkland. It is a breath-taking vision, demonstrating the talents of two of the best-known eighteenth-century British designers: architect and interior designer Robert Adam and landscape gardener Lancelot 'Capability' Brown.[1]

Unlike Danson, Harewood House is still owned by descendants of the family who first built it. Nevertheless, the park and the ground floor of the house are open to the public, as they were for 'polite' visitors, at least, during the eighteenth century. From the stone-paved entrance hall, you walk anti-clockwise through a 'circuit' of public rooms hung with silk damask and filled with family

61

Fig. 3.1: View of Harewood House from across the parkland

portraits, fine oil paintings, antique sculptures and ceramics. One of the most magnificent interiors, and certainly the least changed over the last two centuries, can be found in the music room (see Fig. 3.2). Here, you can see Robert Adam's decorative talents at their best. The design of the ceiling's circular roundels, which display Apollo's muses in flimsy robes, is reflected in the circular patterns on the pink and olive carpet below, while the pale green walls beautifully offset the dark, golden tones of the paintings of classical ruins on the walls.

The twenty-first-century visitor can now also turn clockwise left from the grand entrance hall. Two-hundred years ago, the rooms on this side of the hall would have been private apartments; now, however, they have been converted into a series of exhibition spaces. When I visited at the start of my research twenty years ago, there was a small display entitled '600 years of Royal Sugar Sculpture', which was on loan from the Bowes Museum, in County Durham. Focussing on an obscure, but fascinating, collection of French carved, wooden eighteenth- and nineteenth-century confectioners' moulds, the exhibition showed how finely ground white sugar was mixed with egg whites, or gum, to form a stiff paste, from

Fig. 3.2: The music room at Harewood House

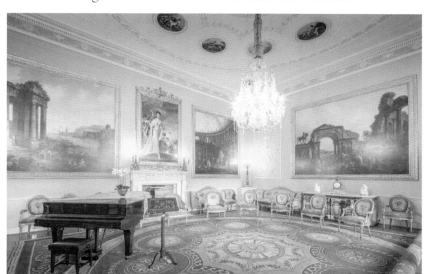

which ornaments were crafted to grace the feast tables of the rich. The creation of these fabulous sugar '*triomfi*' had been a European court tradition stretching back centuries.[2]

The most striking of the exhibits, however, was not part of the Bowes Museum collection. It was housed instead in a small ante-room off the entrance hall. There, on a side table, resplendent in saccharine glory, sat a large, white, iced cake—like a typical British christening or Christmas cake—decorated as a miniature replica of the Robert Adam ceiling in the music room. The link between the architecture and landscape of Harewood House and the culture of sugar in eighteenth-century Britain could not have been better symbolised.

'Trade and Plumb cake forever!'

Of all the colonial Atlantic trading nations of Western Europe— Spain, Portugal, Sweden, Denmark, Holland and France—it was the British who seemed not only to have 'sweet teeth', but who could also afford to buy the imported luxury. Certainly, Britain became the sugar merchants' best customer. In the mid-seventeenth century, sugar had been so rare and expensive that it was only used by the very wealthy; half a century later, however, almost a quarter of Britain's population were regular consumers. Such was the extent of the demand that, by the mid-eighteenth century, sugar was Britain's most valuable import.[3]

Some was used as a sweetener for fashionable hot drinks such as chocolate, coffee and tea.[4] But eighteenth-century cookery books reveal that sugar was already being used, too, for preserving soft summer fruits as jam and as a convenient, if expensive, replacement for honey or carrots in puddings and cakes.[5] Indeed, the number of different types of sugar produced by the refining companies located close to British ports reveals the sheer variety of consumer demand. While strongly flavoured, dark muscavados were preferred for fruitcakes, light brown sugars—eventually known as demeraras—were used for baking sweet buns or sponges. White, close-grained preserving sugar was best for jam, in order not to discolour the fruit, while loaf sugar, cut into small chunks, was designed for table use. But of all the varieties, the finest was the powdery, mechanically crushed confectioner's sugar used to make the sparkling, white icing which ornamented celebratory fruit cakes.

The most famous of these festive confections were Twelfth Day cakes, baked for the feast of the Epiphany on 6 January.[6] The forerunner of today's Christmas cakes, they consisted of a mixture of Mediterranean dried fruit, such as raisins, sultanas (known then as 'plumbs'), citrus peel, dark brown sugar and spices, such as cinnamon, ginger and nutmeg. These expensive imported ingredients were combined with eggs and flour and, sometimes, with French brandy, before baking. After being covered with a layer of 'marchpane'—a mix of ground almonds and sugar now known as marzipan—the rich fruit cake was finally adorned with white icing, then decorated.

With their mixture of homegrown and imported ingredients, the cakes were an edible allegory of eighteenth-century Britain's rapidly expanding, global economic reach. John Newbery, a London publisher, lays out in his popular children's book of 'moral tales', *The Twelfth Day Gift* (1767), how the cake's contents provided a lesson in basic 'oeconomy'. Indeed, the book's frontispiece shows a crowd of children carrying a vast and splendid iced offering through the streets of the City, crying 'Trade and Plumb cake for ever!' (see Fig. 3.3).[7]

Fig. 3.3: Frontispiece of John Newbery's *The Twelfth Day Gift*, 1767

In December and January, these cakes would have formed the centrepiece of the majestic window displays of London's best confectioners, such as Birch and Birch in Cornhill in the City, or The Pineapple in fashionable Berkeley Square to the west. However, unlike homemade, cloth-boiled plum puddings, which shared similar ingredients, the skilled, decorative icing work and the large ovens required meant that Twelfth Day cakes were made only by professionals. Like eighteenth-century writer James Boswell, therefore, the majority of people who passed by these showcase shopfronts could 'partake only by sight'.[8] While many of the 'middling sort' could save up to purchase the expensive imported ingredients for a plum pudding, the glittering white iced cakes were destined for the rich, and, in particular, the families of wealthy London merchants, like the Boyds at Danson and the Lascelles—the patrons of Harewood House.

'Liberty, Britannica, Agriculture and Commerce'

While few records of the building and construction process at Danson House remain, many eighteenth-century building and estate accounts for Harewood were safely deposited in the West Yorkshire Record Office. This rich source of primary evidence, alongside the Lascelles' open acknowledgement of the links between Caribbean slavery and their family's property holdings, means that Harewood House is now one of the best understood examples of West Indian–derived wealth in Britain.[9] And a careful study of the house and grounds also gives us an idea of how such prosperity began to reshape the buildings and, crucially, transform the landscapes of the British Isles more broadly. Before I examine the architecture and design of Harewood, I will first trace the Lascelles' connections with the Caribbean.

Like Augustus Boyd (father of Danson's patron), Henry Lascelles—the founder of the family's fortune and purchaser of the land that would become Harewood—had journeyed to the Caribbean as a young man in the early eighteenth century. Henry, however, came from an already prominent Yorkshire landed family. His grandfather Francis had been a 'republican' Member of Parliament at the time of Oliver Cromwell's 'Western Design'—the Lord Protector's 1655 plan for Britain's expansion in the Spanish Americas. Henry was also not the first member of the extended Lascelles family to make a trans-Atlantic crossing: property records in the Barbados National Archives show an Edward Lascelles purchasing, with two partners, a Barbadian sugar estate as early as 1648, and refer to four other Lascelles brothers from Yorkshire—another Edward, as well as Philip, Robert and William—arriving on the island in 1680.[10] The most successful of these four brothers was Edward, who ran the family business in Bridgetown, Barbados, before going on to manage his family's affairs in the City of London after his return to the UK in 1701. The following year, his daughter Mary became the second wife of another prominent and distantly related Lascelles—Daniel, MP for Northallerton in North Yorkshire.[11]

Henry Lascelles, the Harewood estate's first owner, however, was born to Daniel's first wife, Margaret Metcalfe, who died shortly after Henry's birth in 1690. Like many of his ancestors (and like his elder brother, George, and younger half-brother, another Edward), Henry chose Barbados as the island where he hoped to make his fortune.[12] And he seems to have thrived there, thanks to his close relationship with the Governor, Robert Lowther, a Westmoreland landowner who had also seen the Caribbean as a way to improve his family finances.[13] In 1714, three years after his arrival in the colony and not yet aged twenty-five, Henry Lascelles was appointed to the important post of Collector of Customs in Bridgetown, under Lowther's governorship;[14] one of his first official duties in this position was signing for 5,259 imported 'negro slaves'.[15] In 1729, however, Henry moved back to Britain, following the death of his elder brother, George. By 1738, not only had he taken over the family's West Indian trading business in the City of London, and extended its involvement in slave-shipping and plantation money-lending, but he had also expended £62,000 on the purchase of 3,969 acres of land in the Yorkshire Dales, near to where his family had its roots.[16] This was the estate which would become Harewood.

Yorkshire, at that time, had a prosperous wool trade and, by the mid-eighteenth century, a thriving polite social scene based around the cathedral city of York.[17] However, the life of a provincial landed gentleman held little attraction for Henry, who spent most of his time in London, and rarely, if ever, ventured north. Rather than purchasing the Harewood estate to display status, therefore, Henry seems to have intended his thousands of acres of Yorkshire land to be a safe haven for the profits he had made during his time in the Caribbean. Though returns from eighteenth-century British agriculture were not as high as those from investments in stocks and shares, British financial institutions of the time had a habit of collapsing alarmingly quickly.[18] Grassy hillsides, however, were unlikely to disappear overnight. Growing wheat and raising sheep was also much less risky than sugar planting: there was far less chance of tenant farmers setting fire to the crops, of a French invasion or of a hurricane in the Yorkshire Dales.

It was only when Henry's eldest son, Edwin, inherited the estate after his father's death in 1753 that Harewood began its transformation from an agricultural savings account into a spectacular example of English landscape art. Edwin, who would later become first Baron Harewood, had rather grander architectural ambitions than

Henry. Not content with the existing fifteenth-century manor house, Gawthorpe Hall, which he had inherited along with the estate, Edwin ordered the building to be demolished, and looked, instead, to procure a more fashionable residence.

After early, abortive attempts with young London-based architect, William Chambers, Yorkshire mason-architect John Carr was commissioned to design and build Lascelles' new property. When the external shell of Harewood was finished in the mid-1760s, it looked similar to many other grand country houses started a generation before. There were no complex oval or circular rooms or colonnades, as originally planned by Chambers, just huge, rectangular spaces built around two courtyards. Harewood was later altered, but with its pedimented entrance portico and Venetian windows, it was at the time—like Danson—a British version of Palladio's country houses in the Veneto. Should visitors miss the Palladian allusions to Britain's status as a mercantile superpower, the building's façade was adorned with emblematic medallions representing 'Liberty, Britannia, Agriculture and Commerce', as a printed guide to Harewood from 1819 noted.[19] The extravagantly decorated interiors, however, had a wider range of stylistic influences.[20]

Scots-born architect and designer Robert Adam was the man behind these elaborate interiors. He had presented an architectural plan for the house itself in 1757 but had failed to convince Lascelles of its merits,[21] and, in 1759, had moved on south to London.[22] It was an auspicious time to arrive in the capital. A succession of naval and military victories against the Spanish and French during the Seven Years' War (1756–63) had contributed to growing economic confidence in the country—and a building boom for Britain's elite. One of Adam's first commissions was for the interior of Hatchlands Park in Surrey for Admiral Boscawen, commander of many of these naval battles during the eighteenth century.

Adam also produced interior designs for Spencer House, for a Jamaican heiress (the former wife of the Governor of Jamaica) at Home House, in Portman Square, London, and designs for new country houses for two of the wealthiest and most powerful London-based West India merchants: Richard Oswald, Boyd's lead partner in Bance Island, and Alderman William Beckford, patron of Fonthill Splendens in Wiltshire.[23]

But, in 1763, Adam was again engaged by Lascelles. The designs for Harewood's interiors form part of a large collection of Adam drawings housed in the Sir John Soane's Museum in London. Significantly, the collection comprises drawings from the office of Robert Adam and his elder and younger brothers, John and James, and contains schemes rejected by clients, as well as those actually carried out. The plans show the Adam brothers grappling to find decorative iconographies appropriate to their clients' different international interests.

Adam's decorated plaster ceilings at Hatchlands, for example, contained seahorses and tritons. Nautical motifs, similar to those for Boscawen, were also initially proposed for Harewood, but appear to have been rejected by Lascelles in favour of classical symbols. Nevertheless, a maritime trading theme did run through the interior design of Harewood. One of the large wall paintings in the music room, for example, was of ancient Naples—one of the Roman Empire's prominent seaports—stressing the importance of international trade to the Roman economy and, by inference, to the growing British Empire. Moreover, while the central roundels in the ceiling of the music room depict the classical muses, those in the corners represent Europe, Asia, Africa and, importantly, America—a continent unknown, of course, to ancient Rome.[24]

However, while the decorative motifs and allegorical scenes were derived from the myths of Greece and Rome, the colour schemes were not.[25] The strong reds and vivid blues found on classical remains were rejected in favour of pale greens and pinks. Rather than echoing the buildings of ancient Rome, the glittering white and pastel designs on the walls and ceilings of rooms such as Harewood's main library (see Fig. 3.4) were more akin to the sparkling icing on Twelfth Day cakes. While there is no evidence that Harewood's ceilings were consciously designed to emulate decorated fruitcakes, the resemblance between Adam's interiors and iced confectionary was certainly recognised by his contemporaries.[26] Eighteenth-century novelist and antiquarian (Prime minister Robert Walpole's son) Horace Walpole, for example, used confectioners' terms when he complained that '[Robert] Adam, our favourite, is all gingerbread, filligrane and fanwork'.[27] Meanwhile, Adam's interior designs at Kenwood—the Highgate home of celebrated judge

Fig. 3.4: The main library at Harewood with decorated plaster ceiling

William Murray, first Earl of Mansfield, and his family (including his mixed race great-niece Dido Elizabeth Belle)[28]—earned it the nickname the 'sweet box',[29] with one writer remarking: 'It is quite Twelfth Day style covered all over in panels of fillagree.'[30]

Mahogany and the Caribbean

The subtle allusions to sugar icing are far from the only reference to West Indian wealth in Harewood's interiors. The internal doors— like those at Danson—are made from Caribbean mahogany, likely to have been obtained through its owner's trading connections.[31] As with much of the land in the West Indies, the British sugar colonies had once been covered in tropical rainforests, which had to be cleared to create open land to grow cash crops. Undertaking this task with only seventeenth- and eighteenth-century hand tools would have been an arduous process. One writer of the time explained the difficulties of felling the 'huge and massive trunks, [that] mock the slower growth and softer woods of Europe'.[32] In an evocative phrase, he describes these tropical trees as 'denominated by iron', detailing how the axe of the 'baffled workman … recoiled from his stroke, as if it had met another tool or struck against the material which composed it'.[33]

Nevertheless, the forests produced valuable additional exports for investors in the Caribbean sugar colonies. In 1768, for example, records show that 443,920 feet of mahogany were exported from Jamaica to Britain, together with large quantities of ebony and lignum vitae.[34] For West India merchants, these tropical hardwoods would also have been a useful cargo in the holds of sugar-laden 'West Indiamen', as they could safely be stored below the waterline without risk of damage; if salt water seeped into a sugar barrel, on the other hand, it would ruin the quality of this luxury export.

Some of these tropical timbers were valued primarily for industrial use: lignum vitae, for example, was used in the dyeing industry and in the manufacture of ship's pulleys, where its natural hardness was of great advantage. But the fine, even grain of the timbers—which were not subject to the seasonal growth cycles and uneven lignin deposits of northern hemisphere species—also made them ideal for decorative joinery. Like British oak, timber from the vast mahogany tree could be polished to an attractive, deep shine, while the dense, black heartwood from the centre of an ebony trunk would find use in inlaid marquetry work.

By the mid-eighteenth century, these timbers were often used conspicuously in interiors—the stair balustrades in the expensive new townhouses in the squares west of the City of London are one example—but were so sparingly. Although the rich russet of the balustrade would have made a striking visual statement, the small sections of wood needed to craft an elegant, sinuous rail would have been relatively cheap to acquire in comparison with the large amounts needed to panel a room or construct doors. Contemporary comments on the many 'handsome and massy mahogany doors' at Harewood,[35] therefore, suggest that the sheer amount of timber was an intended, and successful, projection of the family's wealth.[36]

The mahogany dining chairs, and the elaborately inlaid, mahogany marquetry sideboards designed by renowned cabinet-maker Thomas Chippendale would not have gone unnoticed by visitors to Harewood either. In fact, by the mid-eighteenth century, the ownership of mahogany furniture, rather than the more traditional oak, was regarded as one of the hallmarks of gentility.[37] And in a further display of wealth and artistic taste, much of Chippendale's specially commissioned furniture at Harewood, such as the painted chairs in the entrance hall, was designed to co-ordinate with Adam's neo-classical interiors.

The Pinery at Harewood

At Harewood, one of most striking testaments to the Lascelles' Caribbean connections would have been the 'pinery', a vast, heated greenhouse used for growing pineapples, which was located within the walled kitchen gardens. Like the turtle (see Chapter Two), the pineapple occupies an interesting place in the history of West Indian absentees. In eighteenth-century Britain, the fruit was an icon of prosperity which—like intricately fashioned mahogany furniture or the icing on a Twelfth Day cake—clearly alluded to the wealth produced in Britain's West Indian colonies.[38] Unlike sugar cane, which originally had to be transplanted to the West Indies, pineapples were actually native to the pre-colonial Caribbean: in fact, they feature on the seal of Jamaica granted by royal warrant in 1661 following Britain's original capture of the island from the Spanish.[39]

Pineapples were a popular dessert among sugar planters in the Caribbean[40] and, as families became absentees, the spiky-leafed fruits became increasingly sought-after in Britain. However, unlike trunks of mahogany, or even live turtles, pineapples did not travel well in a ship's hold. While the plants themselves were remarkably tough, the chances were that the fruit—which, unlike a banana, does not ripen after picking—would either still be hard, or else fermented and rotten, after a seven-week journey from the West Indies. The difficulty of importing ripe pineapples is hinted at by a recipe in *The Country Housewife and Lady's Director* (1732) for a 'Pineapple Tart' with fruit 'from Barbadoes': instructing the cook to stew the fruit's flesh in sugar and Madeira wine before puréeing and baking, the recipe was clearly designed to transform the unripe produce into an edible, tropical pudding.[41]

The problems associated with transporting pineapples to Britain led to experiments in growing the tropical fruit within the country itself. One of the first people to do so successfully was Matthew

Decker, a Dutch-born City merchant. By the mid-eighteenth century, a pinery was a fashionable accessory for a wealthy landowner. However, raising the fruit in a northern climate was not cheap. The construction of a 'pineapple stove' (one of the names at the time for a heated greenhouse, along with 'stovehouse' or 'hot house') needed copious amounts of glass—an expensive, highly taxed building material—and had to be stocked with plants shipped from the West Indies. Added to this was not only the expense of fuel to heat the greenhouse, but also the constant supervision needed to maintain the hot and humid conditions over the three years the plant took to grow to maturity (see Fig. 3.5). The cost of raising a single pineapple in mid-eighteenth-century Britain has been estimated to be nearly £80, twice the annual wage of a soldier or the price, then,

Fig. 3.5: *Mr Loudon's Improved Pinery*, engraving showing a system for growing pineapples in hothouses, 1810

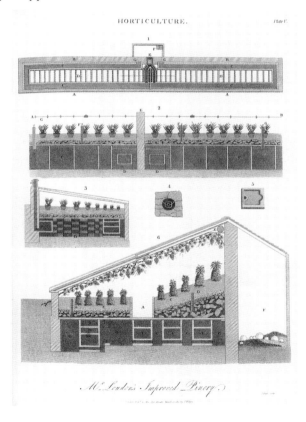

of a new coach.[42] Presenting a pineapple at a dinner—or, as the London-based West India merchant and Ayrshire estate owner Richard Oswald sometimes did, as a gift[43]—would, therefore, have been an extraordinary status symbol.

Sadly, I have been unable to track down any surviving images of the pinery at Harewood, in painting or print, but contemporary accounts give a sense of the majestic character of the building. According to the author of an early-nineteenth-century guide to the house and its grounds, 'at a hundred feet long, thirty feet wide and fifteen feet high',[44] it was for many years the largest heated greenhouse in the country. 'Pineapples had been cut in this house of nearly twelve pounds in weight', one visitor to Harewood enthused, 'and in this hot-house are two very fine granadillas [a close relative of the passionfruit], which seem perfectly at home, and enjoy as much health and vigour as if they were in the island of Jamaica'.[45]

During the eighteenth and nineteenth centuries, a heated greenhouse was, however, not simply a means of producing tropical fruits or blooms to adorn a dining room. Nor was tropical botany just a hobby for a gentleman of leisure: stovehouses such as Lascelles's in Yorkshire and Richard Oswald's in Scotland were also nurseries for new varieties of sugar cane, essential to the profitable development of British plantation colonies. In Chapter Six, we encounter one of the most striking statements of such intent: the huge stone pineapple folly dining room set amid the heated greenhouses at Dunmore Park in Stirling, near Edinburgh.

Harewood's vast, but high maintenance, pineries have long since been demolished. However, the Capability Brown-designed parkland, which is now such a signature of the 'English style' of landscaping, remains, albeit altered from the original design. As we have seen already at Danson, the proceeds of sugar and slavery funded the construction of a huge landscape garden; at Harewood, though, the scale was far grander.

Polite landscapes

Like Boyd's villa at Danson, Edwin Lascelles's new mansion was not built on the site of the original manor house, but near the top of an escarpment overlooking the newly constructed lake. It was one of most prominent spots in the whole of the Harewood estate, and

Brown's landscaping provided it with a dramatic backdrop. Today, the main entrance to Harewood Park is through a triumphal arch from the rebuilt Harewood village. Most contemporary visitors, therefore, miss Brown's original, sweeping approach to the house. However, part of the former drive is a now a publicly accessible footpath, so it is possible to recreate the experience of an eighteenth-century visitor; even walking along this track, rather than driving up it in a coach and horses, is an exhilarating experience. It is rural landscape as pure theatre. There are no tractor sheds, intensive poultry farms, grain silos, nor even ploughed fields in view. All you can see are glimpses of Harewood House and the serpentine lake through the belts of tree plantations and acres of parkland dotted with sheep.

The pragmatic investments into land made by Henry Lascelles were transformed by the designs of Brown into glamorous landscape art. And it is striking how well this 'natural style' adapted to two very different types of British land holdings. Lascelles owned tens of thousands of acres in the uplands of West Yorkshire, whereas Boyd's Kentish estate of Danson was far smaller and in a more densely populated part of England. But the luxurious feeling of calm and space given by the huge undulating lawns is common to both.

In his book *Polite Landscapes*, Tom Williamson argues that the aesthetic origin of the eighteenth-century British landscape park derives from medieval deer parks. These parks—set at some distance from the main house—would have been surrounded by high fences called pales and kept as reserves for the production of venison and timber. Parkland landscapes, like those at Harewood and Danson, though sharing a similar aesthetic of open grassland and belts of trees, were, however, very different. Although eighteenth-century landscaped parks were also used for grazing animals and sometimes raising game birds, fundamentally they were designed to be ornamental. Indeed, as Williamson argues, from the 1760s to the end of that century, 'the possession of land—and the candid, wasteful display of that possession—became an increasingly important marker of status.'[46]

Historically, British landowners had derived much of their income from agricultural rents and the sale of estate produce. A landed family's wealth, therefore, had a direct correlation with the amount of land they owned and farmed. So the transformation of

Fig. 3.6: *Harewood House, Yorkshire, The Seat of the Earl of Harewood*, engraving, 1829

HAREWOOD HOUSE,
YORKSHIRE
The Seat of the Earl of Harewood

tens, or even hundreds, of acres of potential pasture and arable land into lawns or low-intensity grazing was a conspicuous demonstration that the landowner did not have to maximise his agricultural profits. In Williamson's view, this expressed the challenge issued by those who had made their fortunes in 'administration, trade and the law' to the landed wealth of 'traditional feudal families'.[47] By the late eighteenth century, however, the acres of rolling grass would have conveyed another message, too: the family owned—or aspired to own—productive land and wealth elsewhere, likely offering much higher returns.

In the 1750s, as he began his building and landscape projects at Harewood, Edwin Lascelles's vast Yorkshire estate was bringing him an income of just over £2,000 per annum.[48] Though a considerable sum, placing him among England's wealthiest landowners,[49] this was dwarfed by the potential income from a Caribbean sugar plantation.

The Harewood archives show that, in the latter half of the eighteenth century, Lascelles was buying more estates in Barbados and Jamaica. The surviving Caribbean accounts date only from 1805 onwards,[50] however, making a like-for-like comparison with the mid-eighteenth-century income from Harewood difficult. But they do show that, in the years before the abolition of slavery in 1833, the family's Caribbean holdings were making profits of between £9,150 (1805) and £19,459 (1818) per annum.[51] Despite the inflation that would have occurred between the 1750s and 1818, the difference from the Yorkshire estate is nonetheless considerable.

In the case of Danson, however, a more direct comparison is available. A candid letter that John Boyd's son (also called John) wrote to a friend in 1780, after the Danson estate had been increased in size to around 500 acres, sets out in detail the state of family finances:

> I will begin with acquainting you exactly what F's [father's] fortune consists of; First his place in the country, which you have been at; the estate round it is but trifling, about £500 per an .... His estate in St Kitts, very modestly stated at £8000 per an; clear of all charges & deductions ...[52]

John Boyd junior's estimates come a generation after those from Harewood, at a time of high wartime sugar prices. Nevertheless, in investment terms, a Caribbean estate clearly promised far greater returns than British land. Indeed, as we saw in Chapter Two, when building work at Danson temporarily ceased in 1763, Boyd borrowed heavily to purchase a second estate in the former French Caribbean island of Grenada. By 1780, his son noted that, although Boyd still owed £20,000, this new estate was producing 'between £3,000 and £4,000 per an & easily improvable to one half above its present value'.[53] As John junior reflected:

> The expense of a West India Estate is certainly great, but when it is once completely stock'd with slaves, cattle & buildings which is the case with F's, the Rum sold in the Island is enough to defray the charges of keeping it so.[54]

It was not only West Indian absentees, like the Lascelles and Boyds, who were lured by these high returns at the turn of the eighteenth century and who then ploughed their profits back into British landscape parks. The capture of the French sugar colony of Grenada during the Seven Years' War (1756–63) was the catalyst for a new generation of British investors to purchase Caribbean plantations. In the late 1760s, for example, George Amyand—a City merchant, banker and director of the East India Company, owner of Carshalton House in Surrey and of other modest Berkshire landholdings—bought the 254-acre La Taste estate in Grenada. A few years later in 1771, his eldest son George married the heiress of a notable landowning family in the Welsh borders, forging a link between an established 3,875-acre British estate and the sugar plantation he inherited from his father. Accounts from the plantation show that during the 1770s, La Taste was providing nearly as much income as the whole of the British estate, which was more than fifteen times larger. The Grenadan plantation continued to bring in yields of over five times more per acre than the by-then-improved British landholdings up until the 1790s.[55]

It is unlikely that all the 4,000 plus new landscape parks designed and created in Britain in the latter half of the eighteenth century were funded from colonial plantation profits. But it is notable that two of Brown's earliest patrons were George Coventry, sixth Earl of Coventry, at Croome Court, Worcestershire, and Francis Lord Brooke, later the Earl of Warwick, who were both heirs to substantial Caribbean investments made by their forefathers in the previous century. By the mid-1760s, after Britain's victory in the Seven Years' War, Brown's landscape business and those of his protégés had become immensely successful, indeed.[56]

As we have seen, the 'natural style' of landscaping appealed to wealthy eighteenth-century clients for a variety of reasons. Aesthetically, the sinuous curves of the lawns, plantations and 'sheets' of water provided an elegant backdrop to showcase their recently built examples of neo-classical architecture. Moreover, it was a style that adapted well to varying terrains, and the techniques used to compose the landscapes meant that it was difficult to tell whether the estate's owner possessed 200 acres or 20,000. The fashion for such ostentatious uses of precious land, however, was not universally popular. One of the earliest and most influential critics of the elite's craving for parkland landscapes was Oliver

Goldsmith. His poem *The Deserted Village* (1770) took a sombre view of the impact such parks were having on Britain's rural economy. He writes:

> The man of wealth and pride
> Takes up a space that many poor supplied;
> Space for his lake, his park's extended bounds
> Space for his horses, equipage and hounds.[57]

Goldsmith's lines have frequently been quoted in histories of British landscape as a critique of agricultural enclosures.[58] However, it is clear these were not his only, or even main, concern. 'Around the world each needful product flies. // For all the luxuries the world supplies,' he notes in the same poem, thereby linking the consumption of imported luxuries like sugar directly to the changes wrought on the British landscape. It is 'trade's unfeeling train', Goldsmith concludes, that 'usurp[s] the land, and dispossess[es] the swain', as small-scale farmers leave the land and villagers emigrate 'beyond the western main.' He continues on to say that 'Along the lawn, where scatter'd hamlets rose, // Unwieldy wealth and cumbrous pomp repose,' before denouncing: 'Ye friends to truth, ye statesmen who survey // The rich man's joys increase, the poor's decay'.[59]

Goldsmith's poem clearly captured the imagination of the British public, running to five editions in the four months after it was published. His criticisms were also echoed by others, including Henry Mackenzie in his novel *The Man of Feeling* (1771) and John Langhorne in his poem *The Country Justice* (1774).[60] And it was not just the impact of parkland on the British rural poor which caused consternation among many contemporary commentators. Indeed, so close seem to have been the associations between colonial exploitation and the swathes of new parkland that one critic argued it was impossible to contemplate 'natural' landscapes, without 'guilty thoughts' of the plunder of 'Hindoos' or the slavery of 'Negroes'.[61] Jane Austen also refers to the links between these parks and wealth from the colonies in her novel *Mansfield Park* (completed in 1800, but published in 1817), describing how absentee sugar planter Sir Thomas Bertram engages a landscape gardener to improve his English estate. By the latter part of the eighteenth century, the rolling lawns of Danson and Harewood were clearly giving off mixed messages. While to some they were the epitome of good taste, for others they were monuments to ill-gotten fortunes and symbols of rural dispossession.

Although hundreds of miles apart, both the Danson and Harewood estates were closely tied to the elite merchant community in the City of London, the country's largest West India port. However, outside of the capital, western ports such as Bristol, Liverpool, Lancaster, Whitehaven and Glasgow were also becoming important centres for the West India trade. In the next chapter, we therefore move from London towards the Atlantic West and visit the most fashionable destination for polite society in Georgian times: the elegant city of Bath.

4

REFINING THE WORLD

Let Bristol for commerce and dirt be renowned;
At Salisbury, penknives and Scissors be ground,
The towns of Devizes, of Bradford and Frome,
May boast that they can manage better the loom
I believe that they may, but the world to refine
In manners, in dress, in politeness to shine
Oh Bath, let the glory be thine!

Christopher Anstey, *The New Bath Guide* (1766)

In 1987, the entire centre of the small West Country city of Bath was designated a World Heritage Site. The reason for this global accolade was, according to UNESCO, because Bath demonstrated 'a unique combination of outstanding urban architecture, spatial arrangement and social history',[1] which 'harmoniously' connected neo-classical streets and terraces to Roman remains and the surrounding hills. Walking through Bath, the golden limestone façades of the terraced houses that make up most of the urban fabric have a magical quality. It is like stumbling into a glorious Renaissance stage set: a theatrical homage to the work of Palladio and the ancient Roman buildings which inspired his designs.

Like the towns of Tunbridge Wells, Buxton and Harrogate, eighteenth-century Bath was a spa and health resort with an economy almost entirely devoted to the leisure activities of a genteel elite.[2] But, unlike Bath, whose ancient history was lauded even in the 1700s, no-one celebrated the Roman origins of Tunbridge Wells's spa. Nor could Harrogate or Buxton boast of a charitable hospital hung with works by Britain's most fashionable artists, like Bath's Royal Infirmary.[3] Bath, moreover, was the only spa where the shops were 'richer and more extravagant in their show' than those in London, as renowned eighteenth-century potter and entrepreneur Josiah Wedgwood aptly put it.[4] In scale and status, this 'provincial metropolis of fashion, taste and elegance'[5] was unique.

In an apposite allusion, the anonymous author of the allegorical poem *Bath: A Simile* (1789) suggests that the city centre and 'its environs' should be regarded as a huge tea set, or 'Tea Equipage'. This 'Equipage', as the poem describes, is laid out on a naturalistically decorated tray or 'board', alluding to the hilly landscapes in which Bath is located. The city's golden limestone houses are described as 'all of yellow ware', a reference to Josiah Wedgwood's fashionable creamware ceramics. The 'well pav'd' blue lias limestone setts (small paving stones) of Queen's Square are a 'fancy dish' of sweetened bread rolls. The elegant King's Circus—a circular development of terraced houses—is a 'handsome Wedgwood plate'.[6] The 'stone clad' sides and the 'thick yellow stream' of the canalised River Avon are compared to a 'pot of cream',[7] while the quarries in the hills surrounding the town were the sugar bowl. As the poet explains:

> That quarry curiously scoop'd-out,
> Lumps of all size in view,
> Must be the sugar-dish, no doubt,
> And full of sugar too.
>
> From time to time the dish to fill,
> Least empty it should stand;
> Behold in every neighb'ring hill,
> A sugar loaf at hand.[8]

The owner of these quarries, the influential Cornish-born Ralph Allen, made a fortune supplying the distinctive honey-coloured stone used to develop the Georgian spa resort.[9] And the connection made in the poem between Allen's 'lumps' of quarried stone and the consumption of West Indian sugar would certainly not have been lost on Bath's increasingly numerous visitors. For Bath's eighteenth-century development as Britain's pre-eminent urban playground was not just because of its hot springs and Roman remains, but also its proximity to the rapidly expanding port of Bristol. The teatime ritual chosen by the author of *Bath: A Simile* was not just a metaphor for the town's architecture and urban design: the description of English cream, bread and butter, Chinese tea and Caribbean sugar, all displayed on fashionable English ceramics, was a fitting symbol of the wealth produced by British agriculture and manufacturing, as well as of Bristol's growing part in the trans-Atlantic trading economy.

Bristol's historic connections with seventeenth- and eighteenth-century colonial plantations are well documented. Richard Pares's pioneering economic history of the Bristol- and Nevis-based Pinney family, *A West India Fortune*, for example, was published more than half a century ago.[10] Madge Dresser's *Slavery Obscured* (2001)[11] showed how historical locations—from cliffside caves and small-scale sugar refineries, to the neo-classical architecture of Bristol's Queen's Square and the terraces of Clifton (including the elegant house of Caribbean absentee, John Pinney, on George Street, now a museum)—were closely connected to the port's West India trade.[12] More recently, the database of UCL's 'Legacies of British

Fig. 4.1: A view of Bath from Ralph Allen's seat at Prior Park, overlooking the city

Slave-ownership' project has shown how crucial the investment by West India merchants was to the development of other infrastructure in and around Bristol. Bath's intimate links with slavery, however, have so far not been as widely publicised.[13] The classic Pevsner guide to the city's architecture, for example, does not mention the West Indies at all.[14]

But these connections with the Caribbean were instrumental in the city's rise to prominence as a cultural capital. While it was Bristol's sugar works that processed the barrels of raw, dark brown muscovado shipped from the West Indian colonies, Bath, too, refined the products of Britain's Atlantic empire. This chapter will explore Bath's financial, political and cultural connections with the American colonies and, in particular, with the wealthy Caribbean sugar islands. But first, we must turn to Bristol, to investigate the growth of this western port during the eighteenth century and to examine the relationship between the two cities. Bath and Bristol, after all, have always been tied together.

'Avon gliding down the vale'

While Bristol may have been eclipsed as an Atlantic port by cities in north-west England and western Scotland by the late eighteenth century, for much of the 1700s, it was the Severn, rather than the Mersey or the Clyde, that was Britain's second maritime trading gateway, after the Thames. When the anonymous author of *Britannia: A Poem* wrote his patriotic celebration of Britain's imperial ambitions in 1767, his references to these two important rivers still (but only just) reflected reality:

> Commercial Chain! May Thames and Severn hence
> New Kindred gain'd their mutual Aids dispense;
> From Sea to Sea the watry Ways be seen
> And Fleets emit their plenteous Freights between.[15]

Bristol's location near the mouth of the Severn made it well-placed to supply goods for Britain's expanding colonies in the Americas. While voyages to southern ports along the English Channel were, in wartime, vulnerable to naval attacks from rival imperial powers on the continent, Bristol was sheltered by the counties of Devon and Cornwall, which formed a natural barrier reaching well into the Atlantic against enemy fleets. The Severn stretched north from Bristol, via Gloucester, Tewksbury, Worcester and the Shropshire ironworking towns, all the way to Shrewsbury, allowing agricultural produce, timber, ceramics and ironware to be brought downstream for export. Indeed, until the late eighteenth century, the Severn-side counties of Somerset and Gloucestershire were, outside London, two of the most densely populated and highly industrialised areas of England.

Although the economic and logistical benefits of this river contributed to the success of Bristol and its growing Atlantic trade, neither the eighteenth-century city, nor the docks, were actually built on the Severn estuary. Instead, they lay several miles inland, away from the river's huge tidal reach and shifting sands, on the banks of the River Avon. Beyond Bristol, the Avon meanders roughly south-east to the former Somerset textile towns of Bradford-on-Avon and Trowbridge, then passes in a wide loop around Bath. So Bath, too, was joined to the Severn and then to Atlantic by this watery umbilical cord.

If you travel by rail, the close physical connection between Bath and Bristol is laid bare. The railway track follows the route of the section of the 'stone clad' River Avon that was canalised in the early 1720s. Unlike later canal projects, the waterway between Bristol and Bath used the Avon's existing winding course, with weirs and locks built to make this stretch of the river navigable. Today's train passengers, therefore, have a surprisingly pastoral view of the tree-lined river, which meanders through lush water meadows. It is easy to understand the romantic view of the Avon taken by one Bath resident, naval Captain turned diarist Philip Thicknesse, whose writings evoke the dual natural–commercial character of the river at that time:

I look down from my study on a mile and a half of the gentle Avon gliding down the vale; and now and then seeing the swelling bosoms of deep laden barks freighted with merchandise; which I consider as returning messengers, whom I have sent forth to fetch me Tea from Asia, Sugar from America, Wine from France and Fruit from Portugal.[16]

Of course, the river had not been canalised in order to ferry imported luxuries such as tea and sugar from Bristol's quayside to Bath's spa visitors and wealthy inhabitants like Thicknesse, but, more prosaically, to transport woollen cloth and blocks of limestone from Bath's quarries in the other direction, to the rapidly expanding Atlantic port. Indeed, while earlier examples of classical architecture in Bristol, such as Queen's Square, are constructed in brick, later developments—like John Pinney's house on George Street, built after the canalisation of the Avon—tend to be faced in honey-coloured Bath stone.

Nevertheless, investors saw the potential offered by improvements to the Avon's navigation for the development of Bath itself. Wealthy visitors had long been attracted to the town, for both its healing springs and its amusements: as early as 1714, for example, the poet Alexander Pope described how his 'whole day is shar'd by the Pump-Assemblies, the Walkes, the Chocolate houses, Raffling Shops, Plays and medleys'.[17] However, in the first decades of the eighteenth century, Bath was little more than a cluster of gable-roofed, mullion-windowed houses, huddled around the restored fifteenth-century abbey. It was only in 1727, the year after canalisation works on the Avon were completed, that entrepreneurial Herefordshire estate owner, James Brydges, and his designer, John Wood, began drawing up plans for Bath's transformation into a sophisticated resort. And it was then that the link between Bath and the American colonies began.

In his magisterial work *Bath, 1680–1550: A Social History or A Valley of Pleasure, yet a Sink of Iniquity* (1981), historian Ronald Neale describes how Brydges (the Duke of Chandos and Earl of Caernarvon, as he had become by then) had visited Bath in the spring of 1726. Brydges, seeking a cure for 'twitching of the nerves', was accompanied by his wife, who needed help with her 'hysteric fits'. Their visit was not successful, though, as they found their lodgings near the Cross Bath uncongenially 'old' and 'rotten', and unsuitable for a 'person of fashion'.[18] It is likely that their visit to Bath and the West Country, however, was not solely for medical purposes. Brydges had made a fortune from his position as Paymaster General during the War of the Spanish Succession (1701–14). The war, which came to an end with the Treaty of

Utrecht, saw Spain cede Gibraltar and Menorca to Britain, while France was forced to surrender its Canadian territories in Hudson Bay, Newfoundland and Nova Scotia and, in the Caribbean, the island of St Kitts. Crucially, the Treaty also awarded Britain the 'Asiento de Negros', giving it the right to supply the Spanish colonies in the Americas with enslaved Africans, which, over the previous two centuries, had been granted by the Spanish crown to various Atlantic merchants.[19]

With the end of the war in 1714, Brydges, the son of the former British ambassador to Constantinople, looked to invest his newly acquired wealth. He had correctly anticipated that the greatest growth potential was in trade with Britain's new colonies in the New World, Africa and Asia, rather than with traditional trading partners in Europe and the Levant. He therefore bought large holdings in India Stock, South Sea Stock and Africa Bonds,[20] land in Barbados and Jamaica, and several businesses in the West Country, near Bridgewater.[21]

Soon after his initial visit to Bath in 1726, Brydges began acquiring land and leases on buildings there, too. And he was not alone in seeing the potential of the spa's location—a morning's ride from Bristol—and noting how the newly canalised Avon would improve the transportation of consumer goods from the port. Indeed, the majority of the funds invested in Bath's buildings came not from local businesspeople, but through a complex international credit network centred on London.[22] While the supposed healing qualities of Bath's spring waters provided a useful reason to spend time in the resort, it was not difficult for potential investors to ride to Bristol's quays to speak first-hand with merchants about business opportunities in the American colonies. It was fortuitous, therefore, that Bristol's own spa, Hotwells, located at the base of the Clifton Gorge, not only had warm-water springs—useful for 'disorders', where 'Bath waters' were 'improper' or 'hurtful'[23]—but also provided a view of every ship sailing into Bristol's harbour.[24]

Mingling 'with the princes and nobles of the land'

While Bath's medical and spa facilities were one of the reasons absentee West Indians spent time in the city, the city's reputation as a centre of medicine also attracted other professionals from the Caribbean. Many doctors, particularly those trained in Scotland and who had gained experience in the West Indies in the army, navy or on plantations (and who had often, through marriage, gained a stake in the sugar business themselves), practised in Bath.[25] Author, poet and playwright Dr Tobias Smollett, for example, who had worked in Jamaica as a surgeon's assistant after studying medicine at Glasgow University, lived in Bath for a number of years. His 1752 medical paper, *An Essay on the External Use of Water … with Particular Remarks on the Present Method of Using the Mineral Waters at Bath in Somersetshire*, specifically investigated the supposed health-promoting properties of Bath's spa waters.[26]

 Smollett, however, is now better remembered as one of eighteenth-century Britain's first novelists. And his marriage to a Jamaican heiress with a 'comfortable tho' moderate estate' would have helped him secure the financial means to pursue this literary vocation.[27] His description of 1760s Bath in *The Expedition of Humphrey Clinker* is, therefore, not a little disingenuous. He writes:

> Every upstart of fortune, harnessed in the trappings of the mode, presents himself at Bath. Clerks and factors from the East Indies, loaded with the spoil of plundered provinces; planters, negro-drivers, and hucksters, from our American plantations enriched they know not how; agents, commissaries and contractors, who have fattened, in two successive wars on the blood of the nation … all of them hurry to Bath, because here, without any further qualification they can mingle with the princes and nobles of the land.[28]

Historically, the landed elite in Britain, as elsewhere, had used artfully engineered marriages to cement dynastic wealth and power. Indeed, the balls, assemblies and other polite social events that proliferated in provincial Georgian England were primarily stalls in the marriage market. However, if a young woman's—or her family's—ambitions were for a handsome match, then braving a season in Bath was a clever strategy.[29] The magnificent ballroom at Bath's Assembly Rooms, the largest of several in the city, which was built between 1769 and 1771 to designs by John Wood the younger (an earlier design by Robert Adam was rejected as too expensive), was the centre of this 'exchange'.

Perhaps due to its proximity to Bristol's Atlantic port, it appears that the marriage market in eighteenth-century Bath was somewhat more diverse than prospects elsewhere in Britain. In Smollett's novel, the protagonist Matt Bramble, a Welsh border landowner, describes how a ball was opened by a 'Scotch Lord, with a mulatto [mixed race] heiress from St Christopher's and the gay Colonel Tinsel danced all the evening with the daughter of an eminent tin-man from the borough of Southwark'.[30] And in Christopher Anstey's poem *The New Bath Guide*,[31] a landed young man is captivated by the beautiful 'Miss Towzer Simkin' whom he had seen at ball: ''T'is she that has long been the toast of the town,' he eulogises, 'Though all the world knows her complexion is brown'.[32]

A lack of systematic recording makes it difficult to know the extent of inter-racial marriage in eighteenth-century Britain. But it seems that it was not unknown among elite families, particularly those living in the Atlantic West. As Daniel Livesay notes in his book *Children of Uncertain Fortune*, however, the relatively fluid attitudes to race and kinship in the early to mid-eighteenth century did not last long and, by the early years of the nineteenth, these attitudes had hardened and racial discrimination had become more entrenched.[33]

Whether or not Bath's links with Bristol's Atlantic trade made the city more liberal on questions of race than other areas of Britain, the city's proximity to Bristol certainly made the resort the ideal place for a Caribbean absentee to be introduced into English society. The diary of St Kitts planter John Baker, for example, shows how members of his family spent their frequent visits to the city playing cards and dancing, or catching up with gossip from the Caribbean at the Parade CoHo (coffee house).[34] Similarly, the diary of Mary Young—daughter of absentee plantation owner Sir William Young—reveals that, when her father, step-sisters and elder brother had departed for the West Indies on business, she and her mother would also regularly visit the resort. We return to William Young and his significance in the Caribbean in Chapters Seven and Eight.

In painter Thomas Malton's 1775 watercolour *The South Parade, Bath* (see Fig. 4.2), too, one of the elegantly dressed women is carrying a parasol—a small, ornamental version of the sunshades popular in the British Caribbean.

Like his other paintings of Bath—including *The New Assembly Rooms* (1779), *The Circus, Bath* and *Queens Square* (1784)—Thomas Malton's *South Parade* portrays well-dressed couples and families strolling through uncrowded streets and squares. And in contrast with anarchic, sprawling mid-eighteenth-century London, where elegant urban developments were interspersed with the squalor of overcrowded housing and manufacturing industries, Bath was a compact, easily walkable, well-mannered urban centre. Indeed, eighteenth-century Bath can be seen as a model of what Scottish philosopher David Hume (1711–76) envisioned as a contemporary civilised city in his essay *Idea of a perfect Commonwealth*. It is easy to imagine visitors to Bath displaying 'their wit and breeding, their taste in conversation or living',[35] as Hume put it, in the Parade CoHo or the Assembly Rooms. And The Circus—in Malton's painting in which a pair of young women are pictured eyeing two gentlemen dismounting from their horses—would also meet Hume's criterion of providing an environment where both sexes could 'meet in an easy and sociable manner; and the tempers of men, as well as their behaviour, refine apace'.[36]

Fig. 4.2: *The South Parade, Bath*, Thomas Malton, 1775

However, Malton's 1769 painting *The Completion of the Royal Crescent, Bath* (see Fig. 4.3) gives perhaps gives a more realistic impression of the eighteenth-century resort. Despite its apparent visual cohesion, Bath was not built with a planned, unified layout. It is a collage of separate, largely unconnected and often incomplete speculative developments, shaped by accidents of land purchase and constraints of topography, and frequently curtailed by over-ambition and bankruptcy. Along the street and around the corner from formal urban spaces lay scaffolded construction sites.

Pulteney, Brydges and Bayly

As Ronald Neale points out in his illuminating book *Bath: A Social History*, the city's development fell into four main phases, each of which is connected with periods of economic confidence following British colonial gains.[37] The first phase of expansion, between 1726 and 1736, following the canalisation of the Avon, occurred at a time when Bristol was rapidly expanding both as a West India and Africa port.

Fig. 4.3: *The Completion of the Royal Crescent, Bath*, Thomas Malton, c. 1769

In Bath, this era was marked by the collaboration of local architect John Wood with James Brydges, and his striking designs to extend Bath's walled medieval centre, drawing on the planning precedents of a classical Roman town. Wood's 'grand place of Assembly'—Queen's Square—dates from this period. It is a formal, paved quadrilateral, surrounded by terraced houses, the façades of which, when taken together, were designed to look like a Palladian palace. The eruption of hostilities with Spain in the Caribbean from 1739 to 1748 (a conflict known as the War of Jenkins' Ear),[38] however, halted speculative development, and Wood left the city for Bristol, where he designed the Merchants' Exchange on Corn Street.[39]

Five years after the war's end, the second wave of investment into Bath came, from 1753 to 1757, when Britain was competing with other European powers to consolidate and expand its colonial territories—a conflict which eventually culminated in the Seven Years' War (1756–63). It is this period that saw the construction of The Circus, a circular development of terraced houses set around a paved public space. Building work slowed again during the war years, only to resume with vigour at its end.

It is this third period, from 1763 to the start of the American War of Independence in 1776, that saw the construction of the Royal Crescent by Wood's son, also called John. It was also the time when wealth derived from slavery began to be invested into the city. In 1771, at a point when The Crescent was still far from complete, John Wood junior found himself heavily in debt as a result of his development works on the Grand Parade, Pierrepoint Street and Queen's Parade—located to the south of Bath's abbey, along the meadows near the Avon, just outside the old town walls. He was only saved by a loan from Harford Lloyd and John Marchant, two Bristol-based financiers of slave-trading voyages and partners in Bristol Old Bank.[40]

Wood junior was not the only developer during this period to be underwritten by funds derived from African and West Indian trade. Colonial collateral was instrumental in the construction of one of Bath's most renowned monuments, Pulteney Bridge (see Fig. 4.4), which was built between 1769 and 1774 to designs by Robert Adam. Other than James Brydges, the Pulteney family—who were to become the Earls of Bath—were one of the biggest investors in the town's development. Many of the family's papers survive, a few in the Bodleian Library in Oxford, and a far larger number in the Huntington Library in California. They show how in the eighteenth century, like Brydges, William Pulteney also saw the gains to be made from the improvements to the Avon's navigation and from Bath's proximity to an expanding Bristol.

Fig. 4.4: Pulteney Bridge, Bath

In 1727, the year the canalisation works were completed, Pulteney bought a 600-acre manor and agricultural estate at Bathwick, just across the Avon from Bath's Grand Pump Room complex adjacent to the Roman Baths. While it is not clear precisely how Pulteney obtained the money to buy the estate, it appears that he saw British expansion in the Caribbean as one of the keys to his future success. Not only did he have dealings with West India merchants, but a series of personal letters written to Vice-Admiral Edward Vernon (Commander-in-Chief of the West Indies) in Jamaica during the 1739–48 war war reveal that he knew the islands well.[41] However, when Pulteney died in 1764, both his ambition to settle Cuba with 'Americans' and his plan to develop Bathwick were still unfulfilled. And, following the sudden death of his son and heir in 1767, Bathwick may well have remained an area of open fields, were it not for the global financial connections of his niece, Frances, the next heiress.

Seven years previously, Frances had married a Dumfries-born lawyer, William Johnstone. As we shall see in Chapter Six, elite families in this part of west Scotland were heavily involved in colonial development. Indeed, William's brother John was one of Britain's wealthiest East Indian 'nabobs', whilst another brother, George, an officer in the Navy, became the first Governor of Florida. While his brothers attempted to make their fortunes overseas, Johnstone was responsible for investing their remittances back home. Though based in Edinburgh, he improved the family's Scottish estate at Westerhall in Dumfries, and became a partner in a local bank there, which supplied credit for many colonial developments, particularly in the Caribbean. Indeed, through a default on mortgage payments, in 1769, Johnstone himself became the owner of a sugar estate on the island of Grenada,[42] and later purchased another in Tobago.

In the early 1770s, however, he turned his attention to the development of the Pulteney landholdings in Bath. Deciding that a new crossing of the Avon was essential to allow exploitation of the land in Bathwick, Johnstone (who by then had taken the Pulteney family name), after rejecting a bridge designed by Bristol-based Thomas Paty, engaged his fellow Scot, Robert Adam, in 1770.[43] Adam's proposed crossing, influenced by Palladio's unbuilt design for an inhabited bridge in Venice, was extraordinary. At street level it hardly seemed a bridge at all. Over fifteen feet wide and lined with shops and houses on both sides, it extended Bath's urban environment seamlessly over the Avon to the site of future developments at Bathwick. But the conceit came at a price. The complex, three-arched bridge was estimated to cost £10,998, over three times the sum Pulteney (Johnstone) had originally budgeted.[44] In July 1770, not only did the Aldermen of Bath write to Pulteney asking him to 'reconsider his plans', but he was also refused an increased mortgage against the value of the Pulteney estates.[45] However, he was clearly determined not to compromise.

By the end of August, only a month after his initial refusal for a mortgage, a duplicate record held in the archives of the Huntington Library in Pasadena, California, shows that Pulteney had written to Hope & Company in Amsterdam—then Europe's largest banking house—to express how much he was looking forward to meeting the two Hope brothers and thanking them for their loan of £20,000 on his 'Grenadan Estate'.[46] Not only had his brothers' colonial trading links given Pulteney access to international credit at the highest level, it was the personal security of his Caribbean sugar estate which allowed him to build the iconic bridge in Bath.

Pulteney Bridge was completed shortly before the start of the American War of Independence in 1776, when development in Bath had all but ceased. Speculative building did not begin again until the 1780s, when trans-Atlantic trading also recommenced and architect Thomas Baldwin's grand plans for the development of Bathwick itself finally began to be implemented. And it is during this later period, in the concluding decades of the eighteenth century—the fourth great phase of Bath's expansion (1783–93)—that we see perhaps the greatest effects of Caribbean wealth on the city's built fabric.

Indeed, the Pulteneys and Brydges aside, among the most prominent investors in Bath real estate were the Jamaican plantation owners and Scottish West India merchants Nathaniel and Zachariah Bayly, the founders of Bath City Bank.[47] Nathaniel was particularly committed to the development of Grosvenor Place, a site some way north-east of the town centre near the London Road, and lent large sums to developer John Evleigh to create a scheme for a new 'pleasure garden' on the banks of the Avon, overlooked by 140 houses and a hotel. The Bank also part-funded two other Evleigh developments: Somerset Place and Camden Crescent on Lansdown Hill, to the north of the city. All three schemes, however, were abandoned unfinished after the collapse of Bath City Bank in 1793, the year of the revolution in France's largest Caribbean slave colony, St Domingue (now known as Haiti), of Britain's declaration of war on the French Republic, and of Evleigh's own bankruptcy.[48]

The partially built houses of the Somerset Place development were eventually finished in the 1820s, but Nos 1–6 at the western end—which would have completed the sinuous golden terrace—were never built.[49] Camden Crescent was also never fully developed as planned.[50] And only forty-one terraced houses of the 140 originally conceived to surround the new pleasure gardens at Grosvenor Place were constructed. These houses, and the ornate façade of the hotel, still remain just off the London Road to the north-east of the city.[51]

Evleigh was not the only Bath developer to suffer from banking collapses and the crisis in confidence in the wake of the French and Haitian Revolutions. If you cross Pulteney Bridge via Argyll Street and walk along the length of Great Pulteney Street to the small public park at Sydney Gardens (commemorating Britain's new colony in Australia), you reach Beckford Road—the name of another prominent absentee Jamaican family. Halfway along the street, however, the development of five-storey terraces stops abruptly, and the row continues as modest, two-storey Edwardian villas, clearly intended for a very different type of resident.

Between the American War of Independence and the Haitian Revolution, development also continued in nearby Bristol, and in a similar vein. As historian Madge Dresser shows in her book *Slavery Obscured*, West Indian finance was instrumental in the late eighteenth-century development of the Bristol hillside suburb of Clifton.[52] Overlooking, but at once removed from the ships docked below, Clifton was home to many wealthy merchants and West Indian absentees, as well as visitors to the nearby spa at Hotwells. Numerous families of Scottish origin settled there, too, after a period in the Caribbean.[53] This 'continually new accession of Inhabitants' had 'occasioned the Hill to be almost covered with elegant Piles of

Building, and separate Mansions', wrote George Heath, the author of a late-eighteenth-century guide to Bristol. Clifton 'bids fair to become a fine Town', Heath continues.[54] Indeed, if you walk from Bristol's old quaysides through the streets of neo-classical limestone houses of Hotwells, Montpelier, St Paul's and up the hillsides towards Clifton Downs, you could almost be in Bath itself.

Bath and landscape views: The Royal Crescent

One of Bath's most striking physical features is the relationship between the crisp geometry of the limestone-faced architecture and the green amphitheatre-like surrounding hills. In its 1987 World Heritage Site designation, UNESCO pronounced that, in terms of the connection between buildings and landscape, Bath feels 'more akin to the 19th century garden cities' than the 'Renaissance cities' of seventeenth- and eighteenth-century Europe.[55] But this 'harmonious relationship', at least in Bath's earlier building developments, is as much a pragmatic response to site conditions as an aesthetic choice. The city's location in a steep-sided river valley meant that flat land was difficult to come by. Creating formal urban layouts— like the squares of Bloomsbury in London—was, therefore, complex. John Wood the Elder's earliest built scheme, Queen's Square, is set on a slight slope, while the later Circus was constructed on levelled ground. Closer to the abbey, The Parades[56] and Great Pulteney Street were built on top of vast, vaulted basements.

Techniques like these were expensive, and therefore best avoided by speculative developers. Indeed, as the author of *Bath: A Simile* observed, the most noticeable features of many of Bath's streets are not the classically proportioned, smooth ashlar façades, but the rough, stone surfaces of the coursed-rubble flanking walls of each house, that can be seen as the terraces step down the slopes. He writes:

> How the high town a side view shows
> Of pil'd up cups you'll wonder;
> And can't perhaps the low'r suppose,
> As many saucers under.[57]

Wood the Younger's later development at The Royal Crescent (see Fig. 4.5), completed between 1767 and 1775, however, was different. He resolved the problems of recreating neo-classical architectural formality, and minimising elaborate groundworks on a sloping site, by building an open-sided development of terraced houses set along the contours of the hill. Rather than continuing the ceremonial style of The Circus, the terraced houses that formed the curved street of The Royal Crescent were set on one side of the road, open to a view of fields and meadows beyond. There are no surviving records of Wood's intentions for the site, but it bears a resemblance to Wood the Elder's design for Ralph Allen's Palladian villa, Prior Park (completed by 1743), which is situated on a hill overlooking the town from the south. However, the agricultural lands over which The Royal Crescent (see Fig. 4.5) looked out at that time would have been coveted as potential development plots. It was not until the creation of the Royal Victoria Park incorporating the land in front of the terraces, opened by the then Princess Victoria in 1830, that residents of The Crescent were assured of the wide, bucolic views they enjoy today.[58]

Whether by accident or design, The Royal Crescent nevertheless created a unique form of urban layout. Wealthy residents of The Circus, The Parades or Queen's Square looked out of their sash windows onto elegant, neo-classical façades, paved streets and formal gardens. The inhabitants of The Royal Crescent, however— such as Philip Thicknesse, one of the earliest investors in the terraces, who purchased No. 8 in 1768—overlooked open meadows with glimpses of the town centre beyond.[59] Rather than forming part of a dense network of contained urban spaces, this monumental

Fig. 4.5: The Royal Crescent, Bath

composition was connected to the city via a closely framed, semi-rural view.

The Royal Crescent's open-sided layout was to have a profound effect on the subsequent architectural evolution of Bath, and of the Bristol suburb of Clifton, too. The many developments built in the years after the completion of The Crescent demonstrate the value of a curved, single-sided street running along the contours of a hill. Evleigh's hillside Camden Crescent and Somerset Place on Lansdown Hill, Bath, and his Grosvenor Place, designed to overlook the 'pleasure gardens', are prominent examples of how developers used this model to create architectural impact on steep slopes. However, if used as a repeated, closely packed urban layout, the open-sided Crescent would have problems, as the principal façade of one row of terraces would look onto the utilitarian back of another. The terraces at Bath, therefore, not only step down the slope, but are also separated from each other by wide belts of trees and planting. It was not just the elegant appearance of Bath's buildings themselves that enticed potential customers: the aesthetic and pragmatic integration of the architecture into the landscape itself, providing beautiful views over this scenery, would also have been a great attraction.[60]

Indeed, in late Georgian Britain, the simple contemplation of landscape—quite apart from its representation in drawing or painting—came to be regarded as an important genteel pursuit. For the well-educated, to display a 'correct' taste in landscape was a valuable social accomplishment and, in itself, was considered akin to the practice of an art.[61] So by the latter part of the eighteenth century, visitors would have been attracted to Bath as much for the 'picturesque' semi-rural views from the hillsides as for the urban life pictured in Malton's mid-century watercolours. In addition to promenading on the formal Parades in the centre, fashionable visitors also walked to the nearby villages of Lyncombe and Widcombe to the south-east of the city, where quarrying had created extensive cliff-side views.

This fashion for picturesque prospects is gently satirised by Jane Austen in her novel *Northanger Abbey* (completed in 1803, but only published posthumously in 1817). Austen's heroine, Catherine, is given a lecture on the principles of landscape appreciation during a walk up into the hills around Bath with Henry Tilney (son of the pineapple-growing owner of Northanger Abbey, General Tilney). At first Catherine is 'quite lost'. She describes how

> the little which she could understand appeared to contradict the very few notions she had entertained on the matter before. It seemed that if a good view were no longer to be taken from the top of a high hill, and that a clear blue sky were no longer proof of a fine day.[62]

However, as Catherine's companion continues his explanation, 'her attention was so earnest, that he became perfectly satisfied of her having a great deal of natural taste'. Indeed, Catherine proved 'so hopeful a scholar, that when they gained the top of Beechen Cliff, she voluntarily rejected the whole of the city of Bath as unworthy to make part of a landscape'.[63] Catherine's dismissal of the aesthetics of eighteenth-century Britain's most fashionable town, would, no doubt, have drawn wry smiles from Austen's early-nineteenth-century readers. Because, as we shall see in more detail in the next chapter, Bath, alongside Bristol, was where the vogue for picturesque landscape tourism first took hold.

Cultural capital of the Atlantic West

While Bath, of course, was no imperial capital in a political sense, its ability to attract both Britain's landed elite and its colonial adventurers (who, as we have seen, were often younger brothers or cousins of landed families) made it a formidable cultural and economic power base. Bath was not merely a playground for the rich: it was a centre, during the eighteenth century at least, of national cultural importance. It was the 'capital' of the West.

As the renowned economist Adam Smith—based himself in Glasgow, on the Scottish west coast—noted as early as 1776, the success of Britain's colonial expansion in the Americas had caused British overseas trade a 'total change in its direction'.[64] It was westerly Atlantic-facing ports—like Bristol, Liverpool and Glasgow—that saw rapid expansion during the eighteenth century. This was very firmly at the expense of their eastern counterparts, which traded mostly with continental Europe, and by the mid-eighteenth century, in population terms, Bristol had eclipsed Norwich in the east of the country as England's second city. But, I contend, this pivot to the west was not just an economic shift, it was the start of a cultural transformation. Bath's development marked the beginning of what can be described as a change in the 'cultural geography' of the British Isles towards its Atlantic coast and its different physical topography. And this shift also marked a pivotal point in the development of British landscape art.

Despite the country's growing wealth, mid-eighteenth-century Britain was not a particularly propitious place for ambitious artists. There was little royal or church patronage, and most connoisseurs of art—like John Boyd, one of the foremost collectors of the time[65]—preferred to buy paintings by long-established Dutch, French or Italian artists. The exceptions were commissions to provide views of new country houses or portraits of the owner's families, such as Thomas Gainsborough's painting of the elegantly dressed Antiguan plantation owners, *The Byam Family* (see Fig. 4.6), now on display in Bath's Holburne Museum. By the mid-eighteenth century, the large numbers of wealthy and fashionable visitors in Bath meant the city had become a magnet for aspiring British artists seeking potential patrons. The walls of Bath's charitable hospital, The Royal Infirmary, became a public showcase for their work.

Joshua Reynolds (1723–92), for example, was one of the many artists who settled in the city in the boom years of the 1760s, painting portraits of, among others, West Indian absentees Edwin Lascelles of Harewood and Clement Tudway from Wells. Thomas Gainsborough (1727–88), too, was introduced to the resort by the diarist Philip Thicknesse, a former neighbour in Suffolk, who had served in the military in Jamaica and had retired in later life to Bath. As Susan Sloman shows in her book *Gainsborough in Bath*, it was the artist's success as a portraitist, painting illustrious members of society in Suffolk and then Bath—or, as he put it, the 'cursed face business'[66]—that gave him the financial security to experiment artistically and pursue his interests in landscape painting.

As can still be seen today, the hilly topography of Bath and Bristol contrasts with the wide, rolling, arable fields of the eastern and central English counties, with which Suffolk-born-and-raised Gainsborough was familiar. In north Somerset, on the western

Fig. 4.6: *The Byam Family*, Thomas Gainsborough, c. 1762

(and, therefore, mild and wet) scarp slope of the Cotswolds, the limestone geology, together with human activity such as quarrying and mining, have resulted in the distinctive terrains of steep-sided 'coombes', small pastures, thickly wooded hills and precipitous cliffs that characterise the countryside around Bath and Bristol. And it is these hills and valleys that Gainsborough used as inspiration for a series of paintings very different from his portraits of wealthy clients.

The composition of Gainsborough's paintings echoed the seventeenth-century images of the wooded hills between Rome and Naples created by artists such as Nicholas Poussin and Salvator Rosa, then extremely fashionable among Britain's art collectors. However, rather than mythical figures, Gainsborough featured local workers or people, set against the backdrop of Somerset hills and woods. Some of the best examples of this local landscape painting are *Landscape with Rustic Lovers, Two Cows and a Man on a Distant Bridge* (see Fig. 4.7); *Rocky Wooded Landscape with Rustic Lovers, Herdsman and Cows; The Harvest Waggon;* and *Wooded Landscape with Figures, a Cottage and Pool.* At the time, these works were not particularly popular with visitors to Bath: no prints were made from them, and several were unsold at the time of Gainsborough's death in 1788.[67]

However, these classically influenced views of local landscapes seem to have appealed to people who actually lived in the area. Before he left for London in 1774, for example, Gainsborough gave *Rocky Wooded Landscape* to Walter Wiltshire, the prosperous owner of a freight company that had transported many paintings to the capital.[68] And Ralph Allen of Prior Park bought *Wooded Landscape with Figures, a Cottage and Pool.*[69]

Fig. 4.7: *Landscape with Rustic Lovers, Two Cows and a Man on a Distant Bridge*, Thomas Gainsborough, c. 1755–9

This reimagining of the rural areas surrounding the growing towns and cities of the Atlantic West was bound up with a growing trend for landscape touring among the county's elites, a theme I shall develop further in the following chapters. And as we shall see, the development of the Wye Valley, North Wales, the Lake District and the Scottish Highlands as genteel tourist destinations cannot be separated from the rise of Bristol, Liverpool, Lancaster, Whitehaven and Glasgow as prominent Atlantic ports.

5

NATURE'S PROSPECTS

A Creole there is and he lives at a place
Which Nature and Art join together to grace

Monmouthshire Election Rhyme, May 1771

Early one morning in July 1760, a coach left Bath on its way to Hotwells, the fashionable Clifton spa just to the west of Bristol's harbour. On board was 'Miss M' who, a few days later, described her 'agreeable jaunt' in a letter to a friend. But the spa was merely a stop for breakfast and to pick up two more passengers: the true purpose of the expedition was to visit the gardens at Piercefield Park, recently created by Antiguan absentee, Valentine Morris.

Piercefield was situated on the banks of the River Wye near Chepstow, a shipbuilding town on the far side of the Severn estuary. Following their breakfast, Miss M and her companions departed Clifton and set off for Aust, around ten miles to the north of Bristol. Despite treacherous currents, huge tides and hidden sandbars, Aust was a major crossing point on the Bristol Channel and, by the eighteenth century, there were regular ferry services between Aust and Beachley, transporting goods and people across the two-mile stretch of water between the towns and industries of Gloucestershire and Somerset and South Wales, then a largely rural area. It was only in the 1960s that the ferry service ceased, on the opening of the first Severn Bridge, from Aust to Chepstow.

From the perspective of a wealthy woman, whose daily activities in Bath would have been confined to assemblies, teas and balls, this was a 'wild and whimsical' adventure 'abroad', as Miss M describes.[1]

On reaching the coast, the party 'took a little refreshment' at the 'passage house', before driving over 'rocks, amongst sea-weed and I can't tell what' to arrive at their embarkation point. With some drama, Miss M then describes their passage across the Channel, explaining:

> With some difficulty we got into a Stable in which we were to cross the water … Yes, a stable! Littered from one end to the other with dirty straw and filled with as many horses as people. Oh we went most sociably over, Horses, coach and ourselves.[2]

Once arrived in Wales, the party drove to Chepstow, where they went to the 'best Inn to find accommodations'. Lodgings secured for the night, they 'made the best of our way to Persfield [Piercefield], the Seat of Mr MORRIS'. At the time, the house at Piercefield was still the old sixteenth-century manor, and it was only replaced by a more sophisticated residence, designed by John Soane, the architect of the Bank of England, later in the 1790s (see Fig. 5.1). Morris, it seemed, was more concerned with creating landscapes than buildings. Indeed, as Boyd and Lascelles were later to do, Morris had created a fashionable parkland approach to the front of the house.[3] And though the visitors admired the 'waving lawns',[4] it was not the garden itself, but the 'prospects' from it that most interested Miss M and her fellow travellers. For, to the rear of the house, the rolling contours of the park abruptly became a 400-foot cliff, along the edges of which Morris had cut numerous walkways and paths to take advantage of the views. As Miss M exclaimed:

> The Gardens are situated on the *Rocks*, I cannot call the *Banks* of the River *Wye* and cut into Walks, in themselves are excessively beautiful, but the superior beauty of the views they command, so entirely engrosses the eye, that they can be very little heeded.[5]

Several of these walks were towards the cliffs themselves, as they curved around in a vast natural amphitheatre. Miss M thought that these cliffs resembled 'the Ruins of old fortifications',[6] with some covered by the 'most pleasing variety of greens that the eyes can behold'. Some vantage points provided bucolic panoramas of livestock 'grazing on sweet pastures' on the farms that lay below the

Fig. 5.1: Etching of Piercefield from *An Historical Tour in Monmouthshire*, William Coxe, 1801

cliffs, while others allowed views of the nearby ruins of Chepstow Castle (see Fig. 5.2). There was an octagonal temple surrounded by 'Chinese' rails which gave 'an extensive prospect of many counties', Miss M describes; a cave 'from whence are seen the Rocks, the wood, the River, with fine Lawns'; a 'Chinese' bridge giving a 'pretty, confined prospect'; and a spot which afforded a distant glimpse of 'the two passages over the Severn from England to Wales'.[7] Altogether, Morris had fashioned twenty-three different rural 'scenes' for visitors to admire. 'Such a place for the Variety and Beauty of its Prospects I never saw',[8] Miss M marvelled.

The sheer scale of Morris's endeavours proved too much for Miss M and her party. 'The gardens are seven mile round', she laments, 'so our poor old Lady was forced to occupy a Seat just by the house and the rest of us then walked as far as our legs would carry us. We could not compass the whole round but saw all the principal prospects'.[9] Fortunately, after their exhausting tour, one of the visitors was already 'acquainted' with a lady at Valentine Morris's house and

Fig. 5.2: *Chepstow Castle from Piersfield*, Thomas Hearne (© The Trustees of the British Museum. All rights reserved.)

they were invited inside 'to eat a bit of cake and drink a glass of wine', before returning to their inn for the night.

The next day, the party continued their excursion, but this time partly by boat along the steep gorges of the lower reaches of the Wye. Here, the river runs along the north-western edge of the Forest of Dean. During the eighteenth century, the forest was a major source both of mature oak for shipbuilding and small trees to provide charcoal for ironmaking. After visiting the remains of a former monastery, Tintern Abbey, 'the most curious piece of ruins I ever beheld',[10] Miss M and her fellow travellers stopped at the nearby ironworks, where they saw 'the manner of making bar iron and the drawing of wire', before the oarsman rowed them back down the Wye to Piercefield. She chronicles:

> As we rowed along the River we had the pleasure of looking up to
> those beautiful Rocks we had looked down from in Mr. Morris

ground. This Reverse of view made a second enjoyment and we were more sensible of the Height of the mountains in this situation than when we were at the summit of them. So delightful was this Water-Scene, that we all wished a continuance of it.[11]

The party then asked the boatman to return them safely across the Bristol Channel. Coach, horses and servants were dispatched to the ferry, while the 'polite' party had 'the most charming sail to the opposite shore to *England*'. After a reviving drink of tea at the passage house, they returned to Hotwells where they visited the 'Quaker's grotto', a cavern-like folly—including Caribbean shells—built by Bristol West India merchant Thomas Goldney in his garden, before their return to Bath the next day.

Miss M's writing is so evocative and her enthusiasm so infectious that it feels like her trip was made only weeks ago. But she was just one of many hundreds, if not thousands, of people who visited Piercefield during the late eighteenth and early nineteenth centuries. The views from the cliffside walks were described and analysed by some of the most respected writers on landscape aesthetics of the age: from theorists such as Thomas Whateley in his influential *Observations on Modern Gardening*[12] and William Gilpin in his popular treatise on 'picturesque' aesthetics, *Observations on the River Wye*, to poets such as William Wordsworth in *Lines composed a few miles above Tintern Abbey*.[13]

Charles Heath, a printer from the nearby town of Monmouth and the author of a 1793 guidebook to Piercefield—'sold by him in the market place and at all the inns in the county'—was barely exaggerating when he claimed that

> The scenes at Persfield [sic] have been examined by men of such distinguished taste, and the various beauties with which the place is surrounded, pointed out by them with such ability, that in their description the Stranger will find every feature noticed deserving of attention. No part of the kingdom has been more the object of general curiosity, nor seen with greater pleasure.[14]

Today the walks at Piercefield Park are Grade I–listed walks and lawns, the highest form of statutory protection afforded by national legislation in Britain, as an 'early and outstanding example of a "sublime" landscape'.[15] Yet, despite the extent of Piercefield's influence during the eighteenth century, it is little known today outside a small circle of landscape and garden historians.

'Nature so cultivated surrounded by nature so wild'

What could have prompted a young absentee 'creole' (an eighteenth-century term for a European born in the Caribbean colonies), Valentine Morris, to create the cliffside walks that so captivated eighteenth-century Britain's society? Sadly, the break-up of the Piercefield estate means that there are few contemporary records left. And, of these sources, nothing provides any evidence of Morris's aesthetic ambitions. As we shall see, it is the accounts of contemporary visitors, like Miss M and many others, that provide much of the answer.[16]

Of the few present-day studies of Piercefield available, however, two of the most detailed are by a local historian, Ivor Waters.[17] Frustratingly, however, many of the original papers at the Society of Genealogists, on which Waters based his work, have since been mislaid.[18] But fragmentary reports in contemporary newspapers and magazines, together with official records (Morris was later to become Governor of the Caribbean island of St Vincent), also help piece together Morris's family background.

Valentine's great-grandfather, John Morris, had emigrated to Barbados from the village of Tintern[19]—just a few miles upstream on the Wye—soon after the English Civil War (1642–51), to join his uncles Richard and Lewis who had left for the American colonies as indentured servants in the 1630s.[20] It is unclear whether earlier generations of Morrises had invested profits from the West Indies in British land, but the family's Caribbean connections may well explain the Barbados Woods in the hills above Tintern Abbey—one of the curiosities of name which, as I explained in the Introduction, led me to my original thesis.

Valentine was born in 1727 on Antigua, where his father, also named Valentine, owned several sugar estates.[21] Like many other prosperous West Indian families, the Morrises left the Caribbean for Britain at the start of the War of Jenkins' Ear in 1739,[22] and, a year later, Valentine senior used the equity from his Antiguan plantations to purchase Piercefield, a few miles downstream from his family roots in Tintern. He had little time to enjoy retirement in the Wye Valley, however, for in less than two years he was dead.[23]

It was soon obvious that his fifteen-year-old heir was a strong-willed youth, much indulged by his mother and elder sisters. Rejecting his father's instructions that 'he be sent to Leiden [a Dutch university popular with London merchants] for his education' or 'study the common law at one of our inns of court', and that Piercefield be sold to pay legacies,[24] young Valentine read Classics at Cambridge. And contrary to his father's stipulations against early matrimony, at the age of roughly twenty-one he married Mary Mordaunt, a niece of the Earl of Peterborough, with 'no fortune other than beauty, virtue and good sense'.[25] Aided by his lawyer brother-in-law, Morris retained the Piercefield estate in trust. Valentine aimed not to be a City lawyer, nor a London merchant, but a 'gentleman'.

In the first years of their marriage, the couple spent little time at Piercefield. Instead, they preferred the urban delights of Bath, where Valentine was notorious for his passion for 'the gaming tables', his card skills acquired, apparently, during his childhood in the Caribbean.[26] Nevertheless, he was also interested in more genteel cultural pursuits. According to Ivor Waters, after their return from a trip to Antigua in 1753 to inspect their sugar plantations, Morris and his wife turned their attention to landscaping their Welsh country estate. Turning fields into a large lawn would already have established the couple as fashionable landowners. Unlike Danson and Harewood, however, Piercefield also had the striking cliffs over the Wye, which Morris and his wife would use to remarkable effect.

Though nowadays the estate is under multiple different ownerships, it is still crossed by public footpaths, and, with a little persistence and some imagination, it is possible to recreate some of the route taken by Miss M and so many other eighteenth-century visitors. An elegantly drawn fold-out map incorporated in an 1804 guidebook shows a plan of Piercefield in the late 1700s (see Fig. 5.3). The east boundary (on the lower half of the map) is marked by the sinuous curves of the River Wye, and the west by the new Chepstow–Monmouth turnpike road (at the top of the plan). From the road, a sweeping drive leads through parkland towards the mansion house, stables and walled garden (roughly in the centre of the map), located above a great horseshoe-shaped river meander.

Once you have found the village of St Arvan's, just outside Chepstow, it is possible to direct yourself to Piercefield's former grounds with relative ease with a copy of this map. The 'slopes and waving lawns' admired by Miss M now form part of Chepstow's well-known racecourse. A little way from the stands, the toilet blocks and the car parks is a footpath leading to the handsome façade of the house, at the point where the parkland and wooded cliffs meet. The prospect from this spot has hardly changed in the last 250 years. First, there is the wonderful contrast of walking from sunlit open parkland into the cool of the woods. Then comes the sudden, exhilarating realisation that you are standing on the edge of a drop of several hundred feet, making the view of the river and the Welsh border farms below even more extraordinary.

After the initial excitement, however, trying to recapture the experience of Miss M and other tourists becomes more difficult. One

Fig. 5.3: Map of Piercefield from *An Historical Tour in Monmouthshire*, William Coxe, 1801

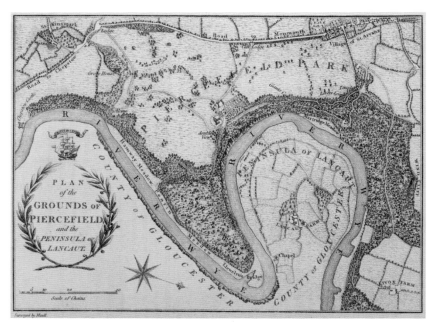

Fig. 5.4: View of the River Wye from the cliffs at Piercefield

eighteenth-century visitor, Arthur Young, for example, described how, after taking in the view from atop the cliffs, you then 'proceed to the temple, a small neat building on the highest part of these grounds and imagination cannot form an idea of anything more beautiful than what appears to your ravished sight from this amazing point of view'.[27] But the temple has long since disappeared, and the 'amazing' aspect is now obscured by foliage. Attempts to follow other descriptions from the time are equally defeating. Indeed, Piercefield's once-famous landscape garden now seems little different from the rest of the yellow-arrowed footpaths and wooded cliffside tracks of the officially designated 'Wye Valley Walk'.

But then you realise: that is exactly the point. In twenty-first-century Britain, and many other Western cultures, following a footpath to admire a renowned 'beauty spot' is regarded as a completely normal thing to do. Large areas of upland in England, Wales and Scotland are designated National Parks or, like the Wye Valley, Areas of Outstanding Natural Beauty. In one of the most highly urbanised and densely populated countries in the world, the aesthetic contemplation of tracts of 'nature' is seen as an individual's right and is protected by law. But, in the mid-eighteenth century, few British people would have chosen to walk along a wooded cliff-face simply for leisure. As the diary of renowned Methodist clergyman John Wesley indicates, woodland like that at Piercefield would generally have been valued not for its beauty, but as a useful natural resource.[28] In an entry written following his visit to Piercefield in 1769, Wesley reflects:

> Through these woods an abundance of serpentine walks are cut, wherein many seats and alcoves are placed; most of which command a surprising prospect of rocks and fields on the other side of the river. And must all these be burned up? What will become of us then, if we set our hearts on them?[29]

Wesley's diary alludes to the fact that the trees lining these Welsh cliffs, like those across most of the valley, had once been a commercial crop used to make charcoal to fuel the local ironworks. Now, however, the woodland was a living picture frame for carefully selected 'scenes' of rural life. 'Nature so cultivated surrounded by nature so wild, compose a lovely landskip together',[30] mused Thomas Whateley, an English politician and writer, upon his visit to Piercefield. The views clearly also entranced the agricultural reformer Arthur Young, who exclaimed, 'The eyes of your imagination are not keen enough to take in this point, which the united talents of a Claud [sic], a Poussin, a Vernet and a Smith would scarcely be able to sketch'.[31] It was high praise from a man chiefly remembered for his advice to landowners on how to improve crop yields.[32]

Poussin, Rosa and Claude

Morris's Caribbean wealth had not only allowed him to convert acres of agricultural land into ornamental lawns, as had been done at Danson and Harewood, but also to transform formerly income-generating woodland into a gallery of landscape art. His cliffside walks and twenty-three prospects at Piercefield were a consummate example of the aesthetic of the 'picturesque', the growing British fashion for appreciating the rural environment according to an ideal found in seventeenth-century Italianate landscape paintings. This picturesque aesthetic was so popular during the late eighteenth and nineteenth centuries that architectural historian David Watkin has labelled it the 'nation's principal contribution to the arts … and European aesthetics'.[33] It had a profound influence on the growth of tourism in the Wye Valley, Cumbria, Wales and upland Scotland, as well as on the design of landscapes, buildings, tourist resorts and even railway infrastructure.

The pioneering account of the growth and influence of the 'picturesque' aesthetic is Christopher Hussey's *The Picturesque: Studies in a Point of View* (1927). As Hussey shows, and to which Arthur Young had alluded in the 1760s, it is the Italianate landscape paintings of Nicholas Poussin, Salvator Rosa and Claude Lorrain that first awoke the growing interest in British natural scenery.[34] Many works by these artists had been brought back to Britain as souvenirs by wealthy elites who had undertaken a Grand Tour around Europe, like Danson's John Boyd. Eighteenth-century art collectors like Boyd regarded landscapes by 'Claude', the commonly used sobriquet of the French painter Claude Lorrain (born Gellée), in particular, in the highest esteem.[35] It is worth pausing for a moment, therefore, to examine one of these paintings carefully to understand more precisely the aesthetic ideals to which Piercefield's prospects were being compared, and it is to Claude that I will turn.

Claude's 1682 painting *Landscape with Ascanius Shooting the Stag of Sylvia*, which now hangs in the Ashmolean Museum in Oxford (see Fig. 5.5), is an instructive example. Contrary to the suggestion made in the title, the painting's main subject is not the beast's actual shooting; the group of hunters in the bottom left form a small and relatively insignificant part of the composition. Instead, the focus is the physical topography: a rocky, heavily wooded bay, scattered with classical ruins looking out to sea, with a mountainous island just visible in the distance. The painting has a high, but semi-enclosed viewpoint, demonstrating how the artist typically structured many of his compositions.

Fig. 5.5: *Landscape with Ascanius Shooting the Stag of Sylvia*, Claude Gellée, 17th century

Each side of the painting is formed from a series of overlapping elements: a ruin, a group of trees or a tower-topped, rocky promontory. These are known as 'coulisses', a term derived from the French word for the scenery wings on either side of a stage. Indeed, like renaissance stage sets, Claude's paintings use false perspective to achieve the effect of distance. However, the French artist's particular skill is that he achieves this not through a gradual diminution in size of the objects within the landscape, but by a series of leaps down from one scale to another, reconciled only by the eye's constant diagonal movement across the picture, as attention is drawn to each object by the sloping lines of the hills. The 'pictorial depth' created by the composition is further aided by Claude's use of colour: the ruins, hunters and animals at the bottom and sides of the painting, in the foreground, are rendered in strong earthy tones, making them appear closer to you, while the sea and mountains beyond are in pale, cooler tints, which helps them recede into the background. Claude's dream-like paintings were, like those of Poussin and Rosa, of imaginary landscapes. While elements would have been sketched from buildings and views Claude had seen during his time in Italy, the painting itself would have been carefully composed in his studio. Wealthy estate owners of Britain's Atlantic West, however, now aspired to make the imaginary real.

Piercefield and the 'picturesque'

Although Boyd's house at Danson is an elegant example of eighteenth-century Palladian design, and Lascelles's parkland succeeded in producing a glorious setting for Harewood House, they were not dissimilar to other grand villas and landscape gardens of the time. In many ways, they typify the patronage of eighteenth-century Britain's landowning elite. But Morris's creation at Piercefield did something different. Rather than merely building a magnificent country house or designing a sweeping stretch of parkland, Morris used the topography of his estate to change the way people perceived the places and industries along the River Wye. Appropriating the natural cliff amphitheatre, and judiciously felling trees to form high viewpoints, he created 'prospects' that reminded educated visitors in the 1700s of fashionable Italianate paintings (or prints of them) they had previously seen.

As agriculturist Arthur Young commented after his visit to Piercefield in 1767, 'In point of striking picturesque views ... Persfield [sic] is exquisite'.[36] While in *Observations of Modern Gardening* (1770), Thomas Whateley argued that landscape gardening was 'superior to landskip [sic] painting as reality to representation'.[37] Whateley admired how Morris' paths and views extended the 'boundary of the place ... beyond the scenes which are thus appropriated to it ... [affording] a greater variety than can generally be found in any garden, the scenery of which is confined to the enclosure'.[38] By providing 'prospects' of distant shipping on the Bristol Channel, of the workings of a Welsh border farm, of ruined castles or of nearby cliff-faces, Morris's twenty-three carefully framed views transformed the ordinary into art.

Inspiration for Morris's endeavours may well have been close at hand. He was not the first person to notice and work to accentuate the aesthetic qualities of the buildings and topography of the lower Wye Valley. Alexander Pope's influential poem on 'taste', *Epistle to Lord Bathurst* (1733), had celebrated the public walks and clifftop 'prospect' created by a local benefactor, John Kyrle, in the late seventeenth century at Ross, a small market town thirty miles upstream. Pope praised Kyrle for spending his 'modest fortune' on public works, in contrast to the boorish figure of 'dissenting merchant' Sir Balaam.

Miss M and her party were also not the first visitors to take boat trips down the River Wye. In the late 1740s, when Valentine Morris senior was in the process of purchasing Piercefield, the new rector of Ross, John Egerton, had built a pleasure boat to allow his friends to see the local landscapes.[39] In a poem of 1742, a Gloucestershire clergyman, the Reverend Sneyd Davies, also described a voyage to Tintern Abbey where he viewed the 'pleasurable sadness' of its 'ruins' and 'follies'.[40] Morris's patronage at Piercefield, therefore, should be seen as part of a cultural change in attitudes to the lower Wye Valley. While the river was clearly still an important trading route, transporting the produce of the Welsh borders to Bristol and beyond, it was also becoming a place of aesthetic pleasure.

'Assisting' views of nature

Morris's more extensive and imaginative use of the natural geology of his estate, of course, was dependent on the substantial wealth he had inherited from his father's Antiguan plantations. True, the wooded cliffs near the ironworks were already covered with small footpaths formed by charcoal burners as they went about their work. But the wide, stone-paved 'walks' built by Morris were not simply muddy tracks.[41] Although Arthur Young regarded them 'merely as an assistance to view the beauties of nature', the creation of properly made paths along the sides of the steep, wooded precipice would have been a demanding feat of construction.

Morris had employed a huge team of 'upwards of one hundred men' to achieve his aesthetic aims.[42] Working on such steep slopes and carefully disposing of the spoil would have involved a complex and exhausting effort. Topsoil and leaf mould had to be taken uphill in heavy buckets or awkward wooden barrows through the woods to the parkland; large rocks, gravel and other waste was laboriously transported to discreet spots to avoid compromising the views. The wonders of Piercefield's famous 'prospects' were, like the 'natural' sweeping lawns, only 'revealed' by the exertions of many men.

But it was a particular combination of wealth, 'gentlemanly' aspirations and, importantly, striking geology that allowed Morris and his wife to create their cliffside walks. John Boyd, for instance, despite his extensive patronage of architecture and landscape, could not have created a living Poussin or Claude at Danson: there were simply no rocks or cliff faces in north Kent to provide the viewpoints. Boyd's own modern Italianate landscape could only be in the form of a painting, *Landscape with Waterfall and Figures*, which he commissioned from French artist Claude-Joseph Vernet to hang on the wall of his salon, featuring 'a large waterfall' and some 'distant views'.[43]

As Miss M's friend, William Shenstone, wrote after his visit to Piercefield, '[I] could not help reflecting on the singular happiness of Mr Morrice [sic], to be possessed at once of a large fortune, one of the finest situations in England and a wife whose taste for rural improvements appears even superior to his own'.[44] However, its fortunate location alone does not explain the extent of Piercefield's influence at the time. To understand why Piercefield captured the collective imagination of British eighteenth-century polite society, it is necessary to look further than Morris's own ambitions and examine the wider historical context.

Two notable features of elite culture in Britain during this period were its increasing mobility, due to the construction of good toll or turnpike roads, and an attitude to domestic privacy that is somewhat different to that of today.[45] For example, while the letters of John Boyd's son show Danson to have been purely a family home, the publication of a 1819 printed guide to Harewood House demonstrates that it was visited by many people who were neither friends, nor servants nor indeed business colleagues of the Lascelles, but strangers unknown to the family.[46] The large number of guides to country houses published in the eighteenth century attests to the fact that visitors were not coming to see the wealthy patron. They would instead be admiring, or indeed critiquing, the architecture of the house, the design of its landscape garden or the provenance and breadth of its art collection.[47]

Part of Piercefield's extraordinary popularity and influence was undoubtedly due to the estate's accessibility from the fashionable resorts of Bath and Bristol Hotwells. Not only could visitors and their coaches use the Aust–Beachley ferry, but from the mid-1750s they could then ride along the new South Wales turnpike roads that Valentine Morris had been instrumental in building, which linked the ferry port to Chepstow, and thence past the entrance to his grounds.[48] Like other West Indian absentees and trans-Atlantic merchants, Morris was a keen promoter of new turnpikes and, as historian Ivor Waters records, helped fund the construction of over 300 miles of new roads in Monmouthshire and Gloucestershire after inheriting Piercefield.

Defining the 'sublime'

Trips along the Wye played a key role in the growth and popularity of the phenomenon of the 'landscape tour',[49] and a further contemporary account attests to Piercefield's wider place in the changing aesthetic views of the time. In the summer of 1759, a year before Miss M's trip, London publisher Robert Dodsley[50] had also travelled

Fig. 5.6: View of Piercefield

'with a polite Party of Gentlemen and ladies'[51] from Bath to Piercefield. Like Miss M, he too had described his visit in some detail in a letter to a friend, concluding that 'the place is certainly of the great and sublime kind'.[52] Dodsley's use of the term 'sublime' is one of its earliest recorded uses to describe the aesthetic qualities of a British landscape. Moreover, it hints at another reason why Piercefield became such a popular destination.

Two years prior to his trip, Dodsley had published a philosophical tract by a young, Irish émigré writer, Edmund Burke, entitled *A Philosophical Enquiry into the Origin of our Ideas of the Sublime and the Beautiful*. Written in 1757, four years after the publication of an earlier work by artist William Hogarth, *Analysis of Beauty*, Burke's *Enquiry* was to become one of the most influential treatises on aesthetics in the English-speaking world.

Burke's originality lay in the importance he placed on the subject's response, rather than the object itself. Beauty was not an innate quality, Burke insisted; instead, it occurred in the eyes and brain of the beholder. Moreover, according to Burke, the sights or objects that generated emotional responses such as fear and awe— that is, 'the sublime'—were as important as the pleasure provided by the 'beautiful'. But for eighteenth-century readers, the most revolutionary of Burke's tenets would have been the suggestion that the aesthetic value of the 'sublime'—characterised by vastness, extremes of height or danger—could equal or even surpass that of well-proportioned and controlled man-made 'beauty'. Although Burke's treatise dealt primarily with abstract aesthetic ideas, not landscape specifically, this was widely interpreted as referring to the natural environment.

Applying Burke's concepts, the delight inspired by the sight of great architectural monuments of the past, for example, could be more than rivalled by the awe engendered by the experience of viewing a majestic mountain—or the thrill, indeed, of standing atop Piercefield's cliffs. Only around a decade after the publication of Burke's treatise, the impact of his ideas on the sublime can already be seen in Arthur Young's assessment of his visit to Piercefield. In what would have been seen as a great accolade, Young commented that Piercefield was 'superiorly sublime'[53] and that it was 'evident that Mr Morris, meant [the walks] … as a means of seeing what nature had already done without any idea of decoration or ornament'.[54]

The opposing categories of the sublime and the beautiful became integral to eighteenth-century discussions about landscape. By the latter half of the century, a true art connoisseur might be found not just examining paintings and prints in London's fashionable galleries or investigating the ruins of ancient Rome, but travelling the uplands of North Wales, Scotland or Westmoreland. And as I examine in more detail in the following chapters, the fashion for celebrating the aesthetics of untamed nature was taken up not just in hilly, remote hinterlands of rapidly expanding Atlantic ports such as Bristol, Lancaster and Glasgow; it was also introduced into Britain's American colonies, allowing them to partake in polite culture, too. While these overseas territories did not have magnificent buildings or fine art of the type found and valued in many European countries, they could boast rivers, cliffs, waterfalls and mountains as 'beautiful' or 'sublime' as any in Europe.

While Burke was writing *A Philosophical Enquiry*, he was also spending time in Bath working on another more obviously commercial project: his book entitled *An Account of the European Settlements in the Americas*. Co-authored with a friend (and possible distant relative), William Burke (later Secretary and Registrar of Guadeloupe), it was also published by Robert Dodsley in the same year as his *Enquiry*, 1757. The section on the West Indies is particularly detailed,[55] and it is here, when discussing the advantages of the sugar islands 'for tempers prejudicial at home',[56] that Burke's own personal Caribbean connections are revealed. His notoriously wayward younger brother Richard was a successful Atlantic merchant, Caribbean land speculator and had held the position of collector of customs in Grenada.[57] 'Those who love risk and hazard,' Burke writes, while dangerous to a 'regular and settled community' can, in the Caribbean, be transformed into men of 'opulence and credit'.[58] Indeed, 'the rashness of hot and visionary men', he argues, contributes to 'the great source of our wealth, our strength, our power'.[59]

The vivid descriptions of the transformative power of a sojourn in the West Indies for men of 'fiery and restless tempers' suggests that—through his brother's adventures—Burke had close experience of such 'tempers' himself. In fact, in 1764, when Burke and his wife (the daughter of a prominent Irish-born Bath doctor) bought a 600-acre country estate and Palladian mansion near Beaconsfield, Buckinghamshire, it was a joint financial investment with his brother Richard and his fellow author William. A decade later, Edmund became a Member of Parliament for Bristol. While Burke's name was made by the success of *A Philosophical Enquiry*, it was profits from Britain's Atlantic colonies that funded his transformation from struggling essayist into landed gentleman.

Observations on the River Wye

Alongside the works of artists like Claude, Burke's treatise provided a theoretical background for the growing interest in the aesthetics of Western landscapes in late-eighteenth-century Britain. The most widely read work on the period specifically critiquing landscape was William Gilpin's short book (albeit with a lengthy title), *Observations on the River Wye and several parts of South Wales, &c: Relative Chiefly to Picturesque Beauty: Made in the Summer of the Year 1770*, published in 1782. Like Burke, Gilpin also had close personal connections with the Atlantic trade: his family were prominent sugar, rum and tobacco traders in the rapidly expanding Cumbrian port of White-haven, as we shall see in the following chapter.

By the 1780s, the fashion for touring the meandering reaches of the lower Wye was, as we have seen, already well-established. Its very popularity convinced Gilpin to publish the notes and sketches that he made during his own visit twelve years before. As he explained in the introduction, he had originally envisaged publishing records of a 'trip made to the lakes and mountains of northern England'—the landscapes of his childhood home in Cumbria—but the 'hazard and expense had rather a formidable appearance'.[60] *Observations on the River Wye*,[61] therefore, was 'a smaller work of the same kind, which might enable me the better to ascertain the expenses of a larger'.[62]

The book was an immediate success, with a second edition published later that year. Examining a facsimile reprint of the 1800 edition, it is not difficult to see why Gilpin's 'little work', proposing a new way of 'examining the face of a country *by the rules of pictur-esque beauty*',[63] should have appealed to Britain's polite public. The book is an illustrated manual with a set of rules for the appreciation of landscape topography. Armed with a copy, any traveller could be a connoisseur of 'natural scenery'. While Gilpin drew on Burke's ideas of the aesthetic importance of directly observing topography and landscape form, *Observations* was far less complex and demanding than *A Philosophical Enquiry*. As Gilpin himself noted, 'Observations of this kind, through the vehicle of description, have the better chance of being founded in truth, as they are not the offspring of theory, but are taken immediately from the scenes of nature as they arise'.[64]

Rather than being a dense theoretical treatise, *Observations* used a descriptive account of a three-day trip along the Wye and a simple explanation of the compositional principles of seventeenth-century Italianate landscape painting—with its use of coulisses, dark detailed foregrounds, and paler backgrounds—to set out precisely how a journey through the borderlands of South Wales could be an aesthetic experience. For example, as Miss M had done more than twenty years before, Gilpin visited the abbey and the ironworks at Tintern. But rather than remarking on the practical techniques of iron production, as she had, Gilpin focuses on their formal aesthetic qualities alone (see Fig. 5.7). He notes how the 'lofty banks' and 'mazy course' of the meandering river helped to compose the image and how the 'pleasing' smoke of the iron furnaces '[was] spreading its thin veil over [the hills] … [which] beautifully breaks their lines, and unites them with the sky'. The coal-loading quay at nearby Lydbrook, too, met with his approval: 'The contrast of all this business, the engines used in lading and unlading, together with the variety of the scene, produce altogether a picturesque assemblage'.[65] For Gilpin, any physical topography, building or industrial development that satisfied the aesthetic principles outlined in *Observations* could itself be construed as 'art'.

Ironically, though, Valentine Morris's famous 'prospects' at Piercefield struck Gilpin as rather overdone. '[T]he situation of Persfield is noble',[66] he commented, noting that '*Little* indeed was left for improvement, but to open walks and views through the woods to the various objects around them'. 'We cannot, however, call these views picturesque', he complained, as 'They are either presented from too high a point or they have little to mark them out

Fig. 5.7: *Tintern Abbey*, William Gilpin, c. 1772

as characteristic; or they do not fall into such composition, as would appear to advantage on canvas'.[67] Despite Gilpin's dismissive remarks, however, the publication of *Observations* only increased the popularity of trips to Piercefield and the Wye. Moreover, the book's success encouraged Gilpin and his publisher to follow through with his original, more ambitious idea of a survey of the highlands of northern England. In 1786, to equally popular acclaim (and with an equally long title), he published his *Observations, Relative Chiefly to Picturesque Beauty, Made in the Year 1772, On several Parts of England; Particularly the Mountains, and Lakes of Cumberland, and Westmoreland*. Three years later, *Observations relative to Picturesque Beauty made in 1776 on several parts of Great Britain; particularly the Highlands of Scotland* was also released.

Gilpin's guides for picturesque touring were a useful accessory for one of late-eighteenth-century Britain's most popular leisure activities.[68] By the end of the century, at least eight pleasure boats— with coverings against the sun and the rain, and with tables for drawing or writing—were carrying tourists back and forth from Ross to Chepstow.[69] Gilpin's writings, like Burke's, provided an intellectual basis for the fashion for landscape tourism in the uplands of the West. And their popularity played a part in forming new, aesthetic ways of thinking about the natural environment. But as Piercefield shows, investment from fortunes founded in Britain's Atlantic colonies was a vital factor underpinning the opening up of the western landscape for such appreciation.[70] And Valentine Morris was not alone in channelling wealth from the trans-Atlantic trade into infrastructure, particularly turnpike roads, in and around Britain's Atlantic ports, as we shall see in the next chapter.

6

CULTIVATING THE REMOTE

'What, have the provincials a relish for turtle?'
Sir, it is amazing how this country improves in turtles and turnpikes;
to which (give me leave to say) we,
from our part of the world, have not a little contributed.

Samuel Foote, *The Patron* (1764)

Your first sight of Penrhyn Castle is the keep tower, its crenelations just visible above the belt of trees and stone wall that surround the grounds (see Fig. 6.1). Through a formidable gatehouse, complete with portcullis and arrow slits, a winding drive leads up a gentle hill to the intimidating grey stone entrance to the castle. If you take a moment to look behind you before stepping into the chill of the vast entrance hall, there is an extraordinary view. To the left you can see the ruins of Beaumaris Castle and, across the Menai Strait, the island of Anglesey, known in Welsh as Ynys Môn (after the Roman name for the island, Mona). To the right are the mountains of Snowdonia, while in the distance you can just make out the cliffs of Penmaenmawr and Conwy Bay, and the Irish Sea, all framed by the trees and lawns which sweep from the fortress walls down to the waters of the Menai Strait. The castle is the centrepiece of a picturesque artistic composition, the focus of a vast, three-dimensional Welsh version of a Claude Lorrain painting.

Unlike Beaumaris and the other majestic castles of North Wales—such as Conway and Harlech, designed in the thirteenth century for Edward I—Penrhyn has no royal or military origins; it was, instead, built as a family home. By the early decades of the

Fig. 6.1: Penrhyn Castle

nineteenth century, when the crenelated country house was designed for Jamaican plantation heir George Hay Dawkins-Pennant,[1] it was no longer just the rugged landscapes and views of South Wales that attracted genteel visitors. The hilly uplands of the north of the country had also become a destination for travellers searching for sublime natural scenery—and the history of Celtic Cymru.[2] A generation before, in the 1790s, when Dawkins-Pennant was still a young man, North Wales was already drawing so many visitors that one frustrated tourist, John Byng, Viscount Torrington (son-in-law of Jamaican heiress and Robert Adam's patron Juliana Lynch), exclaimed in his diary:

> These laced jackets make me sick! And the French Maid!!! And the trunks!!! and the Dressing Gowns!!!! Why if Owen Glandowr [the medieval Welsh independence leader] could see all this and come amongst us looking as grimly as he is painted over the door he would shake the powder from our ears.[3]

Torrington was not the only person to record his experience for posterity; many visitors kept diaries and journals of their Welsh tours, primarily for circulation to friends and colleagues, but in some cases, for wider publication. In his book *The Search for the Picturesque* (1989), landscape historian Malcolm Andrews used such records to map out the exact routes taken by eighteenth-century tourists in North Wales. If you travel to Penrhyn today, via the A5 from Shrewsbury, you will follow the route taken by most visitors of the time. The road winds through the gentle hills near Llangollen until you reach the steep valleys, cliffs and mountains of Snowdonia. On weekdays, at least, there are few other vehicles, and you can still sense the isolation, awe and wonder that seduced so many eighteenth-century visitors to the area. The words of one 'gentleman in Wales', writing in 1767, still capture the feeling: 'by its situation and the great distance that it is from the metropolis, [North Wales] is almost entirely excluded from the advantages of commerce ... an asylum among those impregnable fortresses, built by the hand of nature'.[4]

While North Wales may have been considered remote, it was not as disconnected as this commentator makes out. By the eighteenth century, most tourists would not have been following sheep paths or drovers' tracks but travelling on well-built 'carriageways'. For instance, when Sir Watkin Williams-Wynn visited North Wales in 1771, the five 'gentlemen' and nine servants in his party spent most of their journey following the routes of the new turnpike roads built in the area over the previous twenty years.[5] Among Williams-Wynn's travelling companions was also the topographic artist Paul Sandby, whom he commissioned to illustrate his tour. Sandby's drawings of the trip were published as etchings five years later in *XII Views in North Wales*, which has frequently been credited with establishing North Wales as a tourist destination.

Constructing carriageways

Just as visitors to Piercefield had depended on the creation of stone-flagged paths along the cliff-face, and a good road from the Aust ferry and Chepstow, in North Wales access to 'prospects' had also required substantial financial investment. It is no coincidence that the popularity of landscape tourism in North Wales in the late eighteenth century went hand in hand with the development of a network of well-maintained turnpike roads.[6] Naturally, in order to appreciate the aesthetic qualities of wild and untamed scenery, you had to get there first. Turnpikes, however, were toll roads, where travellers paid fees to cover the costs of building and repair. How could a turnpike in a remote and unpopulated area attract sufficient traffic to make a return on capital and cover the costs of upkeep? The projected revenue from touring landscape aesthetes would hardly have provided sufficient incentive for investors in major construction projects. Moreover, each stretch of turnpike required a special Act of Parliament and a board of trustees to administer it. Who, in such an area, would have had the skills and contacts to organise a venture on this scale?

An early nineteenth-century portrait, hanging in Penrhyn Castle, and depicting George Hay Dawkins-Pennant's second cousin, Richard Pennant—from whom George inherited the estate in 1808—gives a clue (see Fig. 6.2).

In the painting, Pennant, first Baron Penrhyn, born in 1737, a Jamaican absentee planter and prominent Liverpool merchant, poses in front of a red silk curtain, beyond which is a background of

Fig. 6.2: Portrait of Richard Pennant, Henry Thomson, 1790s

130

a steep and rocky mountainside. In one hand he holds a cane and top hat, while the other is pointing to a map, on which is marked a rough triangle in black and red. The red, shorter side of the triangle is the route of the new road which he built from Penrhyn up the slopes of Nant Ffrancon to the mountains beyond. Pennant's road would not have been designed primarily for the benefit of landscape tourists; it was built to allow the efficient exploitation of the slate quarries that lay in the hills of his country estate. But the new highway was not just for hauling slate down to the coast. It was also intended to be the key link in a new system of turnpikes connecting London, via Shrewsbury, to Anglesey and Ireland beyond. It was this road, later improved by renowned Scottish civil engineer Thomas Telford, that still forms the A5's descent from the mountains of Snowdonia to the sea.

Pennant was not the only absentee planter and merchant to become involved in road-building. Valentine Morris, as we have already seen, contributed to the creation of turnpikes near Chepstow; John Boyd and William Young (of whom more in Chapter Seven) both built roads near their newly acquired estates; and Edwin Lascelles played an important role in the creation of a section of the London-bound turnpike in Yorkshire. In Pennant's case, the initial motives for his road-building were clearly commercial. But why should other West Indian plantation owners have been quite so keen to invest in the construction of broken stone and tamped gravel carriageways?

In an era of frequent bank collapses, the physical, material nature of roads was undoubtedly attractive. Some small investors used them effectively as savings accounts, with possible annual returns of up to 4 per cent.[7] But West Indian absentees often had larger amounts of capital and therefore a far wider choice of investment options. These, as we have seen, ranged from risky but potentially highly rewarding colonial enterprises, to the safer, but lower returns of British land. And while the purchase of land conferred social status, roads brought no such cachet. Nevertheless, many Atlantic merchants did invest their profits into transport infrastructure, as well as agricultural improvement of their private estates.[8]

The regional distribution of turnpike networks during the eighteenth century suggests that Britain's expanding Atlantic trade had a strong effect on road formation along the western seaboard. While the earliest turnpikes were around London and in the east of the country, by the mid-eighteenth century, there was a noticeable concentration of road-building in the region bordering the River Severn, near the port of Bristol.[9] During the eighteenth century, the Severn-side counties of Gloucestershire and Worcestershire had the highest population density outside the capital, so it is hardly surprising that there would have been investment in infrastructure in these areas. But could the growing needs of the expanding Atlantic trade have also stimulated the construction of turnpikes in other less populated regions? As we have seen, the success of Bristol as an Atlantic port was an important factor in the growth of the rural South Wales border as a tourist destination for visitors from Bath and Hotwells, with Valentine Morris's enthusiasm for constructing roads facilitating these visits.[10] Pennant's road-building in the north of the country played a similar role in opening up access to the Welsh mountains. But while landscape tourists certainly benefitted from Pennant's turnpikes, the presence of another Atlantic port city, only a few miles along the coast, was the real impetus behind this road construction. That city is Liverpool.

Liverpool's Welsh hinterland

If you take the alternative approach to Penrhyn Castle, along the North Wales Expressway (or A55) from Chester to Bangor, you gain a very different impression of the northern Welsh coast to that from the winding valleys of the A5. You are still very much aware of the mountains to the south, but you also see the wide, flat landscapes to the north: the caravan parks, chemical works and suburbs of the Wirral peninsular. From this perspective, rather than seeming remote, mysterious and otherworldly, Penrhyn Castle and Snowdonia reveal their close connections with the industries of the Mersey, the Dee and the metropolis of Liverpool.

Just as the rise of Bristol to prominence in the early eighteenth century had been the catalyst for development in the south-west and along the Severn, Liverpool's expansion stimulated economic growth along the coast of North Wales. Like Bristol, the port was well-placed to take advantage of the growing trade with Britain's

American colonies, facing west towards the Irish Sea and the Atlantic beyond. But while Bristol's moorings were some way inland, on the River Avon, Liverpool's quays were on the wider Mersey, much nearer the open ocean, thus allowing larger ships to dock. As early as 1723, the town had 'an opulent, flourishing and increasing trade', as Daniel Defoe noted in his work *A Tour thro' the Whole Island of Great Britain*, which not only rivalled Bristol 'in the Trade to Virginia and the English island colonies in America', but was poised eclipse it.[11]

The young Richard Pennant, the future first Baron Penrhyn, moved to England from Jamaica in 1739 with his sugar planter father John Pennant and mother Bonella, a wealthy heiress in her own right. Rather than joining his brothers Samuel and Henry in their London West India House or becoming a merchant in Bristol, however, John chose Liverpool as his base.[12] It was close to his family's roots, as John's grandfather—the first Pennant to emigrate west and buy land in Jamaica—hailed from the Welsh county of Flintshire, just across the River Dee from Liverpool and the Wirral peninsular.[13] John's choice of Liverpool was a shrewd one. By the time Richard had reached adulthood, Defoe's prophecy of Liverpool overtaking Bristol as an Atlantic port had been realised. By 1777, one American visitor counted more than 1,200 ships in Liverpool's harbour and another thirty or forty more in the channel beyond, describing a 'Forest of Masts in the Docks like an American pine-swamp' and noting that 'The trade to Africa is very large & it is ye 3rd if not 2nd place in England'.[14]

Like their southern compatriots, Liverpool's Atlantic merchants were also keen to be regarded as gentlemen, educating their sons at prestigious schools, commissioning art to adorn their houses, and, for the wealthiest, investing profits in British land.[15] As a successful West India trader, John Pennant was no exception. He sent his son to Cambridge and, soon after his graduation, began his search for a country estate on which to 'settle' Richard. The family first considered purchasing Witham, an estate in Wiltshire not far from William Beckford's newly acquired Fonthill Splendens.[16] However, in 1765, Richard married Ann Warburton, the daughter of an English general and the heiress to one portion of the once-substantial Penrhyn estate.[17] Two years later, in 1767, John and his brother

Henry jointly purchased a further part of the estate. That year, Richard also became one of the two MPs at the time for Liverpool.

The Pennants were not alone among Liverpool's Atlantic merchants to invest in North Wales or marry into an existing Welsh land-owning family: John Gladstone, the grandfather of the future British prime minister William Gladstone, bought an estate a few miles to the east of Penrhyn at Gydir; the wealthy Bamford-Hesketh family purchased one further east again at Gwych; and Foster Cuncliffe, grandson of a Lancaster slave-trader and son of a prominent Liverpool merchant, bought Pant-yr-Ochain Hall, near Wrexham. As early as 1760, Anglesey-based scholar of Welsh history (and Holyhead customs controller) Lewis Morris complained that many estates in the vicinity were no longer owned by native Welsh, but were now in the possession of English and Irish 'foreigners'.[18]

By the latter half of the eighteenth century, coastal North Wales was an integral part of Liverpool's economic hinterland, and part of a web of trade across the Irish Sea, linking ports such as Whitehaven, Lancaster, Douglas (on the Isle of Man, a prominent centre for the slave trade), Chester and Dublin to the British colonies on the far side of the Atlantic. Raw linen, for example, was imported from Ireland and bleached in the hills near Denbigh before being shipped to Liverpool—together with cargoes of leather shoes produced in the town—then finally loaded onto ocean-going vessels for export to the West Indies.[19] Copper mines on Anglesey provided the metal for protective cladding for the hulls of oak ships against the ravages of the 'Toledo worm' found in the warm seas of the tropics, as well as the brass for bowls, pans and 'manillas' (horseshoe-shaped items which were used as currency in some parts of West Africa) to trade in Africa. And the land further east along the Dee estuary supplied bricks, lead and wheat to the rapidly expanding port.[20] Far from being 'excluded from the advantages of commerce', as the gentleman visitor to the region had put it, North Wales was closely connected with the expansion of Britain's Atlantic empire.[21]

This influx of new wealth had a profound effect on the northern Welsh coast, particularly the western extremity towards Caernarvon and Anglesey. The profits from the Jamaican plantations and West India trade of the Pennants, for example—just one of the prosperous merchant families which invested in the area—transformed the once-neglected lands around Penrhyn. Soon after he took control of the estate, Richard Pennant invested extensively in the improvement of his agricultural lands by planting hedges and fertilising the soil. He also turned the small-scale slate quarries in the mountainous part of his estate into a major industrial enterprise, shipping slates via Liverpool to ports around the country.[22]

Pennant not only wanted to maximise the potential revenue from his new estate, but also to use his lands to create landscape art. An estate map from 1768 shows the medieval manor at Penrhyn set amid a patchwork of fields, hop yards, woods and wooded pasture; a map from 1804, however, shows that this landscape had been transformed into sweeping belts of grass and trees. These improvement works continued even after George Hay Dawkins-Pennant inherited the estate from Richard in 1808, commissioning architect Thomas Hopper to draw up plans for a magnificent new building. Indeed, a late-eighteenth-century watercolour by Nicholas Pocock (still held in Penrhyn Castle's collection) shows the medieval house reconfigured as a 'picturesque' neo-Norman castle in its new parkland setting, complete with turrets, crenelations and a majestic arched entrance gateway, with a rocky bay forming the distant background. A remote and old-fashioned estate had been transformed beyond recognition into a theatrical castle and landscape that few landowners could surpass.

Establishing the northern Welsh sublime

As at Piercefield, it is the appropriation of the rugged topography beyond the fashionable new parkland that makes the landscape at Penrhyn extraordinary. Just as Morris had used his cliff-top location to create prospects of the Wye Valley half a century before, at Penrhyn, the Pennants were transforming the mountains and cliffs of coastal North Wales into a scenic background for their country estate. Penmaenmawr, a rocky promontory only a few miles from Penrhyn, and which is featured in the middle-distance of Pocock's watercolour, was already an icon of the sublime. This 'Great Headland of Stone', to translate its Welsh name, had first featured in a well-known literary text of the period: the Georgic poem *The*

Seasons (1726), written by a young Scot named George Thompson. In a passage evoking John Milton's seventeenth-century epic poem *Paradise Lost*, Thompson describes a stormy view at this stretch of coast, only too familiar to merchant shipping:

> Amid Carnervon's mountain ranges loud
> The repercussive roar: with mighty crush,
> Into the flashing deep, from the rude rocks
> Of Penmanmaur heaped hideous to the sky.

It was the wealthy estate-owners of the north-west rather than tourists, who first began drawing attention to the area's natural scenery and 'native' Welsh culture, improving their own landholdings to highlight this landscape and commissioning artists to depict it. When the renowned Welsh painter Richard Wilson, for example, first exhibited his works publicly in London in 1761, depicting North Wales as imitation Poussins or Claudes, few people from the capital had actually been to the region.[23] And it was Liverpool ship owner Henry Blundell of Ince Hall who commissioned one of Wilson's best known Italianate visions of North Wales—*Llyn Peris and Dolbadarn Castle* (see Fig. 6.3), now in the National Museum of Wales. It shows the ruined circular keep of the thirteenth-century castle, built by the Welsh leader Llywelyn the Great, at the base of the Llanberis Pass.

Blundell's former estate lies to the north of Liverpool, just inland from Crosby beach. Looking south-west on a clear day, you can see the jagged outline of the blue-grey hills of North Wales in the distance. The cliffs of Penmaenmawr, Penrhyn and Orme's Head are also just visible, and, fifty miles beyond, the peak of Snowdon itself—shown in the background of Wilson's painting in Fig. 6.3. In this painting, however, the aspect—with ruined castle and lake in the foreground—is from the foot of the Llanberis Pass, the most convenient route between coastal Caernarvon, Snowdon and the neighbouring mountains of North Wales. It was a view that would have been familiar to traders dealing in the coarse wool 'negro cloth' or 'Welsh plains', spun and woven in the hill farms and cottages for export, via Liverpool, to the Caribbean to clothe enslaved workers.[24]

Few tourists from the south at the time, though, would have ventured along this then unmade track.

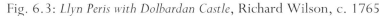

Fig. 6.3: *Llyn Peris with Dolbardan Castle*, Richard Wilson, c. 1765

However, as we have seen, the sketches commissioned by Deeside estate owner Watkin Williams-Wynn (another of Wilson's patrons) of his trip to North Wales and drawn by Paul Sandby helped popularise the idea of leisure travel in North Wales. His description, too, of his terror when one of the horses bolted on a narrow ledge above the sheer cliff face at Penmaenmawr[25] is noteworthy, for he had not only undergone a petrifying, 'sublime' experience, but it had happened in a spot that already had cultural significance.

By the late 1770s, however, access became altogether safer, as the coastal road along the Dee estuary was improved and turnpiked. At the point where the route traversed Penmaenmawr, the road on top of the vertiginous ledge was widened, and a low wall was built at the top of the cliff under the aegis of Richard Pennant. In 1784, one repeat tourist described his wish to pass again over the imposing peak, which was 'within my memory the dread of all travelers'. When arriving at the celebrated site, however, he found that the narrow track along the precipice had been transformed 'into a road to cross with surprise, transport and wonder'.[26]

Although shorn of its dread-inspiring danger, Penmaenmawr was still to become one of the most popular sights on the North Wales tour for visitors from far and wide. In an indication of the cultural significance of this headland, in 1790, a play called *Penmaenmawr, or the Wonders of Wales* was staged in the fashionable north London spa area of Sadler's Wells. A description of the journey along the Penmaenmawr roads from 1810 also shows how anticipated the view from the promontory had become. The author of this account explains: 'We had looked forward to it with much expectation from the accounts of it ... though I doubt much if half of those who mention it have ever seen it'.[27] Like Piercefield's cliffs, Penmaenmawr became an icon of the sublime.

While a visit down the Wye could be comfortably accomplished in a three-day excursion from fashionable Bath, travelling to the mountains of North Wales was a more challenging undertaking. By the late eighteenth-century, however, the tourists who did venture there could not only do so in safety, but also in the luxury of a horse-drawn coach. And comfort would have been no small matter, given that the mountains of North Wales are often subject to strong winds and heavy rains, as the first high ground to meet the prevailing, moisture-laden, south-westerly winds which blow across the Atlantic and the Irish Sea. Even in high summer, Snowdonia is often cold and drenched. The development of roads suitable for coach travel meant that appreciating the natural Welsh scenery was no longer just the privilege of the wealthy new residents of North Wales; any wealthy traveller to the region could now take in the sights in the dry and through a glazed window.[28]

Richard Pennant's road-building also helped to facilitate travel in the region. The completion of his road up Nant Ffrancon, past the slate quarries, transformed what his distant cousin Thomas Pennant described as 'the most dreadful horse-path in Wales worked in the rudest manner into steps along a great length' into a proper carriageway.[29] However, in the latter part of the eighteenth century, unlike in the relatively densely populated Wye Valley, the shelter and warmth afforded by an inn would have been hard to come by for travellers in this part of North Wales. So, in the 1790s, Richard Pennant also built a large hotel at each end of the Nant Ffrancon road for the benefit of travellers to Ireland (which was made an official part of Britain in 1801) and for landscape tourists. References to the '[Capel] Curig Inn' can just be made out at the bottom of the map in Richard Pennant's symbolic portrait (see Fig. 6.2 earlier in the chapter). The location of the Capel Curig Inn—at the intersection of his road and the valley track leading to scenic landscapes of Snowdon and the Llanberis pass, rather than at the junction with the main turnpike road at Betws-y-Coed—suggests that, by the last decade of the eighteenth century, tourists' requirements had now assumed an even greater importance. The site of the inn also provided magnificent views over the Llynnau Mymbyr lake towards Snowdonia.[30]

The coastal end of the road towards Llandygai and Bangor was also attractive for those in search of landscape scenery. In 1810, one traveller described the delight of staying at Pennant's other hotel, the Penrhyn Arms, located not far from the castle itself:

> … we occupied a sitting room with a bow projection, having three windows commanding the most enchanting prospect … the whole bay of Beaumaris, Penmaen Mawr, Orme's Head and the Promontory of Llandudno … too much can't be said in praise of it.[31]

The walk or drive around the Orme's Head peninsula is still popular with visitors, providing spectacular views over the Irish Sea. And it was these investments by the Pennants and other wealthy Atlantic merchants during the late eighteenth and early nineteenth centuries that enabled this part of the North Wales coast to become the fashionable tourist destination it has continued to be to this day.[32]

'Rich improvements' to a 'wild and uncultivated soil'

Further north along the Irish Sea, the historic English counties of Westmoreland and Cumberland (now both part of the modern-day county of Cumbria) also benefitted from the Atlantic trade. The profits made by enslaved labourers in the colonies were key to the transformation of a region that Daniel Defoe had once labelled as 'barren and wild, and of no Use to Man or Beast'[33] into 'the Lakes'—a landscape worthy of polite attention.

The elegant Georgian townhouses and majestic warehouses in the town of Whitehaven are now some of the only reminders of the prosperity of this Cumbrian port during the eighteenth century. And, though its heyday was short as an Atlantic centre for the tobacco and rum trade (rum, a by-product of sugar production was a valuable, secondary export from the Caribbean), the town's wealth was to have a profound effect on the surrounding area.[34] Its successful merchants shared the approach of the Atlantic traders in London, Liverpool and Bristol, investing their profits in land and coastal businesses to give their fortunes a secure base and their families a refined status. As early as 1755, Dr John Dalton—on revisiting the county of his childhood after a thirty-year absence—remarked that the area near Keswick, around twenty miles inland of Whitehaven, demonstrated an 'advantageous comparison of its resent [sic] state with that in which [Dalton] had left it', with 'rich improvements' in a formerly 'wild and uncultivated soil'.[35]

Cumbria's merchants, too, were anxious for their sons to be regarded as gentlemen, and their education included the fashionable subjects of art and landscape appreciation.

Fig. 6.4: *View of Derwent Water, Towards Borrodale, A Lake near Keswick in Cumberland*, Jean Baptist Chatelain, 1752

Picturesque theorist William Gilpin (whom we met in the previous chapter), for example, attended St Bees school, some three miles south of Whitehaven, which employed the Cumberland-raised drawing master John Brown, perhaps the first artist to compare the local hills to Italianate landscape paintings. It was at St Bees that Gilpin received his first drawing lessons and his academic preparation for entrance to Oxford.[36]

Gilpin was born in 1724 at the family home at Scaleby Castle, near Carlisle. His father, Captain John Bernard, was also a talented amateur artist, and had commanded the city's garrison against the 1745 Jacobite uprising. And William's grandfather, also named William, was a powerful land agent to Sir John and Sir James Lowther—proprietors and developers of Whitehaven—and co-owned with his younger brother John a new sugar works in Duke Street in the town.[37] John—William Gilpin the artist's great-uncle—and his son Robert made a fortune from the sugar, tobacco and slave trade, as Whitehaven was transformed from a coal-shipping harbour to trans-Atlantic trading port.

Whitehaven's growth from a village to a town—which, by the mid-eighteenth century, was far greater in size than Cumbria's county city of Carlisle—came just after successful merchant Christopher Lowther inherited the nearby manor of St Bees in 1630. Four years later, Lowther added a pier to Whitehaven's port to allow shipping access for coal exports from his local estates, mainly to Ireland. His son, Sir John Lowther (1642–1706), expanded the family business into the tobacco trade with the American mainland colonies. The 1707 Act of Union between the Kingdom of England (including Wales) and the Kingdom of Scotland, however, led to Glasgow overtaking Whitehaven as the country's pre-eminent tobacco port. So the next in line to the family's fortune, Sir James Lowther (1673–1755), began importing sugar and other commodities from the West Indies into Whitehaven as a substitute, and this was when the port became intimately linked with the slave trade.

Almost uniquely among British seaports, however, Whitehaven was not located at the mouth of a river. This was not a major issue for incoming commodities from the colonies: tobacco and rum shipments to Whitehaven were largely re-exported on ships to other ports, while sugar and snuff (scented, finely ground tobacco

designed for sniffing through the nose) were loaded onto pack animals and distributed inland via the 'snuffpack' rural tracks over the
hills.[38] But, as there was no well-developed road network into the
town in the early decades of the eighteenth century, it was difficult
to transport manufactured goods for outward-bound cargoes for the
American colonies and for slave-trading ships bound for the coast of
West Africa.

The 'snuffpack' routes through the port's hilly, sparsely populated hinterland were, as in North Wales, poor quality. The counties of Cumberland and Westmoreland had lagged far behind in the
development of new turnpike roads, which had started in other
parts of England from the 1660s. That changed, however, in 1739,
with the Whitehaven Harbour Act (which placed new turnpike
roads under the control of a trust); construction of the first new
road began soon after, linking the port with Sir James Lowther's
estates at St Bees. A petition presented to the House of Commons
in 1740 to promote the new turnpikes claimed that there was 'such
increase in carts and wheel carriages as well as loaden horses passing
with goods to and from Whitehaven, that the said roads are become
ruinous and almost impassable in winter'.[39]

Two decades later, eight of Whitehaven's most successful merchants—Gilpin's great-uncle Robert; Peter How; Thomas and
Walter Lutwidge; William Hicks; Thomas Hartley; Richard Kelsick;
and Thomas Patrickson, together with Sir James Lowther—funded
and organised the construction of a network of turnpikes linking
Whitehaven to the nearby towns of Furness, Cockermouth, Penrith,
Keswick, Kendal and Ulverston.[40] And by the early 1770s, nearly
400 new roads had been laid.[41] The creation of these well-built
roads through the previously inaccessible hills meant that, by the
late eighteenth century, Whitehaven was not only linked by shipping routes to Liverpool, Douglas, Dublin, Virginia and the islands
of the Caribbean, but by road to the rest of Britain, too. These road
improvements had, of course, been made for pragmatic reasons, but
they also allowed new visitors to enjoy first-hand the natural scenery, previously only experienced through the medium of a black-
and-white etching.

Arthur Young, for example, visited 'the Lakes' in 1768, as part
of his job surveying 'the state of agricultures, manufactures and

population' in the north of England, and remarked on 'the glory of Keswick Lake … so famous all over England'.[42] It was clearly still a daunting experience, however, as the first new roads had not been designed primarily with landscape tourists in mind. Unlike Piercefield's cliffs, which Young had visited the previous year, the 'wild romantic spots which command the most delicious scenes' could not be reached 'without the most perilous difficulty'.[43] He advised that 'to such points of view, winding paths should be cut in the rock and resting places made for the weary traveler'.[44]

Lancaster and 'the Lakes'

Tourists today—from the south, at least—generally enter the Lake District National Park from the M6 motorway or mainline railway via Kendal. In the late eighteenth century, however, according to the first commercial guidebook to the region published in 1778,[45] many visitors would start their tour on the coast at Hest Bank, three miles west of Lancaster. They would next cross Morecambe Bay— then known as Lancaster Sands—to Cartmel or Ulverston by boat or on foot. 'On a fine day there is no more pleasant sea-side journey in the kingdom. On the right a bold shore deeply indented in some places and opening into bays on others, valleys that stretch far into the country bounded on each side by hanging grounds', exclaimed the author of this guidebook, Ulverston resident Thomas West.[46]

Engaging a local guide was recommended for visitors wishing to traverse the shifting, treacherous channels and sandbars around the bay. As Jamaican absentee William Thomas Beckford noted, during his visit to the area in 1779, 'horrible were the stories told of accidents that had occurred from venturing across at the wrong time of tide'.[47] Indeed, he and his companion reached Ulverston only shortly before the sea 'converted the vast plain of sand we had just passed before into an ocean'.[48] Although popular with tourists, Ulverston was far from a genteel resort; it was, instead, a small port, supplying iron, oats, barley, beans, bark and limestone to the expanding borough of Lancaster.[49]

Unlike Whitehaven, it is not obvious to the casual visitor that Lancaster, too, was once a prominent Atlantic port. But, if you walk down the hill from the castle in the city centre, you reach the mid-eighteenth-century warehouses lining St George's Quay, along the River Lune. Here, the former Customs House has been converted into the Lancaster Maritime Museum, which houses exhibits on the mercantile transformation of Lancaster from a 'town without trade'[50] into a thriving West Indian port. Indeed, as Thomas West noted in the first chapter of his guide, 'The houses are peculiarly neat and handsome, the streets well paved and thronged with inhabitants busied in a prosperous trade to Guinea and the West Indies'.[51]

Lancaster boat-builders turned furniture manufacturers, the Gillows, for example, thrived on the Caribbean trade, making heavy use of imported mahogany wood. One visitor to Lancaster remarked on how 'some very ingenious cabinet makers settle here who fabricate the most excellent and neat goods at remarkably cheap rates which they export to London and the plantations'.[52] Indeed, many of the Gillows's fine mahogany tables, chairs and cabinets—so popular with the lawyers, clerics, merchants and landowners of north-west England—were also sent to the colonies, providing useful, high-value export cargoes for eighteenth-century Lancaster's West India merchants.[53]

By the mid-eighteenth century, Lancaster's thriving Atlantic trade provided the main economic foundation for the whole area.[54] Beans grown near Ulverston, for example, supplied 'food for negroes' during the trans-Atlantic crossing, and one of the main products of the nearby ironworks on the far side of Morecambe at the time were iron cooking pots, or 'Guinea Kettles', for Lancaster's slavers to trade for captives on the west coast of Africa.[55]

As for the local transport network, by the latter part of the eighteenth century, not all newly built roads were being constructed primarily for commercial purposes; some were created as part of the enclosure of what had, up until then, been common land, which facilitated visits to Lancaster and 'the Lakes' beyond.[56] It appears that Arthur Young's plea to improve access to sublime and picturesque views had been heeded. In the 1784 edition of Thomas West's guide, for example, after noting that the state of the roads had improved greatly since the 1760s, the author remarks that 'the gentlemen of this county have set a precedent worthy of imitation in the politest part of the kingdom, by opening, at private expense carriage roads for the ease and safety of such that as visit the country'.[57] And in the late 1780s and 1790s, following the 1786 publication of William Gilpin's *Observations, Relative Chiefly to Picturesque Beauty, Made in the Year 1772, On several Parts of England; Particularly the Mountains, and Lakes of Cumberland, and Westmoreland*, more and more people were doing so.

The shadowy traces of the Atlantic trade would have been apparent to visitors even in the late eighteenth century. Lancaster's traders—the Sawreys, the Bonds and the Rawlinsons, to name but three of the most successful—were from branches of preeminent local families. And while these traders were owners of fine townhouses in the port, their family names were intimately entwined with the nearby hills and valleys—land that some had owned and on which they had farmed for generations.[58] At the frequently visited Lake Windermere, just over thirty miles north of Lancaster, for example, routes between viewpoints, constructed to provide the best picturesque 'prospects', often bore the names of these traders.[59] You can still walk parts of the route, passing signs to Near Sawrey, Far Sawrey and Rawlinson's Nab.[60]

Other connections are less subtle. On Windermere's eastern shore is Storrs Hall, a late-eighteenth-century classical villa extended in the early 1800s by Ulverston-born West India merchant, Sir John Bolton. Further north, near Ullswater, and surrounded by parkland, are the ruins of Lowther Castle, a crenelated country house like Penrhyn, built for the Lowther family on their ancestral land. The project was funded with profits made by the family both from the development of Whitehaven and from their Barbadian sugar plantations.[61] 'To live in such a country seems almost like a continual turtle feast,'[62] exclaimed abolitionist William Wilberforce in 1797, following a visit to the Eusemere Estate, a lakeside farm in the village of Pooley Bridge, on the northern side of Ullswater Lake, owned by fellow anti-slavery campaigner Thomas Clarkson. This observation about the link between the spectacular lakeland views and expensive Caribbean delicacies was certainly apt.[63]

Despite the later decline of Lancaster and Whitehaven's tobacco and sugar trade in the face of competition from the larger ports of Liverpool and Glasgow, the close connections between the 'Lakes' and Atlantic commerce remained until well into the nineteenth

Fig. 6.5: *View of Windermere*, William Gilpin, c. 1762–1783

century. William Wordsworth (son of James Lowther's agent and nephew of a Whitehaven customs collector), born in neighbouring Cockermouth, alluded to these links in his poem *The Brothers* (1800). In it, a 'son of the Lakes' attempts to 'try his fortune on the sea', eventually returning to 'his paternal home' with 'some small wealth Acquir'd by traffic in the Indian Isles'.[64]

Glasgow, the Clyde and beyond

Whitehaven's historic links with the Caribbean are well displayed both in the town's museum and in an atmospheric exhibition, 'The Rum Story', housed in the historic shop, cellars and warehouses of the Jefferson family, prominent Whitehaven sugar and rum merchants. There is now also a memorial at Eusemere, near Penrith, to abolitionist Thomas Clarkson and others involved in the anti-slavery movement. Liverpool, too, has a Museum of Slavery within its Maritime Museum, in which the city's links with the trans-Atlantic trade are made explicit.

In Scotland, however, at the McLean Museum and Art Gallery in Greenock—a former tobacco and sugar port on the Clyde estuary, west of Glasgow—there is, at the time of writing, little acknowledgement of the port's origins. Curators of Glasgow's museums—including the city's Kelvingrove Art Gallery and Museum, built on a country estate once owned by prominent Atlantic merchant Patrick Colquhoun[65]—have, nevertheless, identified objects in their collections that better help to tell the history of Scottish involvement in the plantation colonies. One is an idealised painting of the 'ploughman poet' Robert Burns. Celebrated today as Scotland's national poet, in the summer of 1786 the struggling writer had booked a passage to Jamaica, where he had obtained work as a book-keeper on a sugar plantation. The immediate success of Burns's *Poems, Chiefly in the Scottish Dialect*, published in July 1786 in Kilmarnock, south-west of Glasgow, however, meant that he postponed his voyage.[66] A few months later, rather than itemising hogsheads of sugar in the Caribbean, Burns was being feted by Edinburgh society: the departure 'owre the sea' he had imagined in 'On A Scotch Bard, Gone to the West Indies' did not come to pass.[67]

Many other young Scotsmen also looked to the cash-crop plantations on the far side of the Atlantic. The lure of the sugar and tobacco trade was as strong for those living near the west-facing estuaries of the Firth of Clyde and the Solway Firth (the inlet that forms the English–Scottish border between St Bees Head, near Whitehaven, and the Mull of Galloway), as it was for those on the seaboards of the Severn and Mersey. Indeed, the database of nineteenth-century Caribbean slave compensation records, which forms the foundations of UCL's 'Legacies of British Slave-ownership' project, shows that Scottish owners were a particularly large group of recipients of state money after abolition, with respect to the size of the population. This is partly because, for reasons that I outline in the following chapter, wealthy Scots families became major investors in the Ceded Isles, later known as the Windwards, which were taken by the British during the Seven Years' War (1756–63).[68]

The Scottish elite also aspired to positions in colonial government. Towards the end of the century, in 1795, for example, each of the Ceded Isles, as well as Jamaica and St Lucia, had a Scottish Governor: Lord Balcarres (Jamaica), Henry Hamilton (Dominica), Ninian Home (Grenada), William Lindsay (Tobago) and James Seton (St Vincent).[69] The country's substantial connections with plantation colonies in the Caribbean and Virginia start, though, from the early part of the eighteenth century, and at all levels of society.[70]

As Scottish historians such as the distinguished Sir Tom M. Devine have shown, the disastrous failure of the Darien Venture—Scotland's attempt to establish a 'New Caledonia' on Panama in the 1690s—did not diminish ambitions to participate in trans-Atlantic wealth. The few survivors of this scheme (most died within a year of attempting to settle Panama) fled to the English colony of Jamaica, establishing an early, influential and long-lasting Scottish presence on the island. The financial and political repercussions of the Darien disaster, moreover—including the desire for official access to trade with established English plantation colonies—are widely considered to have contributed to Scotland's union with England and Wales in 1707.[71]

At the turn of the eighteenth century, Scotland was poor in comparison with England, owing to the decline in the Baltic trade, a paucity of quality agricultural land, and a still largely feudal system of landholding. And, while studies are ongoing, it is apparent that wealth remitted from sugar plantations and the wider trans-Atlantic trade in sugar and cotton was an important source of capital for land improvement. It was Jamaican remittances, for instance, that in 1737 allowed John Campbell, the second Duke of Argyll, to eliminate traditional *baile* townships (groups of agricultural smallholdings held in common). In doing so, he created a pool of homeless migrants from land that had now become his personal property on the mainland, on the Western isles of Islay, Tiree and Coll, and, further north, the Isle of Mull.[72]

Like North Wales, these islands were far from the metropolitan hubs of Edinburgh and London, but not so remote for ships sailing from the Caribbean or Virginia on the prevailing south-westerly winds and currents of the northern Atlantic Ocean. Indeed, the west coast of Scotland—and particularly the area near the deep-water estuary of the Firth of Clyde—underwent significant economic change and inward investment following the union with England, and its accompanying official access to English colonies on the far side of the Atlantic. Like Bristol, the old settlement at Glasgow was some way inland along a narrow inlet; improved harbour facilities were therefore built to the west on the navigable waters at Port Glasgow, a former Baltic haven, and further west again at Greenock.[73]

In the early eighteenth century, most Scots lacked the disposable income to buy imported luxuries such as tobacco and sugar (unlike England, which had a large population of the 'middling sort' and which was already a consumer society), and Scotland's Atlantic trade was, therefore, based on exports. By the middle of the century, once struggling Port Glasgow, not best placed to trade with continental Europe, had built on the advantages of a huge, sheltered, west-facing inlet and been transformed into a thriving tobacco *entrepôt*—a facility where tobacco leaf from Virginia was imported and then re-shipped to markets in France and Amsterdam.[74]

There is a wealth of evidence which shows that Scotland became disproportionately dependent on profits remitted from the colonies and the Atlantic trade. Indeed, Devine argues that access to the opportunities afforded by the nascent British Empire renewed the economic strength and resources of the old elite and saved many landed families north of the border from demographic catastrophe.[75] At a different social level, Glasgow's Gaelic Club—founded 'to remind [Highlanders] of Ossian, the melodious and noble prince of poets as well as to converse as friends in the bold and expressive language of heroes in ages past'—was primarily a business forum for the city's Atlantic merchants, where members drank rum punch and enjoyed regular turtle feasts.[76]

The sublime and picturesque in Scotland

In the book so far, I have argued that in the eighteenth century, there was an intimate connection in England and Wales between the wealth derived from sugar and slavery and the development of landscape aesthetics and picturesque tourism. But did the Atlantic trade have a similar effect in Scotland? The answer—inevitably perhaps— is that the situation there was more complex, for reasons of geography, historic land ownership, and the distribution of the country's wealth and population. To understand the influence of trans-Atlantic wealth on the development of landscape tourism and appreciation in Scotland, we must first examine some of the prominent families who invested their riches here.

Fig. 6.6: *Port Glasgow from the South East*, c. 1830 engraving by Joseph Swan, from a painting by J. Fleming

John Boyd's (see Chapter Two) fellow City merchant, Richard Oswald, for example, was one of the many young Scotsmen who flocked to Glasgow as it expanded (see Fig. 6.6). A preacher's son from Caithness, the most north-easterly part of Scotland, the young Oswald moved to Glasgow following his father's death to work as an apprentice to his merchant cousins, Richard and Alexander. These brothers had been living and trading there as early as 1713, when Richard, the elder of the two, had been appointed chief clerk in the Port of Glasgow Customs House.[77] By the time Oswald arrived in Glasgow in 1725, the brothers had established an import–export business trading in tobacco from Virginia, sugar from the Caribbean and the fortified 'Malmsey' wine from Madeira and the Canary Isles, which was particularly popular with planters. They were soon among Glasgow's most successful Atlantic merchants and, during the next decade, Oswald acted as their clerk, first in Glasgow, then in the colonies of Virginia, Carolina and Jamaica. In 1746, the year after the second Jacobite rebellion, he set out on his own to further his career in the City of London.[78]

Two decades later, after establishing his triangular trading foot-print—including the slave-trading consortium that owned Bance island—and marrying a Scottish-Jamaican plantation heiress, Mary Ramsay, Oswald went back to Scotland. But he did not return to his childhood home; instead, in 1764, he bought an estate, Auchincruive, on the River Ayr, south of Kilmarnock,[79] where a vast neo-classical house to designs by Robert Adam was already under construction.[80] Here, on a holding that, at its peak, com-prised more than 80,000 acres, Oswald enclosed fields, planted hedges and introduced new agricultural techniques.

Oswald was not the only Atlantic merchant to invest plantation profits into landed estates in Glasgow's hinterland and south-west Scotland. Ayrshire historian Eric Graham has shown how planta-tions in Jamaica and St Kitts also helped prominent families such as the Hamiltons, Fergussons, Hunter Blairs and Cunynghames at Glengarnock to fund sophisticated lifestyles.[81] Near Dumfries, Oswald's fellow City merchant Alexander Johnston built Carnsalloch House, an elegant, Palladian stone-faced mansion.[82] Still just about standing today as a roofless, fire-damaged ruin, the Venetian win-dows and flanking pavilions shown in historic photographs of Carnsalloch bear a striking resemblance to Adam's original con-cept for Auchincruive.

Further north, successful Glasgow-based merchants, such as the 'Tobacco Lord' James Dunlop and 'Sugar Prince' William MacDowell, followed the example of Whitehaven and Liverpool's Atlantic traders and invested in the purchase of landed estates near the port.[83] And, like Morris at Piercefield and Pennant at Penrhyn, Scotland's improving landowners did not just invest in their own estates; they also funded and organised the laying of new public roads to facilitate better access.[84] Scotland's network of state-funded military roads had originated in the decades after the first Jacobite rising of 1715—the attempt by James Stuart to regain the thrones of Scotland, England and Ireland. A second wave of road-building followed the last major Jacobite rebellion in 1745, strengthening transport links around the English–Scottish border and enabling troops to move more easily to put down insurrections.

By the latter half of the eighteenth century, however, with the growing wealth of Scotland's elite, private finance was increasingly mobilised, as it had been in England. As the authors of a survey of the Scottish transport system in 1775 commented, 'In this country where the making of roads is attended with so much labour and expense … [they] honour the nobility and gentry, who have so judiciously attended to the directing as well as executing'.[85]

Richard Oswald, the owner of plantations and slaves in Virginia, Georgia, Florida and the Caribbean, was a pioneer in this respect. In 1766, shortly after buying Auchincruive, he pressed for an Act of Parliament to establish a trust to build Scotland's first privately financed turnpike road, and was instrumental in the construction of a network of roads near his Ayrshire estate.[86] The result was a transformation of Ayr's transport infrastructure: 100 miles of roads, which did not exist when Oswald bought his estate, were, by his death, arteries connecting various parts of the county to its centre.[87]

Further north in Ayrshire, following his return from his post as Commander-in-Chief of the British forces in North America, including three years as Governor General of Virginia, John Campbell, the fourth Earl of Loudoun, was also organising the construction of new roads near his inherited estate at Loudoun Castle, just east of Kilmarnock. An avid horticulturalist, his landscaping—including trees sent from Virginia—became widely renowned. In 1767, he became president of the county's turnpike trust.[88]

Like North Wales and the Lakes, new investment in roads, principally for commercial motives and to allow access to rural estates, proved vital to tourists in search of sublime and beautiful 'scenery'.[89] As Malcolm Andrews shows in *The Search for the Picturesque*, landscape tourists in the late eighteenth century began their journeys not in Glasgow, however, but Edinburgh, and made their way cross-country to the Falls of the Clyde. Travellers would either take the ferry over the Firth of Forth or, alternatively, follow the coastal road along the Forth's southern shore until they reached Stirling Castle, a popular picturesque tourist site because of its location on a rocky bluff. And, on the way, they could have glimpsed the spectacular stone pineapple folly (see Fig 6.7), built a generation before in 1763 by John Murray, the fourth Earl of Dunmore.

Standing sixty feet high, the enormous pineapple adorns the former hothouses at Dunmore Park, and was constructed just before Murray's departure to become the last colonial Governor of

Fig. 6.7: Former 'pinery' at Dunmore Park, Stirlingshire

Virginia. After US independence in 1776, he became Governor of the Bahamas, where he established pineapple plantations to supply customers on the American mainland.[90]

Travellers could certainly see, too, how landowners were transforming rugged upland landscapes into ornamental parklands, with other whimsical attractions. After moving further on, north of Perth, to visit the newly built 'hermitage' (a cave-like folly) on the Duke of Atholl's landscaped estate, they then continued south-west down the valleys of Loch Tay and Loch Lomond. Here, at the Tayside estate of Kenmore, they could visit a mock 'temple' and use the moveable 'prospect glass' (a small telescope) within it to frame picturesque views of the surrounding landscape.[91] The last major sights were the 'Falls of the Clyde' (see Fig. 6.8)—a collection of

Fig. 6.8: *The Fall of the Clyde, Lanarkshire—Noon*, J. M. W. Turner, 1802

four waterfalls just a few miles from Glasgow—and, from 1786, the palatial cotton mills of New Lanark.[92]

But not all the scenes along their Scottish tour were so pleasant. Between Kenmore and the Clyde, on the grassy meadows adjoining Loch Lomond, they would have seen barefoot women and children laying out sheets of linen to be bleached before export to customers in the West Indies and the mainland American plantations. Plantation owners were the primary market for the cheap, coarse linen made by the rapidly expanding eighteenth-century Scottish textile industries, to clothe their enslaved workers.[93]

'Broken rocks and wild precipices'

The touring route for visitors around the 1770s was set by an influential Welsh naturalist and travel writer,[94] Thomas Pennant of Downing, who visited Scotland in 1769 and heartily recommended the trip: 'They will find the whole country excel[s] in roads, partly military, partly done by statute labour, and much by the munificence of great men'.[95] His journal, *Tour in Scotland*, published in

1772, was illustrated with etchings made from sketches by his travelling companion. Pennant's lively observations made it a compelling narrative. Setting off from Edinburgh, he travelled on the 'Queen's ferry' to the north bank of the Firth of Forth, via Kinross, to Blair Atholl, Macbeth's castle at Scone and Dunkeld, before heading west to Loch Tay and Glasgow.

Like Miss M's journal description of her brief visit 'abroad' to Piercefield and the Wye Valley, made almost a decade before, Pennant's curiosity and excitement is infectious. His first sight of the Scottish borders near Berwick, however, is dispiriting: 'the entrance into Scotland has a very unpromising look … for four or five mile succeeds the black joyless, heathy moor'.[96] Travelling further north to Edinburgh, his journey improves, when he sees 'a city that possesses a boldness and grandeur of situation beyond that I had ever seen'.[97] Like Miss M, he comments on natural scenery, remarking on the rocky outcrops of Arthur's Seat and Salisbury Craigs, near the Old City, describing how 'they exhibit a romantic and wild scene of broken rocks and wild precipices'.[98]

In addition to natural scenery, he also records his observations on the architectural sights of Scotland. He notes the construction of an Edinburgh suburb, New Town, linked to the Old City by a magnificent three-arched bridge over the man-made Nor Loch (now drained),[99] and remarks on the prices of the (as yet uninhabited) grand terraced houses, 'all built in the modern style'.[100] The ease with which Pennant segues between detailed descriptions of birds, animals and their habitats; local industries; renowned historical sites like Macbeth's castle; and, indeed, house prices, is one of the charms of his book.

Later tourists to Scotland, however, were more likely to focus solely on the natural sights, particularly the rugged Highlands.[101] In 1789, twenty years after Pennant's visit, William Gilpin published another book on the picturesque: *Observations, Relative Chiefly to Picturesque Beauty, Made in the Year 1776, on Several Parts of Great Britain; Particularly the High-lands of Scotland*. The work was yet another commercial success and introduced a new, wider Scottish audience to the concept of picturesque scenery. Like his previous publications, Gilpin's narrative focused on the appreciation of picturesque compositions made during his tour.

However, at times, particularly when Gilpin describes the landscapes of the Highlands, the text reads rather more like an instruction manual for an aspirational estate owner. He advises:

> Add trees upon the foreground, tufted woods creeping up the sides of the hills, a castle upon some knoll, and skiffs upon the lake (if there be one) and tho the landscape will still be *sublime*, yet with these additions (if they are happily introduced) the *beautiful* will predominate.[102]

The hills, still at that time home to thousands of subsistence farmers, in Gilpin's eyes, could be transformed into a scenic upland backdrop. And over the next thirty or forty years, many Scottish highland landowners were to heed his advice.

The expansion of the Atlantic trade had not only brought wealth, but wider interest in the Highlands and the western seaboard. One of the earliest English visitors to write about Scotland was Samuel Johnson, the celebrated author of the first dictionary of the English language, who was encouraged to make the trip by his younger Scottish friend (and later biographer) James Boswell. Pennant's keen observer's eye and fluent prose had drawn the admiration of both Johnson and Boswell, and the two men were inspired to make their trip in the summer and autumn of 1773, shortly after Pennant's *Tour* was published. They took, however, a different route: having travelled up the east coast from Edinburgh to St Andrews and Aberdeen, the pair turned west to Inverness, then south-west, past the military fort of St Augustus, before travelling on to Skye and the other western islands.[103]

As they moved across the country, Johnson records his shock at finding that, away from the established Baltic ports on Scotland's north-east coast, currency was still not in regular use. Nevertheless, the influence of the Atlantic trade was apparent even in remote areas: on giving a woman they encountered a shilling, 'she begged for snuff; for snuff is the luxury of a Highland cottage'.[104] Johnson's travels through Scotland's north-western interior were made at the end of a generation of profound cultural dislocation. After the defeat of the second Jacobite Rebellion in 1746, a large number of estates—many of them clan territories in the Highlands—were forfeited to the Crown as a punishment for treason.[105]

Other traditions, too, such as the wearing of clan tartans were prohibited, with punishments including transportation to any of the plantation colonies overseas. The 'Highland Clearances', the mass eviction of tenants from their land, were to follow from 1750, as landowners ruthlessly strove to improve their estates, and would only come to a halt over a century later.

In 1773, at the time of Johnson's visit, however, it appears that little had so far changed physically in the hilly uplands. Although the famed lexicographer uses the term 'cottage' to describe some of the more humble buildings he observed, this was perhaps a misnomer: at that time in the Highlands, before the clearances had really gathered pace, most habitations were the indigenous turf-and-thatch 'blackhouses', so called because of the dark, windowless, smokey—but easily warmed—interiors.[106] Pennant, four years earlier, had also commented disparagingly that 'the habitations of the *Highlanders* … are very small, mean and without windows or chimnies and are the disgrace of *North Britain* as its lakes and rivers are its glory'.[107]

It was only on reaching the west coast, before taking a boat to the Isle of Skye, that Johnson saw familiar building types: 'Having surmounted the hill at last we were told that at Glenelg, on the sea side we should come to a house of lime and slate and glass', he remarked, adding wryly that 'this image of magnificence raised our expectations'.[108] While shocked by the poverty encountered in the uplands, Johnson's visit to the Hebrides seems to have been more to his liking. As there were no inns in that part of Scotland at that time, the pair had to stay with Boswell's local contacts.[109] 'We found nothing but civility, elegance, and plenty', Johnson observed. 'They use silver on all occasions when it is common in England', and the rich breakfasts included tea, coffee, marmalade, conserves, Cheshire cheese, milk, eggs and sugar. The contrast between the 'rough and rocky' landscapes of the Hebridean islands and the generous hospitality they received intrigued him: 'I forgot to inquire how they were supplied with so much exotick luxury'.[110]

After returning to the mainland in Argyll, the pair then travelled cross-country to Loch Lomond, south along the River Leven to Dumbarton (a small port on the north of the Firth of Clyde) and on to Glasgow. They then journeyed south again before staying at

Auchinleck, the newly built Palladian country house on Boswell's family estate in Ayrshire, a few miles east of Auchincruive.[111] Boswell and Johnson's tour through Scotland was made partly by carriage, but also, in the Highlands, on horseback and by small boat. On leaving Inverness, Johnson remarked:

> We were now to bid farewell to the luxury of travelling and to enter a country upon which perhaps no wheel has ever rolled. We could indeed have used our post chaise one day longer along the military road to *Fort Augustus* but we could have hired no horses beyond *Inverness*.[112]

It was only the construction of new roads in the early years of the nineteenth century under the aegis of the Commissioners of Highland Roads and Bridges, established by an Act of Parliament in 1803, that allowed less intrepid travellers to take comfortable coach trips through the dramatic landscapes of the Highlands. The Commission had great political clout, initially including among its members the Speaker of the House of Commons, the Chancellor of the Exchequer and the Lord Advocate of Scotland. However, the key member, until his death in 1805, was Dumfries-born William Johnstone Pulteney, a leading Scottish advocate, West Indian plantation owner and property developer—as we saw in Chapter Four—in the city of Bath.[113]

It was a hugely ambitious infrastructure project, lasting over twenty years and was headed by renowned civil engineer Thomas Telford, once a Dumfries stonemason, whom Pulteney helped to appoint to survey the land and then develop the plan to improve transport links across the Highlands. It included 1,000 bridges and 920 miles of new roads (as well as the sixty-mile-long Caledonian Canal in the Great Glen from Inverness to Fort William, that created a shipping link between the west coast to the east). The task was accomplished through a mix of Government funding, local taxes and contributions by Highland estate owners.

The Highlands and Islands

The improvement in transport and communications coincided with a revolution in land ownership in the western Highlands and Islands.

Fig. 6.9: Taylor and Skinner's 1775 Road Map of Scotland

And, while research is still ongoing, it is clear that wealth derived from plantation slavery, among both the historic clans and the 'new elite' of merchants and proprietors of estates in the Caribbean and North America, was a major contributor to this change.[114]

From historical research to date, the first major slavery-connected land purchase seems to have been the acquisition by Daniel Campbell of the Isle of Islay, and half of Jura, in 1726. Campbell was a Glasgow tobacco and sugar merchant, and slave-trader, and had already bought the Shawfield estate, near Rutherglen, to the south-east of the city. Most of the identified land deals happened from 1790s onwards, however, peaking in the late 1830s—when most of the clearances also took place. And, as historians Iain MacKinnon and Andrew Mackillop have demonstrated, land purchases were accelerated by the compensation payments to slave-owners after slavery was finally abolished by law in 1833.[115] Some of the transactions were vast, including John Walker of Dumfries' investment in the Corrour estate in 1834, in Inverness-shire, where the family's holdings reached 70,000 acres. Walker was the son of a Jamaican returnee, with his own slavery interests. His neighbour James Scarlett (Lord Abinger and Attorney General for England) received compensation for enslaved workers in Jamaica, and built Inverlochy Castle, near Fort William.[116]

Scotland's old nobility also owned Caribbean plantations and were compensated for the freeing of enslaved workers, creating wealth that could be invested in the Highlands and Islands. They included the chief of the MacLeans; members of clans Cameron and Mackintosh; and George Murray, the fifth Earl of Dunmore and son of the creator of the stone pineapple folly near Stirling, who bought over 117,000 acres of land on the Isle of Harris in 1834.[117] In all, historians MacKinnon and Mackillop identify over 455,000 acres of land bought by families with slavery-linked wealth by 1834 in Inverness, Ross, Islay, Jura, Mull and the Western Isles. By 1850, this had nearly doubled to over 850,000 acres, including estates on the Isles of Skye and Raasay—that is, a quarter of the whole land mass of the western Highlands and Islands. And even that is likely to be significant underestimate, as the exact acreage of many of the large land purchases is absent from the records. As MacKinnon and Mackillop remark,

> Hundreds of thousands of people travel through the west Highlands of Scotland to the Hebrides each year …. As they travel through this magnificent tract of the western Highlands it is unlikely these travellers will realise that they are passing estates that were once—and in some cases still are—owned by families who profited from Britain's eighteenth- and nineteenth-century system of plantation and enslavement in its Caribbean colonies.[118]

This wild, romantic 'magnificent tract'—including the grand nineteenth-century crenelated castle at Inverlochy in the foothills of

Ben Nevis, Britain's highest peak—is, of course, also a designed landscape. The sublime views of distant hills, devoid of any 'mean' Highland 'blackhouses' and carefully framed by belts of trees, are not accidental: they are picturesque compositions, as advocated by William Gilpin. Like North Wales, Cumberland and Westmoreland, profits from the plantation trade brought new investment to what had previously been poor, sparsely populated regions. By the early nineteenth century, the Lakes, Snowdonia and the uplands of western Scotland were no longer considered miserable and barren. They were areas where discerning gentlemen or ladies of taste might choose to visit or, indeed, live. As Adam Smith, a former scholar at the University of Glasgow, had foreshadowed in the *Wealth of Nations* (1776), Britain's Atlantic trade had succeeded in 'cultivating the remote'.[119]

7

TAINTED LANDSCAPES

But now far distant from my native soil;
Whose fertile vale ne'er with the Muses rung,
Whose fruits no bard, whose dames no poet sung
Savannahs open, hills rife, floods glide along...

The' ungrateful task a British muse disdains,
Lo! Tortures, racks, whip, famine, gibbets, chains,
Rise on my mind, appall my tear-stain'd eye
Attract my rage, and draw a soul-felt sigh.

Anon., *Jamaica: a poem, in Three Parts* (1777)

In the spring of 1775, a seventeen-year-old British boy set sail for
Jamaica in the hope of creating 'a fortune' in the Caribbean sugar
colonies. But it was not only the lure of potential riches that
attracted him to the West Indies. As he explained in his poem
Jamaica, his ambition was also 'to scan the works of Nature'.[1] He
was not disappointed. 'How blessed is he, who 'midst th' Atlantic
main // Hath rov'd three moons the sugar-isles to gain', he
enthused. His poem continues:

Here glow the plains, cloth'd in eternal green
Here rise the hills, the valleys intervene
While gay plantations on the fancy gain
And tow'ring forests terminate the scene.[2]

The youthful poet, whose name has been lost to history, was
not the only visitor to remark upon the picturesque qualities of
the Caribbean landscape. A year earlier, a Scottish woman named

Janet Schaw had also described her first impressions of Antigua in her own journal:

> … hills, dales and groves, and not a tree, plant or shrub that I had ever seen before; the ground is vastly uneven, but not very high; the sugar canes cover the hills almost to the top and bear a resemblance in colour at least to a rich field of green wheat …. Will you not smile, if after this description, I add that its principal beauty to me is the resemblance it has to Scotland, yes to Scotland, and not only to Scotland in general, but to the Highlands in particular.[3]

By the early 1770s, the concept of picturesque landscape appreciation had arrived in the Caribbean. Indeed, an etching dating from 1769—*A View Of The Town And Harbour Of Montego Bay, In The Parish Of St James', Jamaica, Taken From The Road Leading To St Ann's*, by an unknown engraver but after paintings by John Spilsbury (1730–95)—features a young artist in the foreground sketching amongst the lush undergrowth.[4] And, in his *History of Jamaica* (1774), Edward Long, scion of one of the island's established families, incorporated a picturesque view of rocky cascades. His family archives, held in the British Library and dating from a similar period, contain sketches of a 'prospect of the upper side of a bridge formed by nature' and a couple in riding habits gesturing at a waterfall beyond.[5]

I am not the first historian to address the concept of the 'colonial picturesque' *per se*. In *The Road to Botany Bay* (1988), for instance, Paul Carter argues that 'picturesque tours' played a key cultural role in the early-nineteenth-century British colonisation of Australia.[6] English Literature scholar Sara Suleri, too, has examined how the creation of watercolour landscapes in imperial India allowed wives of British colonial officials to 'understand and order an alien surroundings'[7], while Sue Rainey has shown how images of 'natural wonders' were used to create cultural icons in the independent United States.[8] However, the origins of colonial landscape appreciation began more than half a century before the nineteenth-century examples studied by these authors, and some of the earliest instances of 'picturesque' art in the colonies derive, as we shall see, from Britain's Sugar Isles.

Painting the colonial landscape

In Penrhyn Castle hangs a series of small watercolours of Jamaica (they were in a bedroom corridor when I first visited). Although unsigned and undated, the origins of three of the paintings can be accurately ascertained from a set of etchings of them published in 1778 and now held in the British Library.[9] The etchings identify the watercolour studies as 'drawn on the spot and painted' by George Robertson for plantation owner William Beckford of Somerley in 1774 (see Fig. 7.1 below, and Fig. 7.2 on p. 169). The images would have been well-known among eighteenth-century Britain's artistic cognoscenti: the etchings were issued by John Boydell of Cheapside, at the time the largest and most prestigious print publisher in Britain and continental Europe. Robertson's studies were clearly not just private records of an absentee family's West India estates, but were intended as works upon which prints issued to a wider audience could be based. Indeed, the British Library etchings were once in the topographic collection of King George III.

Robertson's patron, William Beckford of Somerley, was a member of one of Jamaica's wealthiest absentee planter families. However (unlike his cousin and namesake, the builder of Fonthill Abbey, to whom I turn in the next chapter), he was the illegitimate offspring of a fourth son. Although in 1757, at the age of just thirteen, he inherited several Jamaican sugar estates, these were not necessarily the windfall they appeared to be, coming complete with significant debts. Nevertheless, he received a gentleman's education, attending Westminster and Oxford and undertaking an extensive Grand Tour of Europe. In 1774, soon after his marriage to his cousin Charlotte Hay, he returned to his childhood home in Jamaica. It is not recorded whether the newly married couple's return to the West Indies was by choice or out of financial necessity. Given his debt-ridden sugar estates, however, and Beckford's comments that Jamaica was 'Not a place for long term residence for those who have had a liberal education',[10] there is good reason to suggest it was the latter. But why, therefore, were the couple accompanied on their trans-Atlantic voyage by two landscape artists, Robertson and Philip Wickstead, one of renowned German-born painter Johann Zoffany's former pupils?[11]

Fig. 7.1: Watercolour sketch for *A View in the Island of Jamaica of the Bridge crossing the Cabaritta River on the Estate of William Beckford Esq*, George Robertson, c. 1774

The question of why plantation owners might wish to commission artistic depictions of their land has intrigued many art experts. Boydell's prints of Robertson's paintings, for example, have been analysed by several eminent art historians, including K. Dian Kriz, Tim Barringer, Geoff Quilley and Sarah Thomas.[12] In his discussion on the 'representation of British colonial landscapes', Quilley notes that Boydell's prints are significant precisely because of the 'paucity of visual [eighteenth-century] material treating the Caribbean colonies', as West Indians generally chose 'to dissociate their display of cultural refinement from the source of their prosperity'.[13] However, as we have seen, during most of the eighteenth century the sugar isles were viewed—from Britain, at least—primarily as money-making arenas, not places of any inherent artistic or cultural interest to 'polite' society. Given this, it is remarkable that there are any representations of the Caribbean colonies at all.

The art historians above do not examine, moreover, Robertson's original watercolour sketches (hidden away, as they were, in Penrhyn Castle). In these depictions, the island is not a slave colony producing cash crops in the harshest conditions for export, but an idyllic land of ease and plenty: a picturesque landscape of fast-flowing streams, rocky promontories and lush vegetation. These paintings, among the earliest examples of colonial picturesque art, are noticeably different from the prints Boydell made of them. And the changes Boydell made, such as including sanitised depictions of plantation workers, are—as we shall see later in this chapter—significant in understanding the underlying aims and motivations of the Caribbean planters in commissioning the original works.

Of course, many other historic images of Caribbean landscapes do survive, but in a rather different form. In the seventeenth century, 'sea-men going into the West Indies' were officially advised to make 'plots and draughts of prospects of Coasts, Promontories, Islands and Ports marking the bearing and Distances as near as they can'.[14] From the late eighteenth century onwards, this type of information—collated, cross-checked and then finely engraved—formed the basis of the printed *British Admiralty Charts* and *Pilot Books* of the Caribbean. These panoramas and charts of anchorage points and coastal hazards were still (in updated editions) being used, indeed, by sailors until the arrival of satellite navigation.

Robertson's paintings are very different from these imperial topographic and maritime records. The watercolours and etchings are not aids to commercial coastal navigation; they do not provide accurate information for British naval or military commanders. Nor do they even record the form and management of colonial agricultural holdings. They are, instead, images of the financially unproductive parts of a Jamaican plantation, carefully composed to delight a connoisseur of landscape art.

And Robertson and Wickstead (who died in the Caribbean in around 1790) were not the only professional artists to travel to the West Indies. In 1771, the new Captain General and Governor in Chief of the Leewards, Ralph Payne, commissioned the young Thomas Hearne (who was to become one of Britain's most renowned landscape artists) to make twenty watercolour views of the Leewards. And William Young, the newly appointed Scots Antiguan governor of Dominica, engaged Agostino Brunius—an artist in architect Robert Adam's studio—to create a series of paintings of the island.[15]

But why should there have been this unprecedented interest in artistic depiction of Britain's West Indian colonies in the late 1760s and early 1770s?[16] Of course, images of the Caribbean sugar isles had a not insignificant potential market among wealthy absentee owners. But commercial interests alone are insufficient to explain their motives. The answer lies in Britain's colonial expansion in the Caribbean after the Seven Years' War, the vast amount of investment thereafter, and the growing domestic public concern about the trans-Atlantic slave trade in the years that followed.

Reassuring images of stable, profitable communities and paintings of barracks and courthouses, like those produced by Hearne in the Leewards, were useful propaganda—as were Brunius's highly selective and misleading paintings of the so-called 'free-coloureds' in Dominica. But Robertson's images are very different again. His patron Beckford seems anxious to show the Caribbean not only as a place to make money, but a place of cultivation in all senses. Through the artist's depictions, Beckford uses the concept of the 'picturesque' to transform 100-year-old Caribbean slave colonies into living landscape art. And these images, too, were another form of visual propaganda.

The Ceded Isles

Before looking at Robertson's original Jamaican watercolours in a little more detail, it is worth pausing to reflect on what was happening with respect to land management in the British Caribbean at the time, following the wartime capture of the Ceded Isles—the former French colonies of Grenada and the Grenadines, and three 'neutral' islands, Dominica, St Vincent and Tobago (later renamed the Windwards)—which was finalised by the far-reaching Treaty of Paris in 1763. Though tiny in terms of landmass, the British conquest of the Windwards was considered a worthy prize, as the Caribbean was seen as so valuable to the Empire.[17] They were trophies won, however, at great cost to the public purse, and a Commission for Land Sales was set up under the aegis of Scottish Brigadier-General Robert Melville, who assumed overall military and civilian command of the Ceded Isles after the war. Its purpose was to ensure the Crown lands were sold at maximum profit.

But, while there was no shortage of purchasers for coffee and sugar plantations in the former French colony of Grenada, finding

Fig. 7.2: Watercolour sketch for *A View in the Island of Jamaica, of Fort William Estate, With Part of Roaring River Belonging to William Beckford Esq, Near Savannah la Mar*, George Robertson

investors to buy land in Dominica, St Vincent and Tobago was a far more difficult task. These islands had not previously been colonised and were still largely covered in thick tropical rainforest, which had to be cleared before any cash crops could be planted. After an initial enthusiasm for 'sacrificing a few more years in this climate' to leave behind 'a little fortune', James Grainger, the St Kitts-based overseer and author of *The Sugar Cane*, reflected the opinions of many existing colonists and British-based investors and speculators alike when he changed his mind and argued that 'the *first* adventurers there will, *all* be ruined'.[18]

In 1764, Antiguan absentee William Young—the English-educated son of a plantation owner's daughter and a Scottish doctor—was appointed president of the Commission. His father had fled Scotland, like so many others, after the Jacobite rebellion of 1715, and made a new life for himself in the Caribbean.[19] Faced from the beginning with a potential public relations disaster for the government, Young's Commission hastily drew up measures to encourage new investors, including offering interest-free, state-backed loans and undertaking a prominent publicity drive focused on his father's birthplace.[20] The year of Young's appointment, the first of a series of articles appeared in the magazine *The Scotsman*,[21] contrasting the rich fertile soil of the new colonies with the intensively cultivated islands in the Leewards and Barbados.

By this time, there was already a growing understanding of the link between felling tropical rainforests and the degradation of land.[22] As Young explained in *The Scotsman*, 'certain portions of land in wood, will be preserved on the tops of hills and on other convenient places' and to prevent 'that drought, which in these climates is the usual consequence of a total removal of the woods'.[23] But the woods would be kept not just for practical reasons. They were also to help create attractive landscapes, to provide 'publick benefit'.

In the eighteenth century, felling dense woodland was a dangerous and labour-intensive process. More than a century before, in Barbados and the Leewards, it had been predominantly English, Welsh and Irish indentured labourers who had cleared the undergrowth; chopped down the trees; de-limbed the branches; hauled the vast trunks to the coast for export; dug up and removed stumps, roots and stones in order to make fields ready for hoeing; and planted cash crops. In Britain's new Caribbean territories, however, it was to be 'the children of Africa' whom planters would 'drag to the immense forests of our rank climate and there sacrifice them to the felling of trees', as one guide to sugar management, by barrister-turned-plantation owner Clement Caines, documents at the time.[24] Indeed, the demand for labour to create new plantations in Dominica, Tobago and St Vincent in the late 1760s and 1770s contributed to the rapid expansion of the British slave trade at the time—and helps to explain why Richard Oswald and John Boyd's investment in Bance Island proved so lucrative (see Chapter Two).[25]

Young's land sales campaign achieved substantial success, and more than half the land in Dominica was bought by Scots—a pattern repeated in the other islands.[26] Young was also an active investor himself. In 1766, he bought four lots in Queens Bay, Tobago, together with his partner James Stewart. A year later, he sold one of his Antiguan estates, and, in 1768, purchased seventy-six acres of land in the parish of St Andrews in St Vincent, not far from an estate bought by John Trevanion, John Boyd's son-in-law.[27] He subsequently extended the partnership to create two new plantations, Betty's Hope in Antigua and Delaford in Dominica. And while Stewart was to be the overseer, Young provided the 'means for the building, [and for] purchasing stock and slaves', according to correspondence held at Rhodes House, University of Oxford.[28]

By 1767, however, just three years after his appointment as head of the Commission for Land Sales and a year after his own initial land purchases, Young returned to England with sufficient means to purchase a country estate—Delaford, near Iver in Buckinghamshire. One of his first activities was to begin a programme to divert the ancient common tracks and ways that lay near his newly purchased house to create parkland. The next few years saw Young make several journeys between the Caribbean and Britain, travelling back to the West Indies to become Governor of Dominica in 1768. The following year, he was made a Baronet, before venturing back to his English country seat in 1773.[29] In the Caribbean, at his command, enslaved Africans cleared tropical rainforests to provide new fields for sugar cane; by contrast, in Buckinghamshire, farmland was taken out of production in order to create an ornamental landscape park. We return to the now Sir William Young at Delaford Park in the final chapter.

The picturesque, the Caribbean—and the Pacific

Even before George Robertson landed in Jamaica with his patron Beckford in 1774, in the aftermath of Britain's takeover of the Ceded Isles, picturesque depiction of colonial landscapes was already emerging as a trend—primarily as part of British exploration in the Pacific. The first great Pacific expedition, between 1768 and 1771, was undertaken on the research vessel HMS *Endeavour*, under Captain James Cook. On board this ship was a wealthy young man with a passionate interest in botany: the future Sir Joseph Banks, patron of the Royal Botanical Gardens at Kew and president of London's Royal Society, the national academy of sciences, for over forty years. The primary—though at the time unpublicised— purpose of Cook's first voyage to the South Seas was to prospect for new colonial territories in *terra Australis incognita* (the unknown southern land). Many plantation owners hoped that expeditions like these would find suitable bases to supply the Caribbean islands with provisions and potential cash crops.[30]

Interestingly, in May 1767, the year before the HMS *Endeavour* sailed for the Pacific, and after just disembarking from a return voyage to Canada's Newfoundland, Banks had dined with Valentine Morris, after several days spent in the Wye Valley, including a tour of Piercefield.[31] There, he had admired 'the abrupt contrast' between the 'very fine lawn' and 'naked rocks',[32] and remarked in his journal: 'I am more and more convinced that it is far the most beautiful place I ever saw'.[33] From Piercefield, Banks crossed by ferry to Bristol, where he spent several days examining botanical specimens at Clifton Gorge, before travelling to Wells, visiting the nearby caves at Wookey and the spectacular gorge at Cheddar.[34]

There is no record of their dinner conversation at Piercefield but, as a West Indian absentee, Morris would certainly have been curious about Banks's expeditions, past and future. Caribbean investors in the Ceded Isles had already looked to the fishing grounds off Newfoundland and Labrador, on the east coast of Canada, to supply their growing enslaved workforce with protein in the form of salted cod.[35] Their meeting was apparently successful, as Banks would visit Morris again soon after returning from his voyage with Captain Cook.[36] It is quite possible that Banks's trip to the scenic sites of the Welsh borders had stimulated an interest in sublime and picturesque landscapes, indeed, as well as botany.

Banks's retinue on the *Endeavour* included two artists, the Edinburgh-born botanical illustrator Sydney Parkinson and a Scottish landscape painter, Alexander Buchan. Both men died on the voyage, but, a year after his return to Britain, Banks used the sketches they had made during the Pacific expedition to help publicise his account of it. Looking at the engravings made from Parkinson's drawings—of sublime and picturesque sights such mountains and grottos, as well as views of bays and indigenous villages—it is clear that the concept of a landscape tour, as Banks had undertaken at Piercefield, would have been very useful as a way to engage a wider public.[37] In 1772, Banks also commissioned artist George Stubbs (renowned for his portraits of horses) to paint the first Western picture of a kangaroo, from a skin he brought back from Australia. In Stubbs's painting, the kangaroo appears to be in a hilly Welsh landscape. The 'trophy' had been collected from land claimed by Cook in 1770 for Britain, which was renamed New South Wales.[38]

The 'picturesque' as colonial propaganda

Landscape views capture the imagination in ways that topographic surveys and Admiralty charts cannot. But like imperial maps, they also provide important evidence about the politics and society of the time. A picturesque image records an appreciation of topography and vegetation that exists in the mind of the beholder.[39] It is a cultural attitude to land that, in the mid-eighteenth century, still belonged to a certain class of people: those with a knowledge of seventeenth-century French visions of classical Italian landscapes. In short, educated British 'gentlemen'.[40] And this attitude was now being projected to the colonies.

Creating paintings of the 'sublime and picturesque' landscape sites of the Pacific to encourage a wider interest in colonial prospecting expeditions, however, was rather different from aspiring to transform 100-year-old Caribbean colonies into living landscape art. For the sugar islands were, of course, inhabited by thousands of enslaved Africans, whose presence and conditions would have been uncomfortably apparent to visiting travellers. Nowhere in the nascent British Empire would the divisions between elite western 'tourists' and the objects of their gaze have been more sharply pronounced than in the slave colonies of the Caribbean.[41] In an era of growing anti-slavery sentiment in Britain, the 'natural scenery' of the West Indies proved an ambiguous attraction. The anonymous author of the poem *Jamaica*, for example, recalls how he was 'captivated by the beauty of the island [and] the verdure of the country', but 'disgusted with the severity of the inhabitants, the cruelty of the planters and the miseries of the slaves'. As he explained in a preface to his poem, 'the first I endeavour[ed] to celebrate, the last to condemn'.[42] Not all visitors, however, were so torn between the delights of Jamaican landscapes and the deprivations suffered by the majority of the island's inhabitants. Indeed, the aesthetic of the picturesque proved a useful tool for the wealthy, slave-owning, white minority to sanitise the economic structures of the Caribbean and depict the colonies as places of peace and bounty.

George Robertson's paintings are a prominent example of this. As we discussed earlier in the chapter, his watercolours were painted *en plein air* (outdoors, or in the field), and are among the first images of the British colonies to have been made in this way. Until the late eighteenth century, landscape paintings, like portraits, were made in oils: a thin paste of ground-up, solid pigments mixed with various volatile bases that, over days, evaporated to leave a coloured residue. This, clearly, was difficult to do outside. Formal landscape paintings, therefore, were generally painted in the studio from preparatory sketches made in pen and ink or chalk. However, in 1766, a former artist's 'colourman' (the assistant who prepared the paint) named William Reeves had opened a shop near St Paul's Cathedral selling a revolutionary product: boxes of solid pigment bound with a water-soluble gum. Not only did this eliminate the need for tedious grinding and mixing of pigments but, like ink, the paint dried in minutes rather than hours or days. Reeves's convenient 'paintboxes' were ideal for colonial surveyors; indeed, the British Army and the East India Company were among his first customers.[43] But they were also a boon for tourists. Watercolours allowed a landscape tour to be captured on paper in true visual as well as written form.

Robertson revelled in the new medium's ability to record light and colour. He uses a tonal contrast between the yellow ambers of the sunlight and the blue greys of shade to capture the unrelenting intensity of the strong sun and vivid colours of Jamaica. A comparison of these colour studies with the etchings based on them shows that the sense of tropical heat, of the real difference of place which Robertson created, is simply lost in the black-and-white versions.

But some of the variations between Robertson's originals and the later etchings are not simply down to the change of medium; many seem intended to make the scene more familiar to a viewer used to Italianate compositions and European landscapes. For example, in *A View in the Island of Jamaica of the Bridge crossing the River Cobre near Spanish Town*, the cliffs and boulders in the original watercolour study (see Fig. 7.3) are thinly covered by spikey aloes and trailing plants, while in the print (see Fig. 7.4) they are covered in lush

Fig. 7.3: Watercolour sketch for *A View in the Island of Jamaica of the Bridge crossing the River Cobre near Spanish Town*, George Robertson

foliage. The wooded hillside in the background, too, has grown bigger, and the calm river waters of the watercolour have turned into choppy waves. Indeed, the etching looks more like the tree-covered cliffs of Piercefield and the Wye Valley than the hot arid rocks in the original painting.

And it is not only the topography that has changed, but the people, too. The original watercolour shows three enslaved workers, all clad in matching white breeches and shirts. Two, holding hoes, are striding purposefully away from the viewer, while a third has laid his tool down and is sitting on a rock. The figures are spaced apart, and there is a suggestion of an overseer's unseen control. In the etched black-and-white print, however, two convivial groups have been added: a man mounted on a mule pauses to talk to a man and woman, while the solitary man resting on a rock is replaced by two others in animated conversation. There is still an air of purpose—the woman carries a bucket and basket on her head, while one man holds a hoe—but the etching suggests that they are independent smallholders going about their daily business, rather than enslaved plantation workers.

175

Fig. 7.4: *A View in the Island of Jamaica of the Bridge crossing the River Cobre near Spanish Town*, engraved by Daniel Lerpinière after George Robertson, published by John Boydell, 1778. (© The Trustees of the British Museum. All rights reserved.)

It is unlikely that the engravers, Thomas Vivares and Daniel Lerpinière, and the publisher Boydell, were being consciously political. It is more probable that they were simply 'improving' the composition of Robertson's originals to appeal to British or European customers, whose taste in landscape art and appreciation had been formed by engravings of paintings by artists like Poussin and Claude Lorrain.[44] Nevertheless, the prints show how European conventions of picturesque landscape painting could, even inadvertently, create propaganda.

As for landscape artist Thomas Hearne's Caribbean commissions, which were mentioned briefly earlier in the chapter, only three of his formal paintings for Governor Payne of the Leewards are known to have survived. However, the National Museum of Wales holds a pair of pen-and-ink landscape panoramas of eighteenth-century Antiguan sugar plantations, which, though unsigned, display

Hearne's characteristic style.[45] Their wide panoramic format—like that used by naval surveyors—suggest that these were sketches made as preparatory works for paintings commissioned by Payne or by absentee plantation owners. But although they, too, date from the early 1770s, unlike Robertson's carefully framed sketches of Jamaica's lush forested interior, these panoramas give a very different impression of Britain's sugar colonies.

One sketch, *West Aspect of St John's Town, Antigua*, shows the island's capital with its stone cathedral, frigates anchored in the bay and the military fortifications against a backdrop of rolling hills. However, the title is misleading, as the town is far in the distance; it is the sugar harvest that is the focus of the artist's interest. On the extreme right of the sketch is a windmill, but despite the distant flags fluttering in the breeze, it is not in use. Instead, a cattle mill is being used to crush the sugar canes (see Fig. 7.5). Three enslaved women feed the stems into a mechanism of three vertical rollers set on a raised circular platform at the edge of the cane fields. Though stripped to the waist, they are sheltered from the sun by a thatched roof, unlike the two men who drive the four oxen.

Fig. 7.5: Detail of *West Aspect of St John's Town, Antigua*, unattributed, c. 1772

Fig. 7.6: Detail of *West Aspect of St John's Town, Antigua*, unattributed, c. 1772

Another group of five women emerges from the fields to the left (see Fig. 7.6), carrying bundles of canes on their heads. One appears to be questioning the male overseer—dressed in shirt and breeches and carrying a staff or whip—and he gestures towards the mill. It is a reminder that much of the most demanding, and least regarded, plantation work was done by women.

The other panorama in the National Museum of Wales's collection—which is unattributed, but whose style also suggests that it is by Thomas Hearne—is identified as *Jolly Hill Estate, Antigua, belonging to Govn. Morris* (see Fig. 7.7). This is the same Morris who owned Piercefield, which we visited in Chapter Five. Valentine Morris had leased out his Welsh seat and returned to the Caribbean as Governor of the island of St Vincent in 1772, following an expensive and unsuccessful campaign to become a Member of Parliament. Though composed in a similar format to *West Aspect of St John's Town*, this

Fig. 7.7: Detail of *Jolly Hill Estate, Antigua, belonging to Govn. Morris*, unattributed, c. 1772

image is calm and still. There are no signs of work, no oxen, no ships, no people. Groups of birds are used to identify distant landmarks such as Nevis Isle, Gingery Hill and Rotunda Isle.

But the most intriguing feature, framed by two flowering aloes, is not labelled at all. It is a collection of small grass-roofed huts in the top left of the image—the village where Morris's enslaved workers would have lived.

No such settlement appears, however, in Hearne's formal pen-and-ink and watercolour painting of another plantation: *Parham Hill House and Sugar Plantation, Antigua* (see Fig. 7.8). This was painted in 1779, following Hearne's return to Britain, for the Tudways,[46] West Country landowners and Caribbean absentees who lived near the small cathedral city of Wells, south of Bristol. *Parnham Hill House* is composed in the typical rectangle of polite eighteenth-century landscape paintings. The rolling hills of Antigua have been exaggerated into a 'sublime' mountainous backdrop, more akin to the cliffs of St Kitts's Mount Misery.[47] In this image, however, unlike the earlier sketch of *West Aspect of St John's Town*, it is men, not women, who work the fields. In the foreground, a woman walks with a well-dressed male partner and a small child, deftly concealing the horrors of slavery with an

Fig. 7.8: *Parham Hill House and Sugar Plantation, Antigua*, Thomas Hearne, watercolour on paper, 1779 (© The Trustees of the British Museum. All rights reserved.)

image of a reassuring family group. Like the prints of Robertson's Jamaican landscapes, this picturesque pastoral, too, was misleading propaganda.

Post-independence America and the picturesque

When Robertson made his watercolour studies in 1774, Jamaica was the wealthiest of Britain's twenty-six mainland American and Caribbean colonies, including the Ceded Isles. However, five years later, when Hearne painted his picturesque image of Antigua, Britain's empire in the Americas was in the process of splitting, painfully, in two. The conflict now known as the American War of Independence (1775–83) was regarded then by many colonists as a civil war between British subjects.[48] While the thirteen mainland colonies were, of course, to form the independent United States of America, their thirteen Caribbean counterparts remained loyal to Britain. Despite the political divisions and warfare, however, sublime and picturesque natural scenery remained a shared attraction in Britain, the Caribbean and in the USA. Indeed, as I will show later in the chapter, only a few years after the end of the war, plantation owners in the former southern colonies of mainland America were also promoting scenic views.

In Britain, the War of Independence fuelled the fashion for domestic landscape touring. France, intent on disrupting a rival colonial power, had sided with the American 'rebel' colonies in the war. This made it difficult for wealthy young British men to make their traditional coming-of-age Grand Tour around Europe,[49] as the most direct route to the ruins of Imperial Rome was naturally through France. The uplands of the West became an attractive alternative, and Gilpin's *Observations on the River Wye*, published in 1782, therefore found a ready market among aspiring grand tourists, as well as among those of more modest means.[50] The end of the war the following year, moreover, does not seem to have diminished the growing interest in the picturesque: as we have seen, Gilpin's treatises on Cumberland and Westmoreland and on touring the Scottish Highlands were published in 1786 and 1789 and proved tremendously popular.[51]

The following year, London publishers T. & J. Egerton produced the first printed guide to picturesque landscape touring in the Caribbean. 'I wish indeed that I had been possessed of the descriptive pencil and the recording pen of that Elegant Enthusiast who has immortalized the beauties of the Wye and the magnificent variety of the Lakes',[52] reflected the guide's author, George Robertson's former patron William Beckford of Somerley. Beckford's treatise was written while he was bankrupt in a British debtors' prison following a destructive hurricane, which had destroyed most of his income-generating Caribbean plantations, and may explain why no expensive illustrations were included.

Readers of Beckford's guide, the extensively titled *A Descriptive Account of The Island of Jamaica, With Remarks upon the Cultivation of the Sugar-Cane throughout the different Seasons of the Year, and chiefly considered in a Picturesque Point of View*, had to imagine landscapes 'no less romantic than the most wild and beautiful situations of Frascati, Tivoli and Albano'.[53] They had to picture for themselves an island colony where the 'enchanting hues' and 'picturesque and fantastic clouds' of sunsets rivalled those of the Campania of Rome and the environs of

Naples,[54] a place where 'the hand of Nature alone'[55] could excel the works of Claude Lorrain, Nicholas Poussin or Salvator Rosa.[56]

Beckford's book, however, failed to emulate Gilpin's commercial success; the botanist Joseph Banks was one of the few purchasers of the first, limited and only edition.[57] Nevertheless, it seems that his attempt to present Jamaica as a picturesque tourist destination was not an unmitigated failure. A year after Beckford's death in 1799, an unknown patron employed the French engraver James Merigot to produce a set of six enticing, vividly coloured aquatint etchings of Robertson's watercolours.[58] Two years later, Maria Nugent, the wife of Jamaica's new Governor-General, Field-Marshall Sir George Nugent, described rising early, dressing by candlelight and setting of 'with immense party and cavalcade'[59] to visit 'the Walks'—the six-mile-long mountainside track near Spanish Town, described by Beckford in his guide as 'the most romantic, beautiful and picturesque road that I ever saw or could imagine'.[60] Indeed, diarist Daniel McKinnen describes in his *Tour Through the British West Indies*, made as a visitor from England in 1802–3, how the trip had become a tourist attraction: 'the ride through the file of the mountains near Spanish Town … is shown as one of the first objects of curiousity [sic] to a stranger who visits this part of the country'.[61]

'Worth a voyage across the Atlantic'?

The concept of 'sublime and picturesque' landscape touring was well-established in the British Caribbean plantation colonies by the early years of the nineteenth century.[62] It appears, moreover, that the planters and merchants of the states of the American South were also important players in promoting the concept of landscape appreciation in their newly independent country. Despite the divisions sown by the War of Independence, there remained close ties, in terms of family and trading links, between plantation owners in the American South and merchants in the British Caribbean, as well as the British Isles. Together with cargoes of sugar, rice, tobacco and coffee, books, letters and ideas still circulated between them.

Edward Long's *History of Jamaica* (introduced earlier in the chapter), with its illustrations and descriptions of picturesque scenery, was likely the most influential publication.[63] Indeed, tobacco planter, founding father and third US President Thomas Jefferson includes a portrayal of a 'natural bridge … the most sublime of Nature's works', in his *Notes on the State of Virginia* (written in 1781 during the war, see Fig. 7.9), which echoes the description of a 'bridge made by nature' in Long's *History*. Initially circulated in French, Jefferson's *Notes on the State of Virginia* was revised and published in English in London in 1787, four years after the war, and is now considered one of the USA's seminal historical texts.[64] Amidst factual descriptions of Virginia's climate, rivers and creeks, naval and military forces, Jefferson gives an account of the geological formations on his land in the Shenadoah valley, which recall Miss M's description of her visit to Piercefield three decades earlier:

> Though the sides of this bridge are provided in some parts with a parapet of fixed rocks, yet few men have the resolution to walk to them and look over into the abyss. You involuntarily fall on your

Fig. 7.9: Illustration of the 'Natural Bridge' from Thomas Jefferson's *Notes on the State of Virginia*, 3rd American ed., New York: Printed by M. L. & W. A. Davis for Furman & Loudon, opposite the City-Hall, 1801.

A View of the Natural Bridge in Virginia.

hands and feet, creep to the parapet and peep over it … it is impossible for the emotions, arising from the sublime, to be felt beyond what they are here; so beautiful an arch, so elevated, so light, and springing, as it were, up to heaven, the rapture of the spectator is really indescribable.[65]

Like Edward Long, Jefferson used the vocabulary and compositional rules of sublime and picturesque landscape appreciation. As well as describing the emotions occasioned by cascades and caverns, he draws readers' attention to a particular view of the Potomac River at Harper's Creek, near his estate, describing how:

the passage of the Patowmac [sic] through the Blue Ridge is one of the most stupendous scenes in nature … the distant finishing which nature has given to the picture is of a very different character. It is a true-contrast to the fore-ground. It is as placid and delightful as that is wild and tremendous.…[66]

And, in a remark that appears designed to intrigue wealthy British travellers, he mused: 'this scene is worth a voyage across the Atlantic'.[67]

Jefferson, of course, was not the only American with an interest in 'natural scenery'. Some of Edward Long's picturesque views from his *History of Jamaica* had been reproduced in American periodical publications in the early 1780s.[68] And the established audience was such that extracts from Jefferson's *Notes on the State of Virginia* were republished in periodicals such as the *Columbian Magazine* and *The New Haven Gazette*, the same year as its London publication, including his descriptions of the 'natural bridge' and the picturesque view of the Potomac.[69] In the first few years after independence, few citizens of the new country had the wealth and time to partake in landscape touring in a land where distances were so much greater than in Britain or the Caribbean. The widespread distribution of Jefferson's descriptions of the views on his tobacco estate helped, however, to ensure that the concept of scenic appreciation was embedded as a cultural aspiration.[70]

A 'British Atlantic community'

By the 1820s, the concept of landscape touring had firmly taken root among wealthier Americans, particularly the long-established plantation owners of the southern states. They, of course, had the leisure time to escape hot southern summers and travel north to spa towns such as Saratoga (in modern-day New York state) and the shores of the Hudson River.[71] Indeed, the author of one of the first American guidebooks, the highly popular *A Northern Tour: Being A guide to Saratoga, Lake George, Niagara, Canada, Boston, &c. &c.* (1825), the young Henry Gilpin (a relative of William Gilpin and his family in Whitehaven)[72] commented that 'of late years it has become a custom with a large portion of the citizens of the United States, to pass the summer and autumnal months through the northern section of the Union'.[73] Two years after the publication of his book, Gilpin made a trip from Philadelphia to Maryland and Virginia. This was partly for family reasons, but he was also anxious to see the natural sights recorded by Jefferson in his *Notes*, 'a book by-the-bye I have a thousand times regretted that I forgot to bring with me', as Gilpin laments.[74]

On arriving at Jefferson's former plantation (noting, in an aside, the 'immense number of small buildings ... which probably comprise the dwellings of the slaves' at a nearby estate), Gilpin visited the 'natural bridge', Jefferson's Rock ('one of the most stupendous seats in nature'), and the caverns ('the largest is called Washington Hall'), which were clearly then being promoted as tourist destinations. In a testament to the growing popularity of landscape touring in the United States for international travellers, on signing the visitors' book, Gilpin remarked that 'there were many distinguished foreigners ... I was surprised to see so few Americans except those of the immediate neighbourhood'.[75]

The natural sights in the north of the country described in Gilpin's *A Northern Tour*—such as Niagara Falls, later accessible by paddle-steamer from growing northern industrial cities—would ultimately become the most popular tourist destinations. But it is nonetheless clear that the planters and merchants of the slave-owning south, with their long-established colonial shipping links to Britain and the Caribbean, played an important role in the establishment of landscape appreciation in the United States.[76] These planters and merchants formed a community that spanned an entire ocean. Their investments created an Atlantic world linking the west of Britain with the Caribbean and the export-based plantation colonies of mainland America. But it was not just trade in sugar, tobacco, cotton and, of course, enslaved people that linked Britain's Atlantic ports with lands across the sea. They were also connected by shared ideas, including the concept of 'natural scenery'.

Wealthy absentee plantation owners, Atlantic merchants and their descendants had transformed the rugged, rainswept uplands of North Wales, Cumberland, Westmoreland and the Highlands and Islands of western Scotland into 'scenic' backgrounds for new country houses and estates. They provided drawing lessons for their children, commissioned paintings of landscapes, and encouraged a wider appreciation of sublime and picturesque aesthetics. Over the course of half a century, the concept of the landscape tour radically changed the British elite's traditional means of acquiring cultural education and status, the 'Grand Tour' of European art and architecture. The direct experience of raw nature—waterfalls, mountains, caves and dramatic cliffs—was one that could aesthetically equal a visit to the Mediterranean monuments of ancient Greece and Rome. And this sentiment took firm root in the newly independent United States, too. As Henry Gilpin wrote in his introduction to *A Northern Tour*, encouraging wealthy Americans to explore their own land, the 'fair and nobler scenes' where nature 'seems to have exerted more than her ordinary energies' could certainly surpass 'mouldering ruins' in Europe'.[77]

8

THE MOCK TURTLE'S STORY

[The Queen] said to Alice, 'Have you seen the Mock Turtle yet?'
'No,' said Alice. 'I don't even know what a Mock Turtle is.'
'It's the thing Mock Turtle Soup is made from,' said the Queen.
'I never saw one, or heard of one,' said Alice.
'Come on, then,' said the Queen, 'and he shall tell you his history.'

Lewis Carroll (Charles Lutwidge Dodgson),
Alice's Adventures in Wonderland (1865)

If, on a visit to Bath, you leave the Georgian urbanity of the city behind and walk up into the surrounding hills, you will be well rewarded with sweeping panoramas of the city below. Some of best views are to be had from the playing fields at the top of Lansdown Hill. Here, between the cemetery and the football pitches, partly concealed behind a thick hedge, is Beckford's Tower. Designed in 1825 as a library and retreat for Jamaican absentee William Thomas Beckford (son of Lord Mayor William Beckford), the tower once marked the summit of a vast, walled garden known as Beckford's Ride. The Ride began at the rear of Beckford's house in Lansdown Crescent at the northern extremity of eighteenth-century Bath, and stretched for over a mile up the slope of the hill through a series of different picturesque landscape gardens. A gloomy watercolour from 1829—a year or so after the building was finished—shows a lone horse and rider approaching the tower through a fir tree plantation, the focal point of Beckford's private picturesque landscape tour.

While you can still glimpse the rough Gothic entrance gateway to the Ride to the rear of Lansdown Crescent, most of the old landscape is now covered by housing estates. The graves of the surrounding burial ground of Lansdown Cemetery have taken the place of the formal lawns within which the tower was once set, with the stone-winged angels and granite crosses emphasising the tower's severe, almost funereal, exterior. The tower is accessed through a stern, two-storey, stone-faced entrance porch, pierced with small, lattice-covered windows. To the left of the porch is a similar, but single-storey block, while to the right the tower itself rises almost 150 feet. Plain stone, with narrow slit windows at the base, it becomes progressively more ornate as it gets higher, leading towards the richly ornamented viewing gallery at the top.

To reach the Belvidere at the top of the tower, you must climb the winding stone staircase that spirals up inside. The combination of deep pink walls and no central newel gives an extraordinary sensation of shifting and distorting space. You feel compelled to clutch

Fig. 8.1: Beckford's Tower, Belvidere

the iron handrail in an attempt to keep hold of reality. It is a relief when, after 154 steps, you at last reach the top. Here, the panoramic views from the twelve arched, ebony-framed windows are spectacular, and were described by Beckford as 'the finest prospect in Europe'.[1] Indeed, with no sign of the nearby motorway, and with the modern houses concealed by trees or blurred by distance, the vista might well be seen as an enduring allegory of British power, wealth and cultural identity during the Georgian era.

To the south of the tower one can glimpse Aqua Sulis, Britain's eighteenth-century Roman playground; to the west, the dull glint of the Bristol Channel leading to the riches of the trans-Atlantic; to the north, rolling fields of wheat carpet the Wiltshire Downs; while to the south-east, King Alfred's Tower marks out the landscape gardens of Stourhead, the eighteenth-century seat of the Hoares, one of Britain's foremost banking families.

Yet, if this panorama were intended as a visual metaphor, it had already been overtaken by time. In 1789, as we have seen in Chapter Four, Thomas Gainsborough's friend Philip Thicknesse could envisage Bath as the cultural hub of Britain's worldwide empire, transporting the fruits of the colonies from Bristol's quays along the River Avon. But by 1827, when Beckford's Tower was completed, this was no longer the case. The axis of new wealth between London and the Atlantic West had rotated northwards. Bristol's constricted inland moorings had long since been outclassed by the deep-water ports of Liverpool and Glasgow, and colonial venturers and putative investors no longer flocked to Bath and Hotwells in the numbers they had decades before.

Rather than the 'stone-clad sides' of the Avon, it was the new canal between Liverpool and Manchester which now epitomised the wealth created in great part by Britain's trans-Atlantic trade.[2] But Manchester, unlike Bath, was a town of production not consumption—a place to make money from cotton grown in the plantations of the American South and the Caribbean and dispatched in bales to Liverpool. No longer the glittering resort of its mid-eighteenth-century heyday, Bath was becoming a place for invalids and 'genteel' retirees. But, as the stone memorials in the central Abbey and other church graveyards attest, the city continued to attract many West Indians. And of all the absentee sugar planters who spent their twilight years in Bath, none was more notorious than the builder of the tower, the reclusive William Thomas Beckford.

The 'dance of the millions'

The only legitimate son of the powerful Jamaican-born City merchant Alderman William Beckford, William had eschewed business and politics. Like his cousin and namesake, William Beckford of Somerley (see Chapter Seven), Beckford played the role of a cultivated English gentleman. Indeed, the extent of Beckford's inheritance after his father's death—the poet George Byron described him as 'England's wealthiest son'[3]—allowed him to take this role to an audacious extreme. Beckford's lavish patronage of art, architecture, landscapes and, in particular, his construction of a vast country house, Fonthill Abbey in Wiltshire, has made him a popular subject for biographers. He has been the subject of no fewer than fifteen books and seven major exhibitions, making him, arguably, the best known of all West Indian absentees.[4] The level of interest in Beckford is such that in the early 1990s, after several decades of dereliction, Beckford's Tower in Bath was restored and converted into a commemorative museum.[5]

The interior of the tower has been carefully restored to the original designs: vivid crimson and scarlet walls and thick red carpets provide a lavish background to a display of paintings, intricately carved furniture, decorated ceramics and silverware. But, despite the warmth of the colours, the richness of the contents and the far-reaching views, visiting the tower is an oddly claustrophobic experience. It is like being imprisoned inside a colossal, velvet-lined jewellery box. Though far from the last British building or landscape to be funded from the proceeds of Caribbean slavery, the introspective interior, bleak exterior and West Country panoramas make the tower highly symbolic. When architect Henry Goodridge began his designs in 1825, the era of West Indian power and influence in Britain was starting to draw, albeit slowly, to a close.

For more than 150 years, the combination of protectionist trading policies enshrined in the Navigation Acts, slave labour and the British consumer's desire for sugar had meant that the Caribbean colonies were synonymous with great wealth. But, over the course of the nineteenth century, the politics and economics of colonial sugar production were to change, as slavery (in the British Empire at least) and protectionist tariffs were abolished in favour of the 'free trade' advocated by the Glasgow-based economist Adam Smith more than a generation before.

The decline in West Indian fortunes during the nineteenth century was nevertheless slow, as the abolition of the trans-Atlantic British slave trade in 1807 had little immediate impact on the profitability of Caribbean sugar plantations. Slave-owning itself was not outlawed in Britain and its empire until 1833, and it was not difficult for plantation owners to purchase enslaved labour from French, Spanish or Dutch traders. Indeed, as historian Robin Blackburn contends, the ban on the slave trade and the nervousness about investing in plantations in the wake of the establishment of the free republic of Haiti in 1804 (the former French Caribbean colony of St Domingue) brought about a bonanza of spending within Britain itself.[6] Sugar profits were invested into private houses, agricultural estates, roads, lighthouses and docks—in Blackburn's words, this was the British West Indian 'Dance of the Millions'.[7]

Beckford's previous foray into architecture, the extraordinary Fonthill Abbey, is perhaps the most visually spectacular monument of all to these inflated sugar profits. Built between 1797 and 1822 on the Wiltshire country estate he inherited from his father, his new lavish construction replaced the Palladian mansion, Fonthill Splendens, that had been Beckford's childhood home. Contemporary images and written descriptions portray the new manor as a dwelling of astonishing scale. The entrance was through thirty-five-foot-high, pointed-arched double doors. Inside, the hammer-beam oak trusses and stained-glass windows of the seventy-eight-foot-tall hall echoed the architecture of a medieval cathedral, while at the centre of the building rose a 280-foot tower, adorned with intricately carved stone tracery windows. As one overwhelmed visitor remarked, when the house was first opened to the public in 1822, 'the architecture conveyed to the mind of every beholder ideas both of mind and purse, which [Beckford] must have possessed: the first to conceive, and the latter to find means to pay for the execution of so grand a conception'.[8]

Though not meant to be ironic, the comment's timing certainly was. The end of the Napoleonic Wars in 1815 had seen a fall in sugar prices, as supplies of the commodity made from beet grown in continental Europe, as well as cane sugar from Asia and from the Spanish colonies in Cuba, began to be imported into Britain.[9] Even Beckford had found it necessary to curtail his extravagant expenditure, especially after losing two of his Jamaican sugar plantations in 1822 as a result of legal action. Indeed, as a three-shilling *New Guide* to Fonthill made clear, Beckford's decision to 'suddenly throw open'[10] the vast doors of his still unfinished palace that same year to the 'intrusive inspection both of the virtuoso and the tourist'[11] was not made out of choice, but financial necessity.

Beckford's financial situation did not improve, and in 1822, 'The finest effort, which modern art has been able to produce', as the guide to Fonthill described it, was sold to Scottish gunpowder dealer John Farquhar.[12] The subsequent collapse of Fonthill's tower, just three years after the sale (see Fig, 8.2), was a prescient symbol of the coming changes in the fortunes of West Indians. The very foundations of their wealth were beginning to crumble, as new challenges to the institution of slavery were raised in Britain and in the Caribbean colonies themselves. Not for nothing was Fonthill also known as 'Beckford's Folly'.[13] The dance of the millions was coming to an end.

Rebellion and abolition

Organised insurrections by enslaved workers had occurred with regularity throughout the history of British settlement of the Caribbean. As we have seen, the imposing stone military forts on the islands were not built just to deter rival colonial powers. A revolt in 1816, for example, had destroyed much of the Lascelles family's sugar crop on Barbados.[14] However, by the 1820s, rebellions were now beginning to be viewed differently by a British public that was becoming more and more aware of conditions in the Caribbean plantations, and was increasingly vocal about the issue of slavery.[15] No longer were revolts in the sugar colonies always seen as threats to the nation's imperial prosperity; they had instead assumed a profound moral purpose. In 1823, the publicity given to the horrific reprisals meted out by British troops, following a rebellion in Demerara—part of what was to become the sugar colony of

Fig. 8.2: *Ruins of Fonthill Abbey*, lithograph after John Buckler, c. 1825
(© The Trustees of the British Museum. All rights reserved.)

British Guiana in mainland South America—was the catalyst for a renewed campaign in Britain to abolish plantation slavery entirely.[16]

The name of that key battle for the emancipation of enslaved workers is now more readily associated with the light brown, molasses-scented 'demerara' sugar, prized for cake-baking. But the link between state-sanctioned brutality and domestic treats was over a century old by then. During the years following the Demerara Rebellion, echoing campaigns a generation before, more than 100 anti-slavery campaigning groups were set up in Britain, many by married women of the 'middling sort', who forbade their children, and husbands, from eating sweets and cake. Amelie Opie's illustrated children's poem *The Black Man's Lament; Or How To Make Sugar* (1826) is a reminder of how the British ritual of afternoon tea and cake was politicised.[17] The poem explains:

> There is a *beauteous plant*, that grows
> In western India's sultry clime,

Which make, alas! the Black man's woes,
And also makes the White man's crime.

For know, its tall gold stems contain
A sweet rich juice, which White men prize;
And that they may this *sugar* gain,
The Negro toils, and bleeds, and *dies*.[18]

The shift in public opinion followed half a century of argument. In the late eighteenth century, the expansion of the trans-Atlantic slave trade, prompted by the settlement of the Ceded Isles in the 1760s, coincided with a small but growing public awareness drive about the vicissitudes of the plantation economy. The campaigns orchestrated by the abolitionist Granville Sharp from the late 1760s, for example, were among the first to recognise the contradictions between the concept of British liberty and the reality of slave-holding in the American and Caribbean colonies.[19]

Absentee plantation owners, however, including Sir William Young and his eldest son—also named William, who became a Member of Parliament and later the Governor of Tobago until 1815—were vocal in their defence of slavery and the trade itself as an unpleasant necessity. The cruelty and inhumanity described by some observers were, in their opinion, the result of poor management or supervision by individual overseers, rather than systematic abuse, and could be resolved by the introduction of new regulatory legislation.[20]

This opinion that it was individual actions, not the institution of slavery itself, that were the problem is reflected in a small oil portrait of Young, *The Family of Sir William Young* (see Fig. 8.3), painted by the celebrated artist Johann Zoffany in the late 1760s. Hanging today in the Walker Art Gallery in Liverpool, the portrait features Sir William (playing the cello), his son and heir, and the rest of his family—together with a young black footman, who is lifting Young's smallest son onto a horse. In a retort against the abolitionists' arguments, the inclusion of the black page within Zoffany's family portrait transforms the painting from an illustration of domestic arrangements into a political statement: William Young was trying to send the message that he was a 'good master'.[21]

Absentee families frequently brought some of their 'house slaves'[22] to Britain with them. For example, records reveal that an enslaved man, Pero, also known as William Jones, moved to Bristol with Nevis planter John Pinney and his family and continued to work for them—unpaid—for many years.[23] Pero's Bridge, next to which the statue of slave-trader Edward Colston was symbolically thrown into Bristol Harbour during the 2020 'Black Lives Matter' protests, is named after him.

As the eighteenth century drew to a close, debate in Britain over abolition continued to intensify, particularly in the wake of the French Revolution (1789–99) and the slave insurrection in the French Caribbean colony of St Domingue (1791–1804). Even in 1772, in a landmark judgement, the Lord Chief Justice, William Murray, first Earl of Mansfield, had already ruled that a runaway slave could not be forced by his previous owner to return from Britain to the West Indies against his will.[24] The 'Mansfield Judgement' was popularly viewed as freeing slaves in Britain—inaccurately, as those brought to the country were still bound to serve their masters—but it was a seminal case on the road to abolition. It

Fig. 8.3: *The Family of Sir William Young*, Johann Zoffany, c. 1766, oil on canvas

was to be another thirty-five years, however, before the 1807 Slave Trade Act, pressed by the reforming William Wilberforce, officially prohibited the slave trade in the British Empire, and over sixty years until the practice of slave-owning itself was outlawed in the Slavery Abolition Act of 1833.

Compensation and a long-lasting national debt

After almost a decade of campaigning by anti-slavery 'Anti-Saccharist' groups, together with a prolonged insurrection in Jamaica in 1831, the attitudes of Britain's ruling political elite itself were now beginning to change, too.[25] The Jamaican Revolt of 1831 (also known as the Baptist War or the Christmas Uprising), which involved around 60,000 enslaved workers, appears to have marked the political turning point:[26] the possibility of Britain losing its most valuable sugar colony entirely, as France had Haiti, was a daunting threat to the Caribbean planters in Britain's Parliament.

The composition of Parliament was changing, too. The abolition of British colonial slavery was but one of the many political issues under debate at a time when the country's urban industrial population was growing fast. In 1832, what is now commonly referred to as the first Reform Act was passed. It abolished the so-called 'rotten boroughs'—constituencies with few voters, many of which lay in rural English counties—that had been so prized by politically ambitious absentee West Indians in previous decades, and established new electoral districts in the increasingly populous industrial towns and cities. In the three years following this reform, several radical new acts were passed, including the Poor Law Amendment Act, a Factory Act (limiting working hours for children in industry) and, of course, in August 1833, an act to abolish slavery throughout the British colonies.

Near the Cotswold mill town of Stroud, one of the urban manufacturing centres enfranchised by the Reform Act, a local mill owner named Henry Wyatt constructed a huge neo-classical triumphal arch in local limestone to commemorate the Abolition Act, at the entrance to his grounds at Farmhill Park (see Fig. 8.4). And though now the hidden centrepiece of a modern housing estate, it would then have been prominent on the turnpike road. An inscription carved on a tablet set above the arch keystone reads 'Erected to Commemorate the Abolition of Slavery on the British Colonies. The First of August AD MDCXXXIV'. Wyatt was a prominent supporter of the Stroud Anti-Slavery Society, which had put pressure on their newly elected MP to vote for its abolition in Parliament.[27]

The arch is an extraordinary private monument to honour a public act, particularly in an area of Gloucestershire which had so many historic trading links with the Severn and the nearby port of Bristol. Rather than bales of plantation-grown cotton, however, the key trans-Atlantic material needed by Stroud's mill owners was red cochineal, from cactus beetles, to dye the fine 'Stroud-water scarlet', a locally produced wool that clothed the red-coat soldiers of the British Army. Indeed, with the British state as the town's most

Fig. 8.4: Stroud anti-slavery arch

prominent customer, Wyatt's public gesture was perhaps also a canny and timely commercial move.

The daughter of a Jamaican absentee and estate owner at Hope End, near Ledbury, twenty-five miles north of Stroud, Elizabeth Moulton-Barrett (better known as Elizabeth Barrett Browning, the popular Victorian poet), was equally supportive. As she wrote in a letter to a friend: 'Of course you know that the late bill has ruined the West Indians. That is settled. The consternation here is very great. Nevertheless, I am glad, and always shall be, that the Negroes are—virtually free'.[28]

The emancipation of enslaved workers was considered a propaganda coup for the newly reformed British Parliament. In the following years, the abolition of slavery within the British Empire played an important part in creating a sense of nationhood, of the British as the worthy arbiters between the civilised and the uncivilised world.[29] The formidable lobbying power of the parliamentary West India Committee, even in the reformed Parliament, however, had ensured that—contrary to Moulton-Barrett's suggestion—most West Indians were far from ruined: the Abolition Act required British taxpayers to compensate plantation owners for the loss of their valuable 'human stock'.

Elizabeth's father, for example, received £12,453 for the 647 enslaved men, women and children on his Jamaican estates.[30] And in 1836, the heir to Harewood, Henry Lascelles—while assuring his formerly enslaved workers that 'his lordship will continue to feel the greatest anxiety and solicitude for their happiness and welfare'[31]—claimed £26,177, four shillings and four pence for the '1,276 negroes' on his two Jamaican and four Barbadian estates.[32] In total, Caribbean plantation owners received around £20 million in compensation—a vast sum, then equivalent to almost 40 per cent of the British government's annual national budget, and the debts were only fully and finally redeemed in 2015.[33] By contrast, the formerly enslaved workers in the Caribbean received no state aid package, land redistribution or training to help them create their own small farms or businesses. Nor were they even paid: they had to work another four years as bound 'apprentices', before being allowed to receive their liberty.

It appears, moreover, that the much of the state-funded compensation was not reinvested in Caribbean plantations, but in potentially more lucrative opportunities in Britain and elsewhere in the Empire.[34] As UCL's 'Legacies of British Slave-ownership' project reveals, the West Indian penchant for transport infrastructure continued. The construction of many of Britain's railways, and not just Brunel's Great Western between London and Bristol, owes much to investments made by Caribbean plantation owners after receipt of their compensation.[35]

But with less West Indian influence in the reformed Parliament, the trade laws that had protected plantation owners were beginning to be challenged. The Sugar Duties Equalisation Act of 1846 began the process of dismantling protective tariffs. British-based sugar refiners and merchants were no longer required by law to buy sugar grown in British colonies; they could look elsewhere to find the cheapest price. Heavily subsidised German sugar beet and Spanish sugar from vast new estates in Cuba, grown (until 1886) by an enslaved workforce, provided alternative sources. Even with new investment in efficient steam-powered, coal-fired mills, planters in the small British Caribbean sugar islands could not compete.

Within a year of the Act, thirteen West Indian trading companies and two West Indian banks had collapsed.[36] By the time sugar duties were finally equalised in 1852, more than 470 Jamaican plantations had gone out of business.[37] Though sugar consumption in Britain had increased by a third, it was not from the British West Indies. No longer was the Caribbean a place for a young gentleman to 'raise a fortune or create a name'.[38] 'Woe betide the man nowadays who has a West Indian Estate!', sighed absentee George Dasent, the assistant editor of *The Times*, in *Annals of an Eventful Life*, his fictionalised memoir of planter life on St Saccharissa, published (anonymously) in 1870. He reminisced:

> It was not so bad then when brown sugar was eighteen pence a pound … and my father was thought to be a lucky man when it was noised through the Forest of Arden that Old Colonel Ratoon had died in the West Indies and made Squire Halfacre his heir.[39]

Mock-turtle soup

Dasent's *Annals* clearly struck a chord with the British public, and the book ran to several editions.[40] Other British writers, however, regarded the complaints made by West Indians, who looked to the 'good old times before emancipation',[41] with less sympathy. In Lewis Carroll's *Alice's Adventures in Wonderland* (1865), for example, a disconsolate calf-headed, bovine-hoofed 'mock turtle', who 'once was a real turtle', sighs and sits 'sad and lonely on a rock', as he remembers the delights of former days (see Fig. 8.5). 'Beautiful Soup, so rich and green, Waiting in a hot tureen!' the beast sings in a voice 'choked with sobs', as he remembers the exotic delicacies of his youth. 'Who for such dainties would not stoop? Soup of the evening, beautiful Soup!', he laments.[42]

Carroll's comedic depiction of this 'mock turtle' is a gentle satire of the change in the circumstances of some planters. The insinuation is that the declining fortunes of British West Indians meant that they were no longer able to afford imported turtles to make their favourite Caribbean delicacy. Instead, absentees had to make do with 'mock-turtle soup', made—according to nineteenth-century recipes—with a stock of boiled calves' head and feet. Expensive tropical luxuries had been replaced by bovine off-cuts.

Lewis Carroll himself would have been well aware of his own family's connections with the trans-Atlantic trade. Born Charles Lutwidge Dodgson in 1832, the son of a Cheshire vicar, the author of Alice's adventures was the great-great-grandson of Thomas Lutwidge, one of Whitehaven's most prominent tobacco, sugar and slave merchants in the late seventeenth and early eighteenth centuries. Carroll was a frequent visitor to his maternal uncle the Reverend Charles Skeffington Lutwidge (the great-grandson of Thomas Lutwidge) in the village of Holmrook, fifteen miles south of the port, and recorded his Lakeland fell-walking exploits in his diaries.[43]

The unsympathetic protest of Alice's companion the Gryphon to the Mock Turtle's sighs and sobs, 'It's all his fancy, that: he hasn't got no sorrow you know',[44] was a reminder that, for all their complaints, many West Indians had not only survived the structural changes in the British sugar industry, but had done immensely well. Indeed, the agricultural, trading and industrial investments—and marriages—made by many families meant that the by then morally suspect, Caribbean origins of their wealth were well-concealed from public view. And for nearly 150 years, it stayed that way.

Fig. 8.5: *The Mock Turtle, the Gryphon and Alice*, illustration from Lewis Carroll's *Alice in Wonderland*

A bittersweet heritage

In the East End of London, the vast, nearly empty basin of the former West India Docks forms a watery centrepiece to London's eastern financial centre, Canary Wharf. Amid the towering glass-faced office blocks, the majestically solid, brick early-nineteenth-century sugar and rum warehouses, listed Grade I, are poignant reminders of London's former status as Britain's largest West India port. But, despite the Caribbean's historic importance to the city, it is not in the capital that we see the most dramatic architectural statements of the wealth derived from plantation slavery, but in the Atlantic West.

In Bristol Museum and Art Gallery hangs a painting, *View on the Avon at Hotwells*, by an artist named Samuel Jackson. Dating from around 1840, it is the nineteenth-century equivalent of the computer-generated images produced to explain and assess the visual

Fig. 8.6: Detail from *View on the Avon at Hotwells*, Samuel Jackson, c. 1840

impact of major architectural projects today. The oil painting features Isambard Kingdom Brunel's competition-winning proposal from 1831 for an iron suspension bridge over the Avon Gorge, a project that was not actually completed until 1864.[45] To the right, at the top of the gorge, is the Royal York Crescent, where wealthy residents enjoyed sweeping panoramas over the dramatic drop below. At the base of the cliff, by Hotwells, a modern coal-fired paddle-steamer, *The Wye*, takes visitors on a river tour. A richly decorated coach and horses is ferried to Leigh Woods on the opposite bank; while, in the foreground, a cargo of Caribbean turtles is unloaded onto the quayside.

The painting, one of a pair, is a celebration of the intimate relationship between the city's West India trade and picturesque landscapes. It was commissioned by the Society of Merchant Venturers, the group of Atlantic traders and Caribbean plantation owners who did much to create Bristol's spectacular nineteenth-century public realm. The Society's members were not only vitally important in creating and improving docks and transport facilities, but also in funding and organising the construction of the dramatic Clifton Suspension Bridge, and maintaining the adjacent Clifton Downs as a public open space.[46] They were also crucial in introducing the young Brunel to the concept of picturesque landscape aesthetics displayed so markedly in his carefully composed, partially tunnelled section of the Great Western railway between Bath and Bristol.[47]

But perhaps the most significant British cultural legacy of two centuries of wealth from plantation slavery is not to be found in railway tunnels, bridges or landscape parks and gardens; it is instead to be found in our minds. The concept of 'natural scenery' is intimately entwined with that eighteenth-century predatory economy. Valentine Morris's plantation wealth allowed him to transform the cliffs at Piercefield into 'Poussins' and 'Claudes'. It was the merchants and planters of the Atlantic West who popularised the idea that cliffs and mountains, coves and valleys could be viewed as living landscape art. Edmund Burke drew on his brother's trans-Atlantic experiences to codify his theories of the beautiful and the sublime.

The sugar and tobacco merchants of Whitehaven, too, were key to appointing a drawing master at the school William Gilpin and his brothers attended. The turnpike-road-building merchants and planters of the Atlantic West opened up Snowdonia and the Lakes to tourists, and were instrumental in later road-building in the western Scottish Highlands. And it was plantation owners such as Long and Jefferson who promoted the concept of natural scenery on the western seaboard of the Atlantic Ocean, in the Caribbean and Virginia.

But what does this mean for us today? The answer might be found in the Caribbean. On the penultimate day of my visit to the Leeward Islands, our group—mainly composed of archaeologists and academic historians—visited a derelict eighteenth-century sugar works in Nevis's upland interior. Here, the steeply sloping cane fields had been abandoned years before, and we trudged our way up a dirt track in the shade of the forest canopy. After we had inspected the ruined, stone sugar-boiling houses and water reservoirs, we retraced our steps a couple of hundred feet or so to the spot where we were to have our lunch. There, at the top of a high bluff, on a small piece of land that had once been his grandmother's 'provision ground', one of our guides, a retired Nevisian man (having spent his adult life building motorways in Britain) had created a picturesque picnic site.

Carefully framed by lush foliage, he had constructed a small timber cabin, a replica of his grandmother's simple home. Adjacent was the salvaged four-armed mechanism of an early-nineteenth-century cattle-powered sugar mill that had been reworked into a merry-go-round, creating a whirling panorama of forest, distant cane fields and the sea beyond. Like the painting of the Avon Gorge, and indeed the Caribbean shells in the ornamental grotto that inspired my research, this composition linked picturesque scenery with the wealth derived from Caribbean sugar cultivation. But here, the patron was the descendant of the enslaved Africans who once toiled unpaid in the cane fields below. He had quietly transformed a historic symbol of oppressive labour into a garden folly to delight all who visited. He had appropriated a polite eighteenth-century British landscape aesthetic and made it his own.[48]

This personal and inspiring project points to a way forward. Whilst post-colonialism is an integral part of academic research in the humanities, for too long the global connections of Britain's heritage have been concealed from wider public view. For too long, as well, black and ethnic minority people have popularly been regarded as immigrant urban dwellers, having little relationship with Britain's historic buildings and rural landscapes.

In 2020, indeed, a modest project by the National Trust to engage young children with the 'Colonial Countryside' received an extraordinary level of opprobrium from several members of Parliament and in some sections of the British press. And the furore followed outrage from the same quarters after the Trust's publication, in September 2020, of a report, commissioned a year before the Black Lives Matter protests, documenting the links of ninety-three of its historic sites with colonial landholdings.[49] The National Trust found itself in the centre of the ensuing 'culture wars', and the reverberations were still continuing at the time of writing.[50]

But, of course, over a period of more than 300 years of colonisation and empire, much of British history happened overseas. In order, therefore, to truly understand many of the landscapes and much of the eighteenth-, nineteenth- and early-twentieth-century built heritage of the British Isles today, it is not enough to think local. You need to know about the brilliant inventions, the architects and designers, the masons and carpenters, the stone quarries and woods, the writers and artists; but you must also examine patrons and clients in Britain and overseas, and the international structures of historic political power, commerce and trade. And this can, of course, be an uncomfortable process.

And the story of the house and landscapes at Piercefield in the Wye Valley, where this book's journey began, is no exception. In 1779, Valentine Morris had returned in penury from St Vincent after negotiating the island's surrender following a French invasion. Bankrupt, the former colonial governor was forced to sell his extraordinary landscape creation in Wales to George Smith, founder of the local Monmouthshire Bank, who in turn had to sell up following the bank's collapse in a financial crisis in 1792. The estate was then bought by a so-called 'Nabob' returnee from Bengal, Mark Wood, who completed Smith's unfinished alterations to the house, designed in part by John Soane, later the architect of the Bank of England.

A decade on, in 1802, the estate was sold again, this time to Nathaniel Wells, the Bath-based son of a slave-owning St Kitts planter. But unlike previous owners, Wells was mixed race: his mother Juggy had been one of his father's 'house-slaves'. Wells' exceptional life has been well-documented—an example of the tiny minority of mixed race children who were born into slavery but 'granted' their freedom, sent to Britain and educated.[51] His tale is, however, somewhat unsettling: the brutal labour conditions of his siblings and half-siblings, who remained on the plantations, helped to finance Wells' life as a magistrate, Justice of the Peace and county Sheriff, roles typical of the nineteenth-century British provincial elite. Compensation payments to slave-owners, moreover, contributed towards Wells's comfortable retirement in Bath and the substantial legacies he left to his own children.[52]

But surely acknowledging the truth of these entwined histories, difficult as they may be, can also be stimulating and creative? As the vigorous public debates following the Colston statue's theatrical ducking demonstrate, historic landscapes, structures and buildings, as well as sculptures, memorials and paintings, can provide a means of engaging with complex, global histories and identities that is immediate and accessible. Perhaps one day, the woods and walks of Piercefield, together with its ruined mansion, could again be a site of inspiration—a place where those from Britain's large cities, alongside people from country towns, villages, coastal ports and seaside resorts, could together explore a shared, bittersweet heritage.

TIMELINE OF PRINCIPAL CHARACTERS AND EVENTS

1623: English colonisation of the Caribbean begins with the island of St Kitts, followed over the next decade by Barbados, Nevis and Antigua, and, in 1655, by the capture of Jamaica from Spain.

1688: The 'Glorious Revolution', resulting in the deposition of James II as king and his replacement by his daughter Mary II and William III of Orange, to re-stablish the Protestant ascendancy in Britain.

1690: Birth of Henry Lascelles, who moves to Barbados by 1712.

1705: Birth of Richard Oswald, future tobacco and sugar merchant, prominent slave-trader and Crown negotiator, in Scotland.

1707: Acts of Union between England (and Wales) and Scotland to form the United Kingdom of Great Britain.

1713: Birth of Edwin Lascelles, Henry's son, the future first Baron Harewood, in Barbados.

1719: Birth of John Boyd, future patron of Danson Park, in St Kitts.

1725: Birth of William Young, future patron of Delaford Park, in Antigua.

1727: Birth of Valentine Morris, future owner of Piercefield Park, in Antigua; James Brydges, former Paymaster General, and designer John Wood draw up plans for the transformation of Bath, after completion of the Avon canal to Bristol, and the first phase ends in 1739.

1729: Return of Henry Lascelles and family from Barbados to London.

1735: Return of the Boyd family from the Caribbean to London.

1737: Birth of Richard Pennant, future first Baron of Penrhyn, in Jamaica.

1738: Henry Lascelles buys the estate that becomes Harewood.

1739: Start of the War of Jenkins' Ear between Britain and Spain in the Caribbean, which ends in 1748; Valentine Morris's family returns to Britain, and the Pennants to Liverpool.

1740: Valentine Morris's father purchases Piercefield Park in the Wye Valley.

1745: The final major Jacobite rising in Scotland against the Protestant British crown, ending in the rebels' defeat at the battle of Culloden in 1746.

1748: The Boyd family and partners, including Scottish merchant Richard Oswald, purchase the Bance Island slaving fort in Sierra Leone.

1753: John Boyd leases Danson House and, in 1759, purchases the estate outright; Edwin Lascelles inherits Harewood from his father, Henry, and two years later commences plans for a grand country house on the estate; the second phase of Bath's development starts, ending in 1757, following another outbreak of war.

1756: The Seven Years' War starts across Europe and the Atlantic colonies, ending in 1763, with the transfer to Britain of the 'Ceded Isles': Grenada, the Grenadines, Dominica, St Vincent and Tobago.

1757: Publication of Edmund Burke's *A Philosophical Enquiry into the Origin of our Ideas of the Sublime and the Beautiful*.

1759: Richard Oswald buys the Auchincruive estate in Ayrshire, south of Glasgow.

1763: Robert Adam is engaged by Edwin Lascelles on the redesign at Harewood, with landscaping by Lancelot 'Capability' Brown; the third phase of Bath's development begins, ending with war in 1776.

1764: William Young is appointed as Commissioner of Land Sales for the Ceded Isles, and encourages Scottish settlers to buy land on the islands; he buys Delaford in 1767 and becomes Governor of Dominica in 1770.

1772: The 'Mansfield Judgement', ruling that a runaway could not be returned to the West Indies, but enslaved Africans still owe duties to their 'masters'; Valentine Morris becomes Governor of St Vincent's, which is surrendered to the French before his return in 1779.

1774: Publication of Edward Long's picturesque account in his *History of Jamaica*.

1775: Start of the American War of Independence, which ends in 1783 with the secession of Britain's thirteen mainland colonies, while the thirteen in the Caribbean remain loyal to the Empire; Richard Oswald negotiates the peace treaty.

1776: Publication of Adam Smith's *An Inquiry into the Nature and Causes of the Wealth of Nations*.

1781: Publication of the English edition of Thomas Jefferson's *Notes on the State of Virginia*.

1782: Publication of William Gilpin's *Observations on the River Wye and several parts of South Wales*, followed by further books on 'picturesque beauty' in the Lakes and Scotland.

1783: Fourth phase of Bath's classical development begins, coming to a halt unfinished in 1793.

1784: Burdened with debt, Valentine Morris sells Piercefield, and dies five years later. It is bought in 1802 by Nathaniel Wells, the multi-racial son of a St Kitts plantation owner.

1789: Start of the French Revolution, which culminates in the seizure of power by Napoleon in 1799; publication of Olaudah Equiano's *The Interesting Narrative and Other Writings*.

1791: Slave revolution in the French colony of St Domingue (Haiti); two years later, Britain goes to war with Republican France following the execution of King Louis XVI.

1800: Act of Union between Britain and Ireland.

1807: The Slave Trade Act prohibits the slave trade in the British Empire, but not slave-owning.

1815: End of the Napoleonic Wars—which began in 1803—following the French defeat at the Battle of Waterloo. The end of wartime blockades also leads to a collapse in the sugar price, as supplies become more plentiful.

1822: Completion of William Thomas Beckford's lavish Fonthill Abbey in Wiltshire, started in 1797, and immediately sold to pay off debts; the tower at 'Beckford's Folly' collapses three years later.

1826: The slave rebellion in Demerara, in British Guiana, mainland South America, with brutal British reprisals catalysing campaigns at home to abolish slave-owning.

1831: The Jamaican Revolt by enslaved plantation workers, known as the Christmas Uprising or Baptist War, led by preacher Samuel Sharpe.

1833: The Slavery Abolition Act outlaws slave-owning in Britain and the empire, but compensates plantation owners handsomely for the loss of their 'human stock'.

1846: The Sugar Duties Equalisation Act dismantles protective tariffs favouring West Indian owners, a process which takes until 1852, with hundreds of Caribbean sugar plantations collapsing.

NOTES

INTRODUCTION

1. 'Homecoming' from *Uncle Time* by Dennis Scott, © 1973. Reprinted by permission of the University of Pittsburgh Press.
2. Of modest origins, Livingstone spent his youth working in Blantyre cotton mill, near his birthplace on the outskirts of Glasgow, which was owned by a conglomerate of West India merchants. See Stephen Mullen, 'One of Scotia's Sons of Toil: David Livingstone and Blantyre Mill', in Sarah Worden (ed.), *David Livingstone: Man, Myth and Legacy*, Edinburgh: NMS Enterprises, 2012.
3. There is currently debate about the relative extent of slave- and ivory trading from Bagamoyo. See, for example, Steven Fabian, 'East Africa's Gorée: Slave Trade and Slave Tourism in Bagamoyo, Tanzania', *Canadian Journal of African Studies, vol. 47*, no. *1, 2013, pp. 95–114.*
4. *Register of Landscapes Parks and Gardens of Special Historic Interest in Wales*, Gwent, Part 1, Parks and Gardens, 1994, CADW/ICOMOS UK.
5. I have used the terms 'genteel' or 'polite' throughout the book to describe an educated eighteenth-century British elite, as the terms 'upper,' 'middle' or 'lower' class did not then exist. See Amanda Vickery, *The Gentleman's Daughter: Women's Lives in Georgian England*, New Haven, CT and London: Yale University Press, 1998, pp. 14–37.
6. William Wordsworth, *Lines Composed a Few Miles above Tintern Abbey, On Revisiting the Banks of the Wye during a Tour. July 13, 1798*. See Marjorie Levinson, 'Insight and Oversight: reading "Tintern Abbey"', in *Wordsworth's great period poems: Four essays*, Cambridge: Cambridge University Press, 1996, pp. 14–57.
7. 'Uncomfortable Truths: The Shadow of Slave Trading on Contemporary Art' at the Victoria and Albert Museum, London; 'Breaking the Chains' at the British Empire and Commonwealth Museum, Bristol; 'Portraits, People and the Abolition of the Slave Trade' at the National Portrait Gallery, London; 'Abolition 2007' at the Light House, Wolverhampton; and 'Chasing Freedom' at The Royal Naval Museum, Portsmouth were just some of the many exhibitions held to commemorate the abolition of the British slave trade.

8. In 2007, the International Slavery Museum opened in Liverpool within the Maritime Museum, and the Museum of London Docklands added a new gallery, 'London, Sugar & Slavery'. Both Bristol and Lancaster established 'slave trade trails' showing buildings linked to the trade.

9. Katherine Hann and Jacqueline Roy, 'Addressing the Past,' *National Trust Magazine*, Spring 2007, pp. 20–3.

10. See, for example, 'The Scottish Court of Session Digital Archive Project' at The University of Virginia Law Library.

11. For a summary of recent debates, see Catherine Hall, Nicholas Draper and Keith McCelland (eds), *Legacies of British Slave-ownership: Colonial Slavery and the Formation of Victorian Britain*, Cambridge: Cambridge University Press, 2014, pp. 9–15.

12. Kenneth Morgan, *Slavery, Atlantic Trade and the British Economy, 1660–1800*, Cambridge: Cambridge University Press, 2000, pp. 94–8.

13. Richard Pares, quoted in ibid., p. 54. For more information about Fonthill and the Beckford family, see Derek E. Ostergard (ed.), *William Beckford, 1760–1844: An Eye for the Magnificent*, New Haven, CT and London: Yale University Press, 2001; and Perry Gauci, *William Beckford: First Prime Minister of the London Empire*, New Haven, CT and London: Yale University Press, 2013.

14. See Robin Blackburn, *The Making of New World Slavery: From the Baroque to the Modern, 1492–1800*, London and New York: Verso, 1997; and Simon D. Smith, *Slavery, Family and Gentry Capitalism in the British Atlantic: The World of the Lascelles, 1648–1834*, Cambridge: Cambridge University Press, 2006.

15. Anon., *Jamaica: A Poem, in Three Parts. Written in that island, in the year MDCCLXXVI*, London: William Nichol, 1777.

16. See William Beckford, *A Descriptive Account of The Island of Jamaica, With Remarks upon the Cultivation of the Sugar-Cane throughout the different Seasons of the Year, and chiefly considered in a Picturesque Point of View*, London: T. & J. Egerton, 1790, p. vii.

17. Apart from a brief period in Brazil, Dutch nationals tended to be shippers and traders rather than plantation owners. See Blackburn, 1997, op. cit., pp. 192–211.

18. See also Madge Dresser and Andrew Hann (eds), *Slavery and the British Country House*, Swindon: English Heritage, 2013.

19. See David Hancock's study of twenty-three London-based Atlantic merchants, *Citizens of the World: London Merchants and the Integration of the British Atlantic Community*, Cambridge: Cambridge University Press, 1995; and also Nicolas Draper, 'Possessing People: Absentee Slave-Owners within British Society', in Hall, Draper and McCelland (eds), 2014, op. cit., pp. 34–77.

20. C. De Thierry, 'Colonials at Westminster', *United Empire Magazine*, vol. III, January 1912.
21. See Søren Mentz, *The English Gentleman Merchant at Work: Madras and the City of London, 1660–1740*, Copenhagen: Museum Tusculanum, 2006.
22. Indeed, much East India Company trade was carried out within Asia itself: in 1771, for example, the volume of trade between Britain and its American colonies was five times as much as the trade with the East Indies. See Ralph Davis, *The Rise of the English Shipping Industry in the Seventeenth and Eighteenth Centuries*, London and New York: Macmillan, 1962.
23. Sarah Pearsall, *Atlantic Families: Lives and Letters in the Later Eighteenth Century*, Oxford and New York: Oxford University Press, 2008.
24. 'Inventory of Looby's Plantation, Antigua, 1777', in Ivor Waters, *Piercefield on the Banks of the Wye*, Chepstow: Chepstow Society, 1975, p. 7. Inventories are on public display in the Museum of Slavery in Liverpool.
25. Nicholas Draper, 'Slave ownership and the British country house: the records of the Slave Compensation Commission as evidence', in Dresser and Hann (eds), op. cit., 2013, pp. 1–11.
26. See https://historicengland.org.uk/research/inclusive-heritage/the-slave-trade-and-abolition/sites-of-memory/black-lives-in-england/servants/ [accessed December 2021].
27. William Claypole and John Robottom, *Caribbean Story, Book One: Foundations*, Jamaica, Trinidad and Harlow: Longman Caribbean, 1990, pp. 63–9.
28. Blackburn, 1997, op. cit., p. 244.
29. For an overview of this research, see Madge Dresser and Mary Wills, 'The Transatlantic Slave Economy and England's Built Environment: A Research Audit', *Historic England*, no. 247, 2020, available at https://historicengland.org.uk/research/results/reports/247–2020
30. The current Earl speaks openly of his family's past. See, for example, Shingi Marike, 'David Harewood meets the Earl of Harewood: My ancestors were your family's slaves,' *The Sunday Times Magazine*, 17 October 2021.
31. The other three, referred to in the text, but not in as much detail, were: Delaford Park in Buckinghamshire; Lowther Castle in Cumbria; and Dunmore Park, near Stirling in Scotland.
32. Christopher Harvie, *A Floating Commonwealth: Politics, Culture and Technology on Britain's Atlantic Coast, 1860–1930*, Oxford and New York: Oxford University Press, 2008, p. 7.
33. John Scott, *Critical Essays on Some of the Poems of Several English Poets*, cited

in Nigel Everett, *The Tory View of Landscape*, New Haven, CT and London: Yale University Press, 1994, p. 75.

34. Adam Smith, *An Inquiry into the Nature and Causes of The Wealth of Nations*, London: Strahan and Cadell, 1776, vol. II, (first edition), p. 200.

1. THESE CANE OCEAN-ISLES

1. *Montpelier*, Nevis, 2005 brochure. The 2021 website describes it as 'a 300-year-old sugar plantation that now happily embraces effortless luxury'. See https://www.montpeliernevis.com [accessed 16 April 2021].

2. *The Hermitage Inn*, Nevis, 2005 brochure. The 2021 website is more circumspect, preferring the terms 'elegant and authentic'. See https://hermitagenevis.com [accessed 16 April 2021].

3. Quoted from *The Daily Mail* in the 2005 brochure, *The Hermitage Inn*, op. cit.

4. Letterbook of Lascelles and Maxwell, 1743–5, West Yorkshire Record Office, Leeds, 14 November 1743, George Maxwell to James Bruce, Fo. 58.

5. See Richard Grove, *Green Imperialism: Colonial Expansion, Tropical Island Edens and the Origins of Environmentalism, 1600–1860*, Cambridge: Cambridge University Press, 1995.

6. There is extensive literature on the historic architecture and sites of the Caribbean including: David Buisseret, *Historic Architecture of the Caribbean*, London: Heinemann, 1980; Edward Crain, *Historic Architecture of the Caribbean Islands*, Gainesville, FL: University Press of Florida, 1994; Pamela Gosner, *Caribbean Georgian: The Great and Small Houses of the West Indies*, Washington: Three Continents, 1982; and Louis Nelson, *Architecture and Empire in Jamaica*, New Haven, CT and London: Yale University Press, 2016.

7. See also discussions in UNESCO World Heritage Paper 15, 'Caribbean Wooden Treasures: Proceeds of the Thematic Expert Meeting of Wooden Urban Heritage in the Caribbean Region', Georgetown, Guyana, February 2003.

8. Apart from a period in the late nineteenth century, British Caribbean sugar producers received some type of subsidy, whether through state-protected markets as in the eighteenth century, or direct support to producers from the 1930s onwards.

9. See J. R. Ward, *British West Indian Slavery, 1750–1834: The Process of Amelioration*, Oxford: Clarendon Press, 1988, pp. 27–8.

10. See Nelson, 2016, op. cit., for more discussion of the relationship between the architecture of Britain and its Caribbean colonies.

11. There is an extensive literature on the growth of the plantation economy in the British Caribbean, including: Robin Blackburn, *The Making of New World Slavery: From the Baroque to the Modern, 1492–1800*, London and New York: Verso, 1997; Wm. Roger Lewis (ed.), *Oxford History of the British Empire*, Oxford and New York: Oxford University Press, 1998–9, vols I–V; Richard Sheridan, *Sugar and Slavery: An Economic History of the British West Indies, 1623–1775*, Barbados: Canoe Press, 1994; and Barry Higman, *Writing West Indian Histories*, London: Macmillan, 1999.

12. See Russell Menard, *Sweet Negotiations: Sugar, Slavery and Plantation Agriculture in Early Barbados*, Charlottesville, VA: University of Virginia Press, 2006.

13. Algernon E. Aspinall, *West Indian Tales of Old*, London: Duckworth & Co, 1912, p. v.

14. See Blackburn, 1997, op. cit., pp. 315–27.

15. This issue was raised by Raymond Mauney, professor of African history at the Sorbonne, in *Le Guide Bleu: Afrique de l'ouest*, 1958 edition.

16. Melinda Elder, *The Slave Trade and the Economic Development of 18th-century Lancaster*, Halifax: Ryburn, 1992, pp. 51–8.

17. At Jufureh, the village near Fort James featured in Alex Hayley's celebrated novel *Roots*, there was, however, a small museum on the history of the Atlantic slave trade.

18. See Anne Bailey, *African Voices of the Atlantic Slave Trade: Beyond the Silence and the Shame*, Boston, MA: Beacon Press, 2005.

19. In 2011, Fort James was also renamed Kunta Kinteh Island, after the lead character in *Roots*, which charts the story of an enslaved Gambian transported to America in 1767.

20. See Emilie Filou, 'A Pilgrimage to Ghana's Slave Forts', BBC, 13 June 2013, https://www.bbc.com/travel/article/20130610-a-pilgrimage-to-ghanas-slave-forts [accessed October 2021].

21. Talk by Isatu Smith, Commonwealth Heritage Forum, March 2021. Available at: https://www.commonwealthheritage.org [accessed March 2021].

22. Olaudah Equiano, *The Interesting Narrative and other Writings*, (ed. by Vincent Carretta), London: Penguin, 1995, (originally published 1789), p. 55.

23. Vincent Carretta, *Equiano, the African: Biography of a Self-Made Man*, Athens, GA: University of Georgia Press, 2005.

24. Equiano, (ed. by Carretta), 1995, op. cit., p. 58.

25. Ibid., p. 60, as well as subsequent quotes.

26. My thanks to Dr Richard Gilmore of the St. Eustatius Center for

Archaeological Research for his help with information about the history of Oranjestad.

27. Janet Schaw, *Journal of a Lady of Quality: Being the Narrative of a Journey from Scotland to the West Indies, North Carolina and Portugal in the years 1774–1776*, (ed. by Evangeline Walker Andrews), New Haven, CT and London: Yale University Press, 1921, p. 135.

28. Schaw, (ed. by Andrews), 1921, op. cit., p. 135.

29. UNESCO has been running a project there to record the historic sites of the trans-Atlantic slave trade.

30. See Veront Satchell, *Sugar, Slavery and Technological Change: Jamaica, 1760–1830*, Saarbrucken: VDM Verlag, 2010.

31. See John Gilmore, *The Poetics of Empire: A Study of James Grainger's The Sugar Cane*, London: Athlone Press, 2000, pp. 1–15. The verse was the Caribbean's first example of Georgic poetry.

32. Ibid., lines 265–70.

33. Ibid., line 270.

34. The fort is a UNESCO World Heritage Site and archaeological studies have been carried out to document the role that enslaved Africans played in its construction and maintenance.

35. Lowell J. Ragatz, *The Fall of the Planter Class in the British Caribbean, 1763–1833*, New York and London: Century Co., 1929, p. 26.

36. 'The Diary of Thomas Thistlewood', quoted in Ward, 1988, op. cit., pp. 27–8. Also see Douglas Hall, *In Miserable Slavery: Thomas Thistlewood in Jamaica, 1750–86*, Mona, Jamaica: University of the West Indies Press, 1989; and Trevor Burnard, *Mastery, Tyranny and Desire: Thomas Thistlewood and his Slaves in the Anglo-Jamaican World*, Chapel Hill, NC: University of North Carolina Press, 2004.

37. George Maxwell to John Braithwaite, November 1745, in S. D. Smith (ed.), *The Lascelles and Maxwell Letter Book (1739–1769)*, Wakefield: Microform Academic Publishers, 2002.

38. See Lorna Simmonds, 'The Afro-Jamaican and the Internal Marketing System: Kingston, 1780–1834', in Kathleen E. A. Monteith and Glen Richards (eds), *Jamaica in Slavery and Freedom: History, Heritage and Culture*, Kingston: University of the West Indies Press, 2002, pp. 274–90.

39. Schaw, (ed. by Andrews), 1921, op. cit., p. 88.

40. See Barry Higman, *Montpelier, Jamaica: A Plantation Community in Slavery and Freedom, 1739–1912*, Mona, Jamaica: University of the West Indies Press, 1998. See also 'Archaeology and Reconstructive Illustration of Life in the Slave Village at Good Hope Estate', *Friends of the Georgian Society of Jamaica* Webinar, July 2020, available at https://fgsj.org.uk/fgsj-webinar-archaeology%E2%80%A8and%E2%80%A8reconstruct

ive-illustration%E2%80%A8of-life-in-the-slave-village%E2%80%A8at%E2%80%A8good-hope-estate/ [accessed 16 December 2021].

41. George Webbe Dasent, *Annals of an Eventful Life*, London: Hurst and Blackett, 1870, (fifth edition), p. 60.

42. Ibid., p. 80.

43. See Douglas Hall, 'Absentee-Proprietorship in the British West Indies, to about 1850', *Jamaican Historical Review*, vol. 4, no. 15, 1964, pp. 15–35; Draper, op. cit., in Hall, Draper and McLelland (eds), 2014, op. cit., pp. 35–77; and Pearsall, 2008, op. cit.

44. For a more detailed discussion, see Draper, op. cit., in Hall, Draper and McLelland (eds), 2014, op. cit.

45. Daniel McKinnen, *A Tour through the British West Indies, In the Years 1802 and 1803*, London: J. White, 1804, preface.

46. Ibid.

47. Ibid., p. 108.

48. See Nelson, 2016, op. cit.; Tom Concannon, 'The Great Houses of Jamaica', in Morris Cargill (ed.), *Ian Fleming Introduces Jamaica*, London: André Deutsch, 1965, pp. 117–26; Camille Wells, 'The Multistoried House: Twentieth-Century Encounters with the Domestic Architecture of Colonial Virginia', *The Virginia Magazine of History and Biography*, vol. 106, no. 4, 1998, pp. 353–418.

49. McKinnen, 1804, op. cit., p. 108.

2. ARTS AND ELEGANCIES

1. My thanks to Richard Lea of English Heritage for drawing my attention to this.

2. Chris Miele and Richard Lea, 'The House and Park at Danson, London Borough of Bexley: The anatomy of a Georgian Suburban Estate', *English Heritage Historical Analysis and Research Team, Reports and Papers*, 2000.

3. There is no fabric or documentary evidence to suggest that there was originally a chinoiserie element to the wallcovering in the 1700s. See Richard Lea, 'Danson: the "Blue Silk Damask", is this an accurate description of the saloon's original wall covering?', *English Heritage Historical Analysis and Research Team, Reports and Papers*, 2002.

4. See Simon Gikandi, *Slavery and the Culture of Taste*, Princeton, NJ and Oxford, UK: Princeton University Press, 2011, pp. 1–49.

5. For a more detailed account of Augustus and John Boyd's background in St Kitts and their business dealings as London merchants, see Hancock, 1995, op. cit.

6. An undated anonymous map of St Kitts—probably late eighteenth/early

nineteenth century and on display at St Kitts Museum, Basseterre—indicates estates owned by a 'John Boyd' in this area.

7. See Davis, 1962, op. cit.

8. Daniel Defoe, *A Tour thro' the Whole Island of Great Britain*, London: J. Rivington, 1769, vol. II, (seventh edition), p. 157.

9. For more information, see Malachy Postlethwayt, *The African Trade, the Great Pillar and Support of the British Plantation trade in America*, London: s.n., 1745 and *Britain's commercial interest explained and improved*, London: D. Browne, 1757.

10. Malachy Postlethwayt, *The Merchant's Public Counting House: Or, New Mercantile Institution*, London: John and Paul Knapton, 1750, preface. Italics in the original.

11. John Brewer and Roy Porter (eds), *Consumption and the World of Goods*, New York: Routledge, 1993, pp. 1–8.

12. In 1686, Britain traded 67,000 tons of shipping with mainland Europe and 70,000 tons with the Americas. By 1771, this had increased to 105,000 tons and 153,000 tons, respectively. By way of comparison, in the same year, 29,000 tons were traded with the East Indies. See Davis, 1962, op. cit.

13. See Davis, 1962, op. cit., and 'An Abridgement of Several Acts of Parliament relating to the Trade and Navigation of Great Britain to from and in the British Plantations in America', *Laws and Statutes IV Collections and Abridgements*, London, 1739.

14. In this, Boyd and Perchell's firm differed from that of 'factors', who bought goods on their own account and resold them at a profit. See Hancock, 1995, op. cit., pp. 46–7.

15. Other coffee houses included, for example, The Colonial on Threadneedle Street, The Pennsylvania on Birchin Lane, and The New York and The Portugal. See Hancock, 1995, op. cit., p. 89 and p. 308.

16. See John Summerson's classic book on the architecture and planning of London between 1714 and 1830: *Georgian London*, London: Pimlico, 1991 (originally published in 1945).

17. See Hancock, 1995, op. cit. The Crescent was bombed in WWII and the current building is a 1980s replica.

18. For a discussion of the influence of these educational institutions during the eighteenth century, see Linda Colley, *Britons: Forging the Nation, 1707–1837*, London: Pimlico, 1994.

19. For a discussion of the concept of a 'gentleman', see Paul Langford, *A Polite and Commercial People: England, 1727–83*, Oxford and New York: Oxford University Press, 1992; and Douglas Hay and Nicholas Rogers, *Eighteenth-Century English Society: Shuttles and Swords*, Oxford and New

York: Oxford University Press, 1997, pp. 18–36. See also Vickery, 1998, op. cit., pp. 14–37 for an investigation of 'gentility'.

20. Daniel Defoe, *The Compleat Gentleman: Edited for the First Time from the Author's Autograph Manuscript in the British Museum, with Introduction, Notes, and Index*, (ed. by Karl D. Bülbring), London: David Nutt, 1890.

21. Ibid., p. 254.

22. Ibid., p. 256. See also Hancock, 1995, op. cit., pp. 281–2.

23. Defoe, (ed. by Bülbring), 1890, op. cit., p. 258.

24. Robert Maxwell to Thomas Finlay, 17 May 1744, in Smith (ed.), 2002, op. cit.

25. For the social status of the planter vis-à-vis attitudes to new wealth, see James Raven, *Judging New Wealth: Popular Publishing and Responses to Commerce in England, 1750–1800*, Oxford and New York: Oxford University Press, 1992, p. 208 and pp. 221–48.

26. Barbecue derives from the Spanish word 'barbecoa', a corruption of the word 'barabicu' in the Arawak language native to the Caribbean. 'Barabicu' was the name for a raised wooden grate used to smoke food. The term was first used in Europe by returning Spanish explorers in the early sixteenth century.

27. Samuel Foote, *The Patron: A Comedy in Three Acts*, Dublin: P. Wilson, 1764, Act I Scene I.

28. Richard Cumberland, *The West Indian: A Comedy*, Dublin: P. & W. Wilson, 1771, Act I Scene III.

29. Anon., *City Biography: Memoirs of the Aldermen of London*, London: s.n., 1800.

30. See Janet Clarkson, *Soup: A Global History, London*: Reaktion, 2010, pp. 115–18.

31. See Jeremy Black, *The British Abroad: The Grand Tour in the Eighteenth Century*, Stroud: Sutton, 1992.

32. Marcus Binney, Sir Robert Taylor: *From Rococo to Neoclassicism*, London: Allen & Unwin, 1984.

33. See Lewis Namier and John Brooke, *The History of Parliament (The House of Commons), 1754–1790*, London: HMSO, 1964. St Kitts absentee Ralph Payne (1739–1807), Governor of the Leeward islands, also made the Grand Tour in his youth.

34. See Miele and Lea, 2000, op. cit., Appendix for a list of paintings and sculptures owned by Boyd, who became one of eighteenth-century Britain's foremost art collectors. Thanks to David Solkin, of the Courtauld Institute, too, for pointing out the significance of his collection.

35. See Hancock, 1995, op. cit., pp. 170–213. It is likely that John's social connections would have been valuable in gaining the introductions for

these contracts, making Augustus's shrewd investment in his gentle-manly education worthwhile.

36. The consortium was led by the City tobacco and sugar merchanting firm Grant, Sargent & Oswald, a Scots-led partnership between Sir Alexander Grant (1705–72), John Sargent (1714–91) and Richard Oswald (1705–84), with the involvement of Grenadines plantation owner John Mill (1710–71). Grant later became an MP for Inverness; Sargent a director of the Bank of England and an MP; and Oswald, to whom we return in Chapter Six, the chief British negotiator for the 1783 Treaty of Paris, the settlement which formally ended the American War of Independence.

37. Hancock, 1995, op. cit., p. 174.

38. Ibid., p. 213. For more background on trans-Atlantic slave-trading voyages, see the Slave Voyages website, available at https://www.slave-voyages.org [accessed 16 December 2021].

39. See Boyd family accounts (formerly Drummonds Bank), Royal Bank of Scotland Archives, London, DR/427/160.

40. Danson Deeds, Bexley Local Studies Centre, Bexley, DAN, 3 July 1753.

41. Ibid.

42. For a discussion of the growth of 'suburban' seats around eighteenth-century London, see Robert Fishman, *Bourgeois Utopia: The Rise and Fall of Suburbia*, New York: Basic Books Inc., 1997.

43. Hancock, 1995, op. cit., p. 287.

44. For discussions of the eighteenth-century British concepts of 'taste' and 'elegance', see, for example, Jules Lubbock, *The Tyranny of Taste: The Politics of Architecture and Design in Britain, 1550–1960*, New Haven, CT and London: Yale University Press, 1995, pp. 10–174; and Amanda Vickery, 1998, op. cit., pp. 161–94.

45. For a wider discussion of Palladio and his influence, see James Ackerman, *Palladio*, London: Penguin, 1977, (second edition); and Reinhard Bentmann and Michael Muller, *The Villa as Hegemonic Architecture*, New Haven, CT and London: Yale University Press, 1992 (English translation of *Die Villa als Herrschaftsarchitektur*). The latter argues that Palladio's appeal to the Venetians lay in their quest, following the loss of their Eastern empire, to establish the legitimacy of Venice's rule over the Italian mainland. The Palladian style was rooted in Roman antiquity, conferring the appearance of longevity, and therefore of an imperial right to rule over its dominions.

46. See, for instance, Colley, 1994, op. cit., p. 168.

47. See also Charles Saumarez Smith, 'Supply and Demand in English Country House Building, 1660–1740', *The Oxford Art Journal*, vol. 11, no. 2, 1988, pp. 3–9. In this he suggests how Palladianism may have

been used to disguise a structural shift in the composition of the English elite.

48. Colley, 1994, op. cit., pp. 168–70. One of Palladio's most enthusiastic advocates in the early years of the eighteenth century was Richard Boyle, Lord Burlington, heir to a Yorkshire estate and 'plantations' near the Irish Atlantic port of Cork.

49. See, for example James Gibb, *Rules for Drawing the Several Parts of Architecture* (1732); Robert Morris, *Architectural Remembrancer* (1751); Isaac Ware, *The Complete Body of Architecture* (1756); and William Chambers, *A Treatise on Civil Architecture* (1759).

50. The sash windows at Danson, with their fine mouldings and elegant folding internal shutters, are very different from the leaded light casements, chunky timber transoms and mullions and rough external shutters found in Palladio's villas.

51. See Miele and Lea, 2000, op. cit., pp. 94–7.

52. Typical is an agreement from 12 August 1761 for the lease and release of 12.5 acres 'in Consideration £166.13.4 in India Stock yielding £10 per annum interest', Danson Deeds, Bexley Local Studies Centre, DAN 109, 110 and 115.

53. Hay and Rogers, 1997, op. cit., p. 28.

54. See Miele and Lea, 2000, op. cit., p. 100.

55. Tom Williamson, *Polite Landscapes*; *Gardens and Society in Eighteenth-Century England*, Stroud: Sutton, 1995, p. 85.

56. Unconventionally, the plan in the image runs south to north, hence not using these geographical terms in the description, to avoid confusion.

57. The term 'paddock' was sometimes also used.

58. Williamson, 1995, op. cit., p. 89.

59. Miele and Lea, 2000, op. cit., p. 18.

3. TRADE AND PLUMB CAKE

1. The house also had a substantial refurbishment in the 1840s, when terraces and formal gardens were introduced.

2. See Ivan P. Day, *Royal Sugar Sculpture: 600 years of Splendour*, Barnard Castle: The Bowes Museum, 2002.

3. See James Walvin, *Fruits of Empire: Exotic Produce and British Taste, 1660–1800*, London: Macmillan, 1997; and Blackburn, 1997, op. cit., p. 272.

4. Walvin, 1997, op. cit., p. 144.

5. Alan Davidson, *Oxford Companion to Food*, Oxford and New York: Oxford University Press, 2006, (second edition).

6. See Bridget Henisch, *Cake and Characters*: *An English Christmas Tradition*, London: Prospect, 1984.

7. John Newbery, *The Twelfth Day Gift*, London, 1774, (third edition).

8. James Boswell, quoted in Henisch, 1984, op. cit., p. 174. We encounter Boswell again later, touring Scotland with his friend, the writer Samuel Johnson, in Chapter Six.

9. The Lascelles archives at York have been extensively researched by historian James Walvin and his team at the nearby University of York. See, for example, James Walvin, *Black Ivory: A History of British Slavery*, London: Harper Collins, 1992. A collaboration between Harewood House and the Borthwick Institute for Archives, part of the Library of the University of York, has also provided access to the Lascelles Slavery Archive. Available at https://www.york.ac.uk/projects/harewood-slavery/index.html

10. For a history of the Lascelles's involvement in Barbados, see Smith, 2006, op. cit.; and, for instance, J. W. Fortescue (ed.), 'Calendar of State Papers Colonial, America and West Indies', London: His Majesty's Stationery Office, 1904, entry for 28 August 1698. Available from *British History Online*, http://www.british-history.ac.uk/cal-state-papers/colonial/america-west-indies/vol15 [accessed 13 December 2021].

11. See Smith, 2006, op. cit., p. 51.

12. As with many landed families, through the propensity to intermarry and give the same forenames to multiple offspring, the Lascelles's family tree can be confusing. Henry (1690–1753), the most successful of Daniel's children, was the inaugural patron of the estate which would become Harewood. It was inherited by his son Edwin (1713–95), who built the house itself. Edwin was the first and last Baron Harewood, and he died childless. So, the estate then passed to Henry's nephew Edward (1740–1820), first Earl Harewood, son of his younger half-brother. The second Earl Harewood was Edward's son, also named Henry Lascelles (1767–1841).

13. J. V. Beckett, 'Inheritance and fortune in the eighteenth century: the rise of Sir James Lowther, Earl of Lonsdale' in *Transactions of the Cumberland and Westmoreland Antiquarian Society*, vol. 87, series 2, 1987, pp. 171–8.

14. William A. Shaw and F. H. Slingsby (eds), *Calendar of Treasury Books, Volume 29, 1714–1715*, London: Her Majesty's Stationery Office, 1957, pt. 11, Barbados Out Letters (Customs) XVI, p. 102. Available from *British History Online*, https://www.british-history.ac.uk/cal-treasury-books/vol29

15. Cecil Headlam (ed.), *Calendar of State Papers Colonial, America and West Indies: Volume 28, 1714–1715*, London: Her Majesty's Stationery Office, 1928, entry from 24 April 1714, item 654.vi, p. 327. Available from

British History Online, https://www.british-history.ac.uk/cal-state-papers/colonial/america-west-indies/vol28

16. Harewood Archives, Survey 14A, 1738/9, West Yorkshire Record Office, Leeds.
17. See Vickery, 1998, op. cit., pp. 226–9.
18. See Hay and Rogers, 1997, op. cit., for the relative returns of investments in stocks and land.
19. John Jewell, *The Tourist's Companion and Guide to the Antiquities of Harewood*, Leeds: B. Dewhirst, 1819.
20. See Gikandi, 2011, op. cit., pp. 60–2 for comments on the contrast between sober 'polite' exteriors and extravagantly decorated interiors.
21. See Alistair Rowan, *Bob the Roman: Heroic Antiquity & the Architecture of Robert Adam*, London: Soane Gallery, 2003; and also Eileen Harris, *The Genius of Robert Adam: His Interiors*, New Haven, CT and London: Yale University Press, 2001.
22. Adam had tried to persuade him to incorporate two circular colonnaded courtyards into the plans of Harewood. See Mary Mauchline, *Harewood House*, London: David & Charles, 1974, pp. 101–8.
23. See Hancock, 1995, op. cit., pp. 320–81.
24. Jewell, 1819, op. cit., p. 30.
25. Harris, 2001, op. cit. See also Adriano Aymonimo, 'The True Style of Antique Decoration: Agostino Brunius and the Adam style at Kedleston Hall and Syon House', in Colin Thorn (ed.), *Robert Adam and His Brothers: New Light on Britain's Leading Architectural Family*, Swindon: Historic England, 2019.
26. The ceiling decorations at Harewood are also different technically from seventeenth- and early-eighteenth-century plaster ceilings. Rather than hand-moulded and sculpted plaster, they used repetitive, cast ornaments set in carved moulds, not unlike those used for sugar decorations. See Geoffrey Beard, *Stucco and Decorative Plasterwork in Europe*, London: Thames and Hudson, 1983, p. 32.
27. Horace Walpole quoted in Henisch, 1984, op. cit. p. 112.
28. For more background see English Heritage, 'Dido Elizabeth Belle', n.d., https://www.english-heritage.org.uk/learn/histories/women-in-history/dido-belle/ [accessed October 2021]. We refer to Mansfield further in Chapter Eight, regarding the abolition of the slave trade.
29. Ignatius Sancho, *Letters*, quoted in Henisch, 1984, op. cit., p. 113.
30. *Civil Engineering and Architectural Journal 1*, 1838, p. 337; also quoted in Henisch, 1984, op. cit., p. 161.
31. For a more detailed discussion see Jennifer L. Anderson, *Mahogany: The Costs of Luxury in Early America*, Cambridge, MA: Harvard University Press, 2012.

32. Clement Caines, *Letters on the Cultivation of the Otaheite*, Cane, London: Messrs. Robinson, 1801, p. 252.
33. Ibid.
34. Figures from Bryan Edwards, *The History, Civil and Commercial of the West Indies*, London: John Stockdale, 1807, (fourth edition).
35. Jewell, 1819, op. cit., p. 17.
36. The design of the library bookcases at Danson is notable for its use of large, flat panels of the tropical hardwood—a form of construction then impossible in native oak, as it would have distorted, if not held in place by a frame.
37. See Vickery, 1998, op. cit., p. 161.
38. See Fran Beauman, *The Pineapple: King of Fruits*, London: Chatto & Windus, 2005, pp. 112–15.
39. Pineapples, or *ananas* (derived from the word *nanas*, meaning 'excellent fruit' in the Tupi language native to South America), originated in South America and were introduced to the Caribbean islands by the migrating Carib peoples, from whom the islands take their name. For a short synopsis, see the *Social History of the Pineapple*, by Hoag Levins, 2009, https://www.levins.com/pineapple.html [accessed December 2021].
40. Schaw, (ed. by Andrews), 1921, op. cit., 9 August 1774.
41. Richard Bradley, *The Country Housewife and Lady's Director, in the Management of a House and the Delights and Profits of a Farm*, London: Woodman and Lyon, 1732, part II, p. 94. And the 'Pineapple Tart' was followed by another West Indian–derived recipe: instructions for dressing the giblets of a sea turtle.
42. See Beauman, 2005, op. cit., p. 85.
43. See Hancock, 1995, op. cit., pp. 379–80. See also Susanne Seymour, Stephen Daniels and Charles Watkins, 'Estate and empire: Sir George Cornewall's management of Moccas, Herefordshire and La Taste, Grenada, 1771–1819', *Journal of Historical Geography*, vol. 24, issue 3, 1998, pp. 313–51, (p. 343).
44. Jewell, 1819, op. cit., p. 20.
45. Ibid.
46. Williamson, 1995, op. cit., p. 24.
47. Ibid.
48. The 'moot rent' from the 3,969 Yorkshire acres in 1739 was £2,172 per annum excluding taxes. See Harewood Archives, Survey 14A, 1738/9, West Yorkshire Record Office, Leeds.
49. During this period most English landed gentry earned between £400 and £1,000 per year. See Hay and Rogers, 1997, op. cit., pp. 19–21.
50. See Harewood Archives, Ac.c 2677/10, 29 June 1786, 'Bargain and Sale of Premises in Barbados', William Daling to Edwin Lascelles, West

Yorkshire Record Office, Leeds; and also Harewood Archives, Ac.c, Box 7/119, 'West Indies Accounts'.

51. Harewood Archives, WI/Bundle 1, 'Accounts and Miscellaneous Papers, 1790–1748', West Yorkshire Record Office, Leeds.
52. Pollard family papers (Additional Manuscripts, Hardwicke Papers, vol. CCCV11), folio 35, 517, 8 February 1780, John Boyd (Junior), British Library, London.
53. Ibid.
54. Ibid.
55. Seymour, Daniels and Watkins, 1998, op. cit., p. 323.
56. David Brown, 'Lancelot Brown and His Associates', *Garden History: Journal of the Garden History Society*, vol. 29, no. 1, summer 2001, pp. 2–11.
57. Oliver Goldsmith, *The Deserted Village*, 1770, (ed. by Desmond Egan), The Curragh, Ireland: Goldsmith Press, 1978, (facsimile edition).
58. See Williamson, 1995, op. cit., p. 24, for a critical overview of this debate.
59. Goldsmith, (ed. by Egan), 1978, op. cit., p. 24.
60. Nigel Everett, *The Tory View of Landscape*, New Haven, CT and London: Yale University Press, 1994, pp. 70–82.
61. John Scott, *Critical Essays*, 1785, quoted in ibid.

4. REFINING THE WORLD

1. UNESCO, 'City of Bath, http:/whc.unesco.org/en/list/428 [accessed May 2021].
2. See Vickery, 1998, op. cit., pp. 269–92.
3. The hospital, now known as The Royal National Hospital for Rheumatic Diseases, still contains a small eighteenth-century art collection.
4. Josiah Wedgwood, 1763, quoted in Susan Sloman, *Gainsborough in Bath*, New Haven, CT and London: Yale University Press, 2002, p. 9.
5. George Heath, *The New History, Survey and Description of the City and Suburbs of Bristol, or complete Guide*, Bristol: W. Matthews, 1794, p. 215.
6. Anon., *Bath: A Simile*, London: *s.n.*, 1789.
7. Ibid.
8. Ibid.
9. See Hancock, 1995, op. cit., p. 223–4; and also Jerom Murch, *Ralph Allen, John Palmer and the English Post Office*, London: Longmans, 1880; and Frank Staff, *The Transatlantic Mail*, Lawrence, MA: Quarterman, 1980. Allen's Bath townhouse and original post office in Terrace Walk (refaced and extended by Wood in 1727) is now a museum. His 'cross

post' system, linking provincial towns, also contributed to the development of a 'culture of the West'. The first post boats to the West Indies sailed from Falmouth in Cornwall, and, with the 'cross post', the mail no longer had to go via London.

10. Richard Pares, *A West India Fortune*, London: Longmans, Green & Co, 1950.

11. Madge Dresser, *Slavery Obscured: The Social History of the Slave Trade in an English Provincial Port*, London: Continuum, 2001.

12. See visitbristol.co.uk/site/the slave trade trail. In 2007, Bristol Museums and Galleries established an exhibition and 'sugar trail' in The Georgian House, John Pinney's former home.

13. Derrick Knight, *Gentlemen of Fortune: The Men who Made their Fortunes in Britain's Slave Colonies*, London: Frederick Muller, 1978, p. 81.

14. Michael Forsyth, *Bath: Pevsner Architectural Guides*, New Haven, CT and London: Yale University Press, 2003.

15. Anon., *Britannia: A Poem*, London, 1767, p. 15.

16. Philip Thicknesse, *Memoirs and Anecdotes of Phillip Thicknesse*, London: *s.n.*, 1788, vol. II, p. 302. An adventurer, Thicknesse served in the military in Jamaica and later became Lt.-Governor of Landguard Fort, at Felixstowe in Suffolk, where he befriended the painter Thomas Gainsborough, before moving to Bath.

17. Alexander Pope to Martha Blount, 6 October 1714, quoted in R. S. Neale, *Bath: A Social History, 1680–1850 or A Valley of Pleasure, yet a Sink of Iniquity*, London: Routledge, 1981, p. 12.

18. Quoted in Neale, 1981, op. cit., p. 131.

19. The 'Asiento de Negros' system was established after Spain's colonisation of the Caribbean, with the first licence granted in 1518. Britain gave up its rights to supply 4,800 slaves a year at the Treaty of Madrid (1750) after the War of Jenkins' Ear (1739–48) against the Spanish in the West Indies. But the acquisition of the Asiento was a seminal step in Britain's involvement in the slave trade.

20. Neale,1981, op. cit., p. 127. On 28 September 1720, Brydges possessed £141,000 in India Stock and £40,000 in Africa Bonds.

21. The family owned the Hope and Middleton plantations in Jamaica. See also Close Rolls (Barbados), The National Archives, Public Record Office, Kew; the Bodleian Library, Gough MSS, Somersetshire, *Copies of papers relating to a scheme in the West Indies*, 1723, HMC Principal family and estates collections A-K, 1996 (44a) (Stowe Collections); and Huntington Library, CA. Stowe Collection, ST 58/vol. 9: Incoming Brydges Correspondence, 1711.

22. Neale, 1981, op. cit., pp. 122–31.

23. Heath, 1794, op. cit., pp. 98–109.

24. Ibid.

25. Douglas Hamilton, *Scotland, the Caribbean and the Atlantic World, 1750–1820*, Manchester: Manchester University Press, 2005, pp. 112–34.

26. Quoted in Lewis Mansfield Knapp, *Tobias Smollett: Doctor of Men and Manners*, Princeton, NJ: Princeton University Press, 1949, p. 219. See also Alan Karras, *Sojourners in the Sun: Scottish Migrants in Jamaica and the Chesapeake, 1740–1800*, Ithaca, NY and London: Cornell University Press, 1993; and Richard Sheridan, *Doctors and Slaves: A Medical and Demographic History of Slavery in the British West Indies, 1680–1834*, Cambridge: Cambridge University Press, 2009.

27. Knapp, 1949, op. cit., p. 219.

28. Tobias Smollett, *The Expedition of Humphrey Clinker*, (ed. by Thomas R. Preston), Athens, GA: University of Georgia Press, 1900, (originally published in 1771), p. 36.

29. See Vickery, 1998, op. cit., p. 265 for a more detailed discussion.

30. Smollett, 1900, op. cit., p. 47.

31. Christopher Anstey, *The new Bath guide: or, memoirs of the B-r-d family. In a series of poetical epistles*, Dublin: *s.n.*, 1766, (reprint in 1978 of 1820 edition), p. 18.

32. Anstey, 1766, op. cit., p. 33.

33. Daniel Livesay, *Children of Uncertain Fortune: Mixed Race Jamaicans in Britain and the Atlantic Family, 1733–1833*, Chapel Hill, NC: University of North Carolina Press, 2018.

34. John Baker (ed. by Philip Yorke), *The Diary of John Baker, 1751–1778*, London: Hutchinson, 1931, pp. 107–9 and pp. 247–9.

35. David Hume, *Essays*, Essay XIV, 'Idea of a perfect Commonwealth', quoted in Miles Ogborn, *Spaces of Modernity: London's Geographies, 1680–1780*, New York and London: Guildford Press, 1998, p. 116.

36. Ibid.

37. Neale, 1981, op. cit., p. 44.

38. The name refers to Robert Jenkins, captain of a British merchantman, whose ear was cut off by the Spanish coast guard on boarding his ship for a contraband check. The incident happened in 1731, but seven years later, to drum up support for war, Jenkins was theatrically brought before Parliament, minus his ear.

39. Heath, 1794, op. cit., p. 102.

40. Neale, 1981, op. cit., p. 162.

41. See *A letter to a Certain Eminent British Sailor Occasion'd by his Specimen of Naked Truth*, London: M. Moore, 1749. Available at https://archive.org/details/lettertocertaine00zealuoft

42. The Baccaye (later Westerhall) Estate, Grenada, and Port Royal Estate, Tobago.

43. William Adam, Robert's father, had previously designed a five-arched, stone bridge over the River Tay, near Aberfeldy in Scotland, in 1733, as part of General George Wade's road-building programme to improve military communications in case of a further Scottish revolt after the 1715 Jacobite rebellion. See Historic England, 'Pulteney Bridge', https://historicengland.org.uk/listing/the-list/list-entry/1394514 [accessed October 2021].

44. Pulteney Papers, Box 8: Spa, The Huntington Library, Pasadena, California (now searchable online).

45. Ibid., Box 8: Bath 30 July 1770: Aldermen and Council of Bath—W. Pulteney.

46. Ibid., Box 8: Spa, Germany 27 August 1770: to Messrs Hope & Co (unsigned duplicate record).

47. Neale describes the investments, but does not pick up the West Indian links (Brian Edwards, author of *A History Civil and Commercial of the West Indies*, was their nephew). Neale, 1981, op. cit., pp. 246–56. See Zachary Bayly's page on UCL's 'Legacies of British Slave-ownership' project website, available at https://www.ucl.ac.uk/lbs/person/view/2146652013 [accessed October 2021].

48. Several other British banks with prominent Caribbean connections including the Monmouthshire Bank also collapsed during this time. See Robin Blackburn, *The Overthrow of Colonial Slavery, 1776–1848*, London and New York: Verso, 1988, pp. 213–60 for a wider discussion of the crisis.

49. See Historic England, 'NOS 5–20 (CONSEC) AND ATTACHED WALL AND RAILINGS', https://historicengland.org.uk/listing/the-list/list-entry/1394986 [accessed October 2021].

50. See Historic England, 'NOS. 6–21 AND ATTACHED RAILINGS AND VAULTS', https://historicengland.org.uk/listing/the-list/list-entry/1395191 [accessed October 2021].

51. See Historic England, 'NOS. 1–41 AND ATTACHED AREA RAILINGS', https://historicengland.org.uk/listing/the-list/list-entry/1396090 [accessed October 2021].

52. Dresser, 2001, op. cit.

53. Hamilton, 2005, op. cit., pp. 213–15.

54. George Heath, *The Bristol Guide; Being A Complete and Ancient and Modern History of this City of Bristol: Including a Description of the Interesting Curiosities of its Vicinity*, Bristol: J. Mathews, 1815, (third edition, revised and considerably enlarged by Bristoliensis), p. 248–9.

55. See UNESCO, 'City of Bath', http:/whc.unesco.org/en/list/428 [accessed December 2021].

56. See Forsyth, 2003, op. cit., pp. 24–7.

57. Anon., *Bath: A Simile*, op. cit.

58. For background, see Robin Whalley, 'The Royal Victoria Park', *Bath History*, vol. V, n.d., pp. 147–69, available at https://historyofbath. org/images/BathHistory/Vol%2005%20-%2007.%20Whalley%20 -%20The%20Royal%20Victoria%20Park.pdf [accessed October 2021].

59. The landscaping of the Royal Crescent and the trees in the Circus are nineteenth-century additions.

60. See Peter Leach, 'The House with a view in late eighteenth century England: a preliminary inquiry', *The Georgian Group Journal*, vol. XVI, 2008, pp. 117–28.

61. See John Barrell, *The Idea of the Landscape and Sense of Place, 1730–1840*, Cambridge: Cambridge University Press, 1972.

62. Jane Austen, *Northanger Abbey*, London: *s.n.*, 1906 (originally published in 1817), p. 110.

63. Ibid.

64. Smith, 1776, op. cit., book IV, p. 200.

65. Again, see Hancock, 1995, op. cit., appendix, for details of Boyd's collection.

66. Quoted in Susan Sloman, *Gainsborough in Bath*, New Haven, CT and London: Yale University Press, 2002, p. 58.

67. Ibid., Chapter 7, 'Nature sat for Mr Gainsborough'. Gainsborough revisited the theme of peasants and cottagers in his later years. See Hugh Belsey, *Gainsborough's Cottage Doors: An Insight into the Artist's Last Decade*, London: Paul Holberton, 2013.

68. See *Rocky Wooded Landscape with Rustic Lovers, Herdsman and Cows*, Art Collections Online, https://museum.wales/art/online/?action=show_ item&item=2181 [accessed October 2021].

69. See discussion and analysis by Philip Mould: http://www.historicalpor-traits.com/Gallery.asp?Page=Item&ItemID=1290&Desc=Wooded-landscape-%7C-Thomas-Gainsborough-RA [accessed October 2021].

5. NATURE'S PROSPECTS

1. Thomas Hull, *Select Letters between the late Duchess of Somerset, Lady Luxborough and others*, London: *s.n.*, 1778, Miss M to W. Shenstone, 21 July 1760, pp. 285–94. This quote is from p. 286.

2. Ibid., p. 287.

3. There are no records to show when construction started, but the fact that Miss M could see a completed lawn in 1760 suggests that Piercefield was an early example of new parkland landscaping.

4. Hull, 1778, op. cit., p. 288.

5. Ibid. Italics in the original.

6. Ibid.

7. Ibid., Dodesley to W. Shenstone, letter LXVII, 12 October 1759, p. 265.

8. Hull, 1778, op. cit.

9. Ibid., p. 288.

10. Ibid., p. 289.

11. Ibid.

12. Thomas Whateley, *Observations on Modern Gardening*, Dublin: James Williams, 1770.

13. William Wordsworth, *Lines composed a few miles above Tintern Abbey, on revisiting the Banks of the Wye during a tour: July thirteenth, 1798*.

14. Charles Heath, *Descriptive Accounts of Persfield and Chepstow, including Caerwent, and the Passages; also, the Road to Bristol and Gloucester; Interspersed with Local and Interesting Particulars*, Monmouth: *s.n.*, 1793, p. i.

15. Cadw/ICOMOS, 'Piercefield Park and the Wyndcliff', *Register of Parks and Gardens of Special Historic Interest in Wales*, available at https://web.archive.org/web/20160304001555/http://www.coflein.gov.uk/pdf/CPG298/# [accessed January 2022].

16. See, for example, Elisabeth Whittle, 'All these enchanting Scenes', *Journal of Garden History*, vol. 24, issue 1, 1996, pp. 148–61; Stephen Spending, 'One Among the Many: Popular Aesthetics, Polite Culture and the Country House Landscape', in Dana Arnold (ed.), *The Georgian Country House: Architecture, Landscape and Society*, Stroud: Sutton, 2003, pp. 61–78; and Seymour, Daniels and Watkins, 1998, op. cit.

17. Ivor Waters, *Piercefield on the Banks of the Wye*, Chepstow: Chepstow Society, 1975 and *The Unfortunate Valentine Morris*, Chepstow: Chepstow Society, 1964.

18. Papers of Morris family of Antigua (Ac. no. 22138), The Society of Genealogists Archives, London.

19. Ibid., family tree of the Morris family, drawn up by J. R. Thompson in 1928.

20. John Hotten (ed.), *The Original Lists of Persons of Quality: Emigrants; Religious Exiles; Political Rebels; Serving Men Sold for a Term of Years; Apprentices; Children Stolen; Maidens Pressed; and Others Who Went From Great Britain to the American Plantations, 1600–1700*, New York: Empire State Book Co., 1931.

21. Waters, 1964, op. cit., p. 2.

22. Ibid.

23. Extracts from the will of Colonel Valentine Morris in *The History of the Island of Antigua, One of the Leeward Caribbees in the West Indies, From the*

First Settlement in 1635 to the Present Time, London: Mitchell and Hughers, 1896, vol. II.

24. Obituary of Valentine Morris in *The Gentleman's Magazine*, September 1789, pp. 862–4.
25. Ibid.
26. Ibid.
27. Arthur Young, *A Six Weeks Tour though the Southern Counties of England and Wales*, London: W. Nicholl, 1769, (second edition), p. 166.
28. Five years after his visit to Piercefield, Wesley produced a pamphlet *Thoughts Upon Slavery*, criticising the viciousness of plantation life. See David Dabydeen, John Gilmore and Cecily Jones (eds), *The Oxford Companion to Black British History*, Oxford and New York: Oxford University Press, 2007, p. 514.
29. John Wesley, *Journal*, 25 August 1769, quoted in Waters, 1964, op. cit., p. 17.
30. Whateley, 1770, op. cit., p. 241.
31. Young, 1769, op. cit., p. 170.
32. Young's tour was principally made to examine agriculture in Britain following riots and food shortages in 1766.
33. David Watkin, *The English Vision; The Picturesque in Architecture, Landscape and Garden Design*, London: John Murray, 1982, p. vii.
34. Christopher Hussey, *The Picturesque: Studies in a Point of View*, London: Frank Cass, 1967, (new impression with preface by the author, originally published in 1927), p. 7. Boyd owned at least five paintings by Poussin and one by Rosa. See Hancock, 1995, op. cit., appendix.
35. See, for example, Michael Kitson, *The Art of Claude Lorrain*, (exhibition catalogue), 1969, London: Arts Council of Great Britain, 1969.
36. Young, 1769, op. cit., p. 174.
37. Whateley, 1770, op. cit., p. 1.
38. Ibid., p. 236.
39. Heath, 1793, op. cit. See also David Jacques, *Georgian Gardens: The Reign of Nature*, London: Batsford, 1983, p. 63.
40. See Malcolm Andrews, *The Search for the Picturesque: Landscape Aesthetics and Tourism in Britain, 1760–1880*, Aldershot: Scholar, 1989, pp. 89–92.
41. See Roland Trafford-Roberts, *An Assessment of the Historic and Picturesque Viewpoints in the Wye Valley*, report commissioned for the Wye Valley Area of Outstanding Natural Beauty, February 2001.
42. Charles Heath, quoted in Waters, 1964, op. cit., p. 8.
43. Richard Lea, 'Danson, The Saloon Paintings: works by Claude Joseph Vernet, George Barret and Elias Martin', *English Heritage Historical Analysis and Research Team, Reports and Papers*, no. 64, 2003, p. 8.
44. Hull, 1778, op. cit.

45. See Dario Castiglione and Lesley Sharpe (eds), *Shifting the Boundaries: Transformation of the Languages of Public and Private in the Eighteenth Century*, Liverpool: Liverpool University Press, 1995.

46. See Jewell, 1819, op. cit.

47. John Harris, 'English Country House Guides, 1740–1840,' in John Summerson (ed.), *Concerning Architecture. Essays on architectural writers and writing, presented to Nicholas Pevsner*, London: Allen Lane, 1968, pp. 58–74.

48. Obituary of Valentine Morris in *The Gentleman's Magazine*, op. cit.

49. See Andrews, 1989, op. cit.

50. Dodsley himself had strong links with the Caribbean, having served as a footman to Robert Lowther, the former Governor of Barbados.

51. Hull, 1778, op. cit., Dodsley to Shenstone, letter LXVII, 12 October 1759, p. 265.

52. Ibid.

53. Hull, 1778, op. cit., p. 192.

54. Young, 1769, op. cit., p. 175.

55. As well as accounts of the differing British islands, climate and weather, there are technical descriptions of sugar cultivation and processing, and political commentary, with chapters entitled 'Observations on taxing the colonies' and 'State of the Negros in the West Indies, Danger from them'.

56. Edmund Burke and William Burke, *An Account of the European Settlements in America*, London: R. & J. Dodesly, 1757, vol. II, Chapter VII.

57. Burke and Burke, 1757, op. cit., vol. II, p. 107.

58. Ibid., p. 108.

59. Ibid.

60. William Gilpin, *Observations on the River Wye and several parts of South Wales, &c: Relative Chiefly to Picturesque Beauty: Made in the Summer of the Year 1770*, London: T. Cadell and W. Davies, 1800, (fifth edition, originally published in 1782), p. v.

61. Gilpin was a friend of Thomas Whateley and the pioneering British landscape artist Alexander Cozens (drawing master at Eton and private tutor to Jamaican absentee William Beckford); the title of Gilpin's work clearly resembles Whateley's earlier book *Observations on Modern Gardening* (1772).

62. Gilpin, 1800, op. cit., pp. v–vi.

63. Ibid., p. 1. Italics in the original.

64. Ibid., pp. 1–2.

65. Gilpin, 1800, op. cit., pp. 19–22, 36.

66. Ibid., p. 58.

67. Ibid., pp. 58–9.

68. The fashion for picturesque touring in the West was satirised by William

Combe in his poem *The tour of Doctor Syntax in search of the picturesque*, London, 1812.

69. Andrews, 1989, op. cit., p. 89.
70. Cockermouth-born William Wordsworth, too, had intimate family connections with the Atlantic trade through his father and his brother, while prominent 'picturesque' theorist Richard Payne-Knight came from a Shropshire family with trading interests in Bristol and in St Kitts in the Caribbean.

6. CULTIVATING THE REMOTE

1. For more on the family background and inheritance, see UCL's 'Legacies of British Slave-ownership' database, https://www.ucl.ac.uk/lbs/person/view/22227 [accessed July 2021]. On the abolition of slavery, Dawkins-Pennant was awarded £14,683, 17s, 2d (about £1.3 million in 2020) for freeing 764 enslaved people from four Jamaican plantations.
2. See, for example, David Solkin's biography of the North Wales–born painter, *Richard Wilson: The Landscape of Reaction*, London: Tate Gallery, 1982; and also Michael Freeman's website Early Tourists in Wales: 18th and 19th tourists' comments about Wales, https://sublimewales.wordpress.com [accessed April 2021].
3. Viscount Torrington, *A tour to North Wales*, 1793, in John Byng, *The Torrington Diaries, containing the tours through England and Wales of the Hon. John Byng between the years 1781 and 1794*, (ed. by C. Bruyn Andrews), London: Eyre & Spottiswoode, 1936, vol. 3, p. 250.
4. 'A Gentleman in Wales 1767', quoted in Solkin, 1982, op. cit., p. 265. See also Freeman, *Early Tourists in Wales*, op. cit.
5. From Wynnstay, they went west to Bala, then turned north to Caernarvon, crossed to Anglesey, and returned via Conway and Holywell. See also Richard Moore-Colyer, *Roads and Trackways of Wales*, Ashbourne: Landmark Publishing, 2001, p. 139.
6. See Alexander McCreery, *Turnpike Roads and the Spatial Culture of London, 1756–1830*, PhD thesis, University College London, 2004, especially Chapter 4.3, 'Turnpikes and the Development of Picturesque Aesthetics', pp. 200–16.
7. See B. Buchanan, 'The Evolution of the English Turnpike Trusts', *Economic History Review*, vol. 39, no. 2, 1986, pp. 223–43.
8. Hancock, 1995, op. cit., Chapter Nine, 'The urge to improve', pp. 279–319.
9. See Eric Pawson, *Transport and Economy: The Turnpike Roads of Eighteenth Century Britain*, London, New York and San Francisco: Academic Press,

1977, especially Chapter Six, 'The Spatial Diffusion of the Turnpike System'.

10. Valentine Morris promoted the first Turnpike Bill in Monmouthshire in 1754 and was trustee for the construction of several turnpike roads in the area, directing the construction of new routes and a toll house. See Ivor Waters, *Turnpike Roads: The Chepstow and New Passage Turnpike Districts*, Chepstow: Moss Rose Press, 1985.

11. Daniel Defoe, *A Tour thro' the Whole Island of Great Britain*, London: S. Birt and T. Osborne, 1748, vol. III, p. 236.

12. Jean Lindsay, 'The Pennants and Jamaica 1665–1808: The Growth and Organisation of the Pennant Estates', *Transactions of the Caernarvonshire Historical Society*, no. 43, 1982.

13. John's grandfather, Richard's great-grandfather, was Gifford Pennant, who migrated to Jamaica, having been garrisoned there immediately after the island's capture from the Spanish in 1655.

14. Peter Oliver, *Journey of a Voyage to England*, British Library, Egerton Manuscripts, 2,673, vol. I f. 18, Summer 1777.

15. See Pat Starkey (ed.), *Riches into Art: Liverpool Collectors, 1770–1880*, Liverpool: Liverpool University Press, 1993.

16. Witham was eventually bought by Alderman William Beckford, who erected a house designed by Robert Adam. See Robert Wilson-North and Stephen Porter, 'Witham, Somerset: From Carthusian Monastery to Country House to Gothic Folly', *Architectural History*, vol. 40, 1997, p. 93.

17. Richard's wife was the daughter of General Hugh Warburton. Her grandfather Sir George Warburton had been an MP for Cheshire until 1722.

18. See the *Letters of Lewis, Richard, William and John Morris of Anglesey, 1728–65* (ed. John H Davies), Aberystwyth, 1907 for descriptions of the development of North Wales. For Liverpool merchant connections to the trans-Atlantic trade, see 'Read the Signs–Street Names in Liverpool Connected to the Trade in Enslaved Africans', Historic England, available at https://historicengland.org.uk/research/inclusive-heritage/the-slave-trade-and-abolition/read-the-signs/ [accessed 21 December 2021].

19. Samuel Lewis, *A Topographical History of Wales*, Denbighshire: *s.n.*, 1849. Irish landowner Thomas Fitzmaurice built a classical style, crescent-shaped bleachery at Lleweni with a pavilion at either end.

20. See Thomas Pennant, *A Tour in Wales*, London: Benjamin White, 1784, vol. 1, p. 1.

21. See also Chris Evans, 'Welsh Copper: What, When and Where?' in

Louise Miskell (ed.), *New Perspectives in Welsh Industrial History*, Cardiff: University of Wales Press, 2020, pp. 25–47.

22. *1801 agreement with Samuel Worthington, Michael Humble and Samuel Holland of Liverpool to supply slates from Penrhyn Quarry*, Penrhyn MSS, 2034.

23. Solkin, 1982, op. cit., p. 225.

24. See Chris Evans, 'From Sheep to Sugar: Welsh Wool and Slavery', an NLHF supported project exploring the production and the trade routes for the fabric Welsh Plains, available at http://www.welshplains.cymru [accessed December 2021].

25. Andrews, 1989, op. cit., p. 131.

26. Ibid.

27. John Fischer (ed.), *Tours in Wales by John Fenton, 1804–1813*, 23 July 1810, London: *s.n.*, 1917, p. 201.

28. Coach access would have been particularly advantageous to women tourists: riding side-saddle, as required by the social mores of 'polite' eighteenth-century society, would have been uncomfortable on a long journey.

29. Pennant, 1784, op. cit., vol. II, p. 153. (Thomas Pennant, heir to an estate near Holywell, was a distant cousin of Richard Pennant).

30. See 'Capel Curig Inn', Early Tourists in Wales: 18th and 19th century tourists' comments about Wales, https://sublimewales.wordpress.com/practicalities/accommodation/inns/capel-curig-inn/capel-curig-inn/ [accessed October 2021].

31. Fischer (ed.), 1917, op. cit., p. 209.

32. In 2021, the estates around Penrhyn Castle formed part of the Slate Landscape of Northwest Wales, which was awarded World Heritage Site status by UNESCO.

33. Defoe, 1748, op. cit., p. 255.

34. See J. V. Beckett, *Coal and Tobacco: The Lowthers and the Economic Development of West Cumberland, 1660–1760*, Cambridge: Cambridge University Press, 1981 for the background to Whitehaven's growth from coal port to a provincial Atlantic trading centre.

35. Rev. John Dalton, December, 1754, in Andrews, 1989, op. cit., p. 176.

36. See Andrews, 1989, op. cit., p. 177 and John Brown, *A Description of the Lake at Keswick (And the adjacent Country) In Cumberland Communicated in a Letter to a Friend, by a late popular Writer*, Kendal: J. Hodgson, 1771.

37. The sugar works was disposed of in 1751. See local historian Nev. Ramsden, 'Whitehaven Merchant Families', Rum Butter, http://rum-butter.info/gen/cumb/families/merchant-families-of-whitehaven. Shortly after, William Gilpin did his MA at Oxford and started teaching in Cheam, Surrey. His final position as Rector of Boldre, in

Hampshire, may well have been acquired through family trading net-works, as the owners of the Boldre estate, the Morants, were also Jamaican plantation owners. His younger brother Sir Joseph Dacre Appleby Gilpin (1745–1834) is also recorded as owning 200 acres at Queen's Bay, Tobago. See UCL 'Legacies of British Slave-ownership' project, https://www.ucl.ac.uk/lbs/person/view/2146632829 [accessed October 2021].

38. See Paul Hindle, *Roads and Tracks of the Lake District*, Milnthorpe: Cicerone Press, 1998.

39. Commons Journal, xxiii, 433, quoted in Beckett, 1981, op. cit., p. 172. For Lowther's Barbadian links see, J. V. Beckett,1987, op. cit., pp. 171–8.

40. Beckett, 1987, op. cit., pp. 173–7.

41. See Hindle, 1998, op. cit., for a thorough account of road-building around the Lake District.

42. Arthur Young, *A Six Months Tour through the North of England*, London: W. Strahan, 1770, p. 155. His remarks on the manufacture of fabrics 'chiefly from West Indian cotton' in Manchester and the importance of fabric exports in 'low priced goods' to North America and 'fine ones to the West Indies' are also of interest, p. 244.

43. Ibid, p. 155.

44. Ibid.

45. Thomas West, *Guide to the Lakes in Cumberland, Westmorland, and Lancashire*, London: W. Pennington, 1812, (tenth edition).

46. Ibid., pp. 26–7.

47. William Thomas Beckford, 1779, cited in Boyd Alexander, *England's Wealthiest Son*, London: Centaur, 1962, p. 72.

48. Ibid.

49. Elder, 1992, op. cit.

50. Defoe, *A Tour thro' the Whole Island of Great Britain*.

51. West, 1812, op. cit., p. 23.

52. Thomas Pennant, *A Tour in Scotland*, cited in Melinda Elder, 1992, op. cit., p. 122.

53. See Elder, 1992, op. cit.

54. See ibid. again for details of the economic importance of the slaving industry to the whole area.

55. See the entry for 'Guinea kettles' in *The Oxford Companion to Black British History*, Oxford and New York: Oxford University Press, 2007. The West India and Africa trade declined sharply towards the end of the eigh-teenth century, in part because of new laws governing slave-trading. Many merchants, however, continued their trade from Liverpool.

56. Few eighteenth-century tourists visited the western valleys of Wasdale

and Ennerdale as there was no road access until the mid-nineteenth century. See Ian Gregory and Sally Bushell, 'Analysing 18-Century Tourism in the English Lake District', *Spatial Humanities: Texts, GIS and Places*, Research Project 2012–16, University of Lancaster. Available at https://www.lancaster.ac.uk/fass/projects/spatialhum.wordpress [accessed August 2021]. And Ian Whyte, *Transforming Fell and Valley: Landscape and Parliamentary Enclosure in North West England*, Lancaster: Centre for North-West Regional Studies, 2003.

57. West, 1812, op. cit., p. 2.

58. See, for example, Melinda Elder, *A Georgian Merchant's House in Lancaster: John Rawlinson, A West-Indies Trader and Gillow Client*, 2020, https://lahs.archaeologyuk.org/Contrebis/elderrawlinson.pdf [accessed May 2021].

59. See Andrews, 1989, op. cit., pp. 157–60.

60. For more details about the Rawlinson family, see their profile pages on UCL's Centre for the Study of the Legacies of British Slavery database, available at https://www.ucl.ac.uk/lbs/person/view/2146648567 [accessed May 2021].

61. Beckett, 1987, op. cit., p. 174.

62. Duke University, Special Collections, Papers of William Wilberforce, William Smith etc. William Wilberforce Letters 1796–99, Box 1, Folder 5.

63. See 'Clarkson Memorial', Friends of the Ullswater Way, available at https://www.ullswaterheritage.org/heritage-trail/clarkson-memorial [accessed September 2021].

64. See Michael Wiley, *Romantic Geography: Wordsworth and Anglo-European Space*, Basingstoke: Palgrave, 1998, pp. 99–101.

65. Colquhoun was a partner of tobacco merchant Alexander Spiers and founded the Tontine Coffee House, home to Glasgow's West India Club. See https://glasgowmuseumsslavery.co.uk/about [accessed July 2021].

66. See G. Carruthers, 'Burns and Slavery', in J. Rodger and G. Carruthers (eds), *Fickle Man: Robert Burns in the 21st Century*, Muir of Ord, Scotland: Sandstone Press, 2009. See also 'Robert Burns, Slavery and Abolition: Contextualising the Abandoned Jamaica Sojourn in 1786', Editing Robert Burns for the 21st Century, https://burnsc21.glasgow.ac.uk/robert-burns-slavery-and-abolition-contextualising-the-abandoned-jamaica-sojourn-in-1786 [accessed August 2001].

67. See https://ceilidhclub.com/on-a-scotch-bard-gone-to-the-west-indies [accessed August 2021]

68. The Ceded Isles comprised Grenada, the Grenadines, Dominica, St Vincent and Tobago.

69. See Hamilton, 2005, op. cit.

70. See Tom M. Devine (ed.), *Recovering Scotland's Slavery Past*: *The Caribbean*

Connection, Edinburgh: Edinburgh University Press, 2015 and also the National Library of Scotland's wide list of articles, books and theses on the Scots and the West Indies, https://digital.nls.uk/travels-of-henrietta-liston/pdfs/scots-and-west-indies-resources.pdf [accessed August 2021].

71. Devine, 2015, op. cit.

72. Hamilton, 2005, op. cit., p. 39. See also Iain MacKinnon and Andrew Mackillop, 'Plantation slavery and landownership in the west Highlands and Islands: legacies and lessons', *Economic History Society*, 18 May 2020, https://ehs.org.uk/plantation-slavery-and-landownership-in-the-west-highlands-and-islands-legacies-and-lessons/ [accessed January 2022].

73. Tom M. Devine and Gordon Jackson (eds), *Glasgow Vol 1: Beginnings to 1830*, Manchester: Manchester University Press, 1995.

74. See Devine and Jackson, 1995, op. cit.

75. Devine, 2015, op. cit.

76. See Douglas Hamilton, *Patronage and Profit: Scottish Networks in the West Indies*, unpublished PhD thesis, University of Aberdeen, 2001, p. 39.

77. See Hancock, 1995, op. cit.

78. Hancock, 1995, op. cit., p. 64 and footnote 54.

79. David Hancock, 'Oswald, Richard', *Oxford Dictionary of National Biography*, Oxford and New York: Oxford University Press, (online edition), available at https://www.oxforddnb.com/view/10.1093/ref:odnb/9780198614128.001.0001/odnb-9780198614128-e-20924 [accessed August 2021].

80. Hancock, 1995, op. cit., pp. 332–47.

81. See Eric J. Graham and Tom Barclay, 'The early transatlantic trade of Ayr, 1640–1730', *Ayrshire Archaeological and Natural History Society*, 2005; and Eric J. Graham, 'Burns & the Sugar Plantocracy of Ayrshire', *Ayrshire Monographs*, vol. 36, Ayrshire Archaeological and Natural History Society, 2009.

82. Hancock, 1995, op. cit., p. 321, note 4. Attributed to Isaac Ware, the principal elevations, are, however, very similar to Adam's drawings for Auchincruive.

83. For more background, see Anthony Cooke, 'An Elite Revisited: Glasgow West India Merchants, 1783–1877', *Journal of Scottish Historical Studies*, vol. 32, no. 2, November 2012, pp. 127–65 and Stuart Nisbet, 'Early Glasgow Sugar Plantations in the Caribbean', *Scottish Archaeological Journal*, vol. 31, no. 1–2, October 2009, pp. 115–36.

84. Tom M. Devine, 'Glasgow Colonial Merchants and Land, 1770–1815', 'Glasgow Colonial Merchants and Land, 1770–1815', in J. T. Ward and R. G. Wilson (eds.), *Land and Industry: The Landed Estate and the Industrial Revolution*, Newton Abbot: David & Charles, 1971.

85. George Taylor and Andrew Skinner, *The Traveller's Pocket Book or Abstract of Taylor and Skinners Survey of the Roads of Scotland*, 1775, p. 6.

86. Hancock, 1995, op. cit., p. 300.

87. See Neil Davidson, *The Origins of Scottish Nationhood*, London: Pluto Press, 2000, p. 108. Oswald became the lead negotiator in 1782, on the British side, of the Treaty of Paris to end the American War of Independence and died in 1784 at Auchincruive.

88. The source of all Loudoun's funds is unclear. Earlier in the century, his father's correspondence reveals the struggles to make their Ayrshire estate profitable. See Burn, W. L. 'The Ayrshire Lands of the Campbells of Loudoun during the Eighteenth Century', *Agricultural History*, vol. 10, no. 2, 1936, pp. 84–90. Also notably involved in the turnpike trusts was the Ayrshire-born civil engineer John Loudon McAdam, later inventor of the revolutionary 'Tarmacadam' road-building method.

89. Christopher Dingwall makes the case for the importance of 'sublime gardening' at country seats in Scotland from the mid-eighteenth century. See Christopher Dingwall, 'Gardens in the wild', *Garden History: Journal of the Garden History Society*, vol. 22, no. 2, 1994, pp. 133–56.

90. See Public Record Office, Kew (CO 23, *Original Correspondence relating to the Bahamas* 24, 271); and also Anon., *The Pineapple Industry of the Bahamas: A booklet of the archives exhibition held at the Art Gallery, Jumbey Village*, Bahamas Public Record Office, 1977, as well as Beauman, 2005, op. cit.; and Andrew Jackson O'Shaughnessy, *An Empire Divided: The American Revolution and the British Caribbean*, Philadelphia, PA: University of Pennsylvania Press, 2000.

91. Andrews, 1989, op. cit., pp. 215–17.

92. By the 1770s, as well as from the American mainland, cotton was imported to Glasgow from Scottish-owned plantations in Grenada, Tobago and St Croix, Carricou, Mustique and Demerara. See Hamilton, 2005, op. cit., pp. 202–4. Founded by industrialist David Dale, in partnership with spinning frame inventor Richard Arkwright, New Lanark is now a UNESCO World Heritage Site. Notwithstanding the mills' reliance on slave-produced cotton, in 1791,Dale became chair of the newly established Glasgow Society for the Abolition of the Slave Trade.

93. Tom M. Devine, *Scotland's Empire, 1600–1815*, London: Allen Lane, 2003, pp. 325–40.

94. Andrews, 1989, op. cit.

95. Thomas Pennant, *A Tour in Scotland*, London: Benjamin White, 1772, p. 90. Pennant is a traditional north Welsh surname and Thomas hailed from Downing Hall at Whitford in Flintshire, near the River Dee estuary, forty miles east of his contemporary Richard Pennant at Penrhyn Castle.

96. Ibid., p. 42.

97. Ibid., p. 48.

98. Pennant, 1772, op. cit.

99. The bridge, designed by William Mylne (who was also constructing a crossing over the Clyde in Glasgow), collapsed still unfinished in 1769, and was only completed in 1772. It was then rebuilt again in the 1890s to a new design.

100. Pennant, 1772, op. cit., p. 5.

101. See discussion in Kazumi Kanatsu, *Picturesque Tours in Scotland: Forming an Idea of the British Nation*, PhD thesis, University of York, September 2000, available at https://etheses.whiterose.ac.uk/14179/1/341825.pdf [accessed March 2021].

102. William Gilpin, *Observations, Relative Chiefly to Picturesque Beauty, Made in the Year 1776, on Several Parts of Great Britain; Particularly the High-lands of Scotland*, London: R. Blamire, 1792, (second edition, originally published in 1789), vol. II, p. 122. Italics in the original.

103. Johnson's *A Journey to the Western Islands of Scotland* was published in 1775 and Boswell's *A Journal of a Tour to the Hebrides* a decade later in 1785.

104. Samuel Johnson, *A Journey to the Western Islands of Scotland*, London: T. Cadell and W. Davies, 1816, (new edition, originally published in 1775), p. 37.

105. The majority of forfeited estates had been auctioned off in the 1750s, but thirteen continued to belong to the British Crown under the charge of the Commissioners for the Annexed Estates, who had 'improved' them—before returning them, minus the costs of improvement, from the 1780s onwards.

106. See Daniel Maudlin, *The Highland House Transformed*: *Architecture and Identity on the Edge of Britain, 1700–1850*, Dundee: Dundee University Press, 2009.

107. Pennant, 1772, op. cit., p. 81. Italics in the original.

108. Johnson, 1816, op. cit., p. 57.

109. For more discussion on inns, see Daniel Maudlin and Bernard. Herman (eds), *Building the British Atlantic World: Spaces, Places, and Material Culture, 1600–1850*, Chapel Hill, NC: University of North Carolina Press, 2016.

110. Johnson, 1816, op. cit., pp. 67–8.

111. Boswell's father was a noted Edinburgh lawyer. Further research is needed, though, to clarify if he was involved in the contractual organisation of Scots investment in the Ceded Isles during this period.

112. Johnson, 1816, op. cit., p. 31. Italics in the original.

113. See Parliamentary Archives: Highland Roads and Bridges Commission,

1803–1862 and the Caledonian Canal Commission, 1803–1822 and A. R. B. Haldane, *New Ways through the Glens*, London: Thomas Nelson & Sons, 1962.

114. David Alston notes the importance of Highland investors in the later, mainland Caribbean colonies of Demerara, Essequibo and Berbice, former Dutch possessions until 1796. See David Alston, '"The habits of these creatures in clinging one to the other": Enslaved Africans, Scots and the Plantations of Guyana', in Devine (ed.), 2015, op. cit., pp. 99–123.

115. See MacKinnon and Mackillop, 2020, op. cit. Available online at https://www.communitylandscotland.org.uk/plantation-slavery-and-landownership-in-the-west-highlands-and-islands-legacies-and-lessons/ [accessed August 2021]. I am greatly indebted here to their summary, drawing on records from UCL's 'Legacies of British Slave-ownership' project, Tom M. Devine's research into property ownership and land sales from 1800–60 and other work, including Eric Richards, *The Highland Clearances*, Edinburgh: Birlinn, 2013.

116. MacKinnon and Mackillop, 2020, op. cit., p. 16.

117. MacKinnon and Mackillop, 2020, op. cit., Annex of Sources, p. 6. I have based the following calculations on land deals by the cited dates, which are listed in the paper's Annex. By the end of the nineteenth century, the authors estimate that around one third of the total land had been bought by families with slavery-connected wealth and put the total investments at just over £120 million, or £1 billion in today's terms, based on economic historians' accepted calculation methods.

118. See MacKinnon and Mackillop, 2020, op. cit., p. 3.

119. Adam Smith, 1776, op. cit., vol. II, pp. 265–9.

7. TAINTED LANDSCAPES

1. Anon., *Jamaica: A Poem, in Three Parts. Written in that island, in the year MDCCLXXVI*, London: William Nichol, 1777.

2. Ibid.

3. Schaw, (ed. by Andrews), 1921, op. cit., p. 74. Schaw's manuscript journal describing her trans-Atlantic voyage with her brother on the *Jamaica Packet* from the Firth of Forth was donated to the British Museum in the nineteenth century. The edited version was published in 1921. However, the editors do not say why Schaw chose to travel to the Caribbean. But the impression she gives was that she travelled simply to see what the colonies were like for herself. She was, in effect, a tourist.

4. The image is one of a series of four anonymous 'scenes' of Jamaican

harbours, published in London by Spilsbury between 1769 and 1770, British Library, Maps, K Top. 123.53.2.

5. British Library, Additional Manuscripts, Long family papers 27, 968.

6. Paul Carter, *The Road to Botany Bay: An Essay in Spatial History*, London and Boston, MA: Faber and Faber, 1987, p. 255.

7. Sara Suleri, *The Rhetoric of English India*, Chicago, IL: University of Chicago Press, 1992. See also Barbara Maria Stafford, *Voyage into Substance: Art, Science, Nature and the Illustrated Travel Account, 1760–1840*, Cambridge, MA: MIT Press, 1984.

8. Sue Rainey, *Creating Picturesque America: Monument to the Natural and Cultural Landscape*, Nashville, TN: Vanderbilt University Press, 1994.

9. My thanks to the National Trust for licensing the images for this book. They have been attributed at Penrhyn to the painter John Cleveley (1747–86), but this is an innocent mistake. John and his twin brother Robert received some training in watercolours under Paul Sandby (of The Royal Military Academy Woolwich) and John travelled with Joseph Banks to the Hebrides and Orkney. He was also subsequently employed to produce engravings from sketches made on Cook's second voyage to the South Seas (1772–5). Neither, however, went on the expedition and, while Robert sailed to the Caribbean on board the naval vessel *Asia* (c. 1776–7), there are no records of John travelling there. His work focussed on marine imagery, rather than landscape, and it was George Robertson who accompanied William Beckford to Jamaica. The three paintings which are identifiable as by George Robertson are: *A View in the Island of Jamaica of the Bridge Across Cabaritta River in the Estate of William Beckford Esq*; *A View in the Island of Jamaica, of Fort William Estate, With Part of the Roaring River Belonging to William Beckford Esq, Near Savannah la Mar;* and *A View in the Island of Jamaica of the Bridge Across Rio Cobre near Spanish Town*, engraved by Daniel Lerpinière, British Library, Topographic Works, West Indies seventeenth and eighteenth Century, Maps CXX111, 54 a-e. See also https://www.britishmuseum.org/collection/object/P_1853-0112-105 [accessed November 2021].

10. William Beckford, *A Description of the Island of Jamaica*, London, 1790, p. 44.

11. Information from *The Dictionary of National Biography:* William Beckford of Somerley.

12. See Tim Barringer, 'Picturesque prospects and the labour of the enslaved', in Tim Barringer, Gillian Forrester and Barbaro Martinez-Ruiz (eds), *Art and Emancipation in Jamaica: Isaac Belisario and His Worlds*, New Haven, CT and London: Yale University Press, 2007. See also Geoff Quilley, 'Pastoral plantations: the slave trade and the representation of British colonial landscape in the late eighteenth century', in Geoff

Quilley and Kay Dian Kriz (eds), *An Economy of Colour: Visual Culture and the Atlantic World*, Manchester: Manchester University Press, 2003, pp. 106–28. Also see the John Carter Brown Collection at Brown University, Providence, Rhode Island.

13. Quilley and Kriz (eds), 2003, op. cit., p. 107.

14. *Philosophical Transactions of the Royal Society*, 1660, vol. 1, cited in Bernard Smith, *European Vision and the South Pacific*, New Haven, CT and London: Yale University Press, 1985, p. 8.

15. See, for example, Aymonino, op. cit., in Thorn (ed.), op. cit., 2019, pp. 104–23; Sarah Thomas, *Witnessing Slavery: Art and Travel in the Age of Abolition*, New Haven, CT and London: Yale University Press, 2019, pp. 66–7; and also Amanda Bagneris, *Colouring the Caribbean: Race and the Art of Agostino Brunius*, Manchester: Manchester University Press, 2018.

16. Albert Moritz argues that the first picturesque images of Britain's Atlantic colonies were the *Great Cohoes Falls* (in New York State), produced in 1761 from paintings made by the British topological artist Paul Sandby. However, Sandby—who was to accompany Joseph Banks on a tour of South Wales and illustrate Sir Watkin Williams-Wynn's celebrated own tour of North Wales—had not actually travelled to America himself. The paintings were instead based on sketches made by Thomas Pownell, a former Governor of the Massachusetts Bay Colony, just prior to his return to England in 1759. See Albert Moritz, *America: The Picturesque in Nineteenth Century Engraving*, New York: New Trend, 1983.

17. Indeed, such was their value that the French were willing to hand over their territory in Canada to recover the islands of Guadeloupe and Martinique, which were also taken by the British in 1761.

18. James Grainger to Thomas Percy, 29 February 1766, quoted in Gilmore, 2000, op. cit., p. 20. Italics in the original.

19. William had been sent to school in England and in 1746, five years after his father's death, inherited two plantations on the island. In 1748, aged twenty-three, he mortgaged both, Body Pond and Road Estate, for just over £3,500 and by 1760, he had raised £7,000 against his Caribbean estates. Rhodes House, Young Manuscripts, MS W. Ind. t.1, vol. 1, fol. 4.

20. Hamilton, 2005, op. cit., pp. 93–5 and PRO: CO 106/9(246–253): *Account Sales of plantation allotments in the islands of Tobago, Dominica and St Vincent, March to May 1767.*

21. W. Young: 'Considerations which may tend to promote the Settlement of our new West-India Colonies, by Encouraging individuals to embark in the undertaking', *The Scotsman*, 26 May 1764, p. 283; 27 April 1765, p. 216; and 28 August 1766, p. 443.

22. Richard Grove, *Green Imperialism: Colonial Expansion, Tropical Island Edens and the Origins of Environmentalism, 1600–1860*, Cambridge: Cambridge University Press, 1995, pp. 133–5.

23. William Young in *The Scotsman*. The Commission, however, was not entirely successful, as many colonists took a hostile view of primeval woodland, viewing it superstitiously as a promoter of disease and 'insanitary winds', and he was forced to modify his instructions to allow more agricultural land.

24. Clement Caines, 1801, op. cit., p. 252.

25. For background see Mark Hauser, 'The Infrastructure of Nature's Island: Settlements, Networks and Economy in Colonial Domenica', *International Journal of Historical Archaeology*, vol. 19, no, 3, 2015, pp. 601–22; and Olaf Janzen, *War and Trade in Eighteenth-Century Newfoundland*, Liverpool: Liverpool University Press, 2013.

26. See Hamilton, 2005, op. cit., pp. 93–5 and PRO: CO 106/9 (246–253): *Account Sales of plantation allotments in the islands of Tobago, Dominica and St Vincent, March to May 1767.*

27. *Report of Committees of Legislature appointed by both Houses in Nov 1796* (compensation claimants after the French invasion and slave insurrection), Rhodes House Young Manuscripts, MS W., Ind. t.1, vol. 5.

28. Rhodes House, University of Oxford, Young Manuscripts vol. 4, Tobago, William Young, 1798 Appeal to King and Council, ff. 26–27.

29. Young returned after taking part in the First Carib War (1769–73), an insurrection by the native populace against British colonial land demands on the island of St Vincent, to which he went in 1772.

30. See discussion in David Mackay, *In the Wake of Cook: Exploration, Science and Empire, 1780–1801*, London: Croom Helm, 1985, p. 29. It was during one such mission to Tahiti two decades later, for example—with the aim of collecting and transporting breadfruit to the West Indies as food for enslaved workers—that an infamous mutiny on the HMS *Bounty* took place. In 1789, as the ship travelled back to Britain from Polynesia, a number of disaffected crewmen seized control of the vessel from its captain and set him and eighteen other loyalist sailors adrift. See Julia Bruce, 'Banks and Breadfruit', *RSA Journal*, vol. 141, no. 5444, November 1993, pp. 817–20. It was not until 1793 that breadfruit plants were successfully transferred to the botanic gardens in St Vincent, the Bath settlement in the central highlands of Jamaica, and thence onwards to the Royal Botanic Gardens at Kew.

31. Banks's trip to the Wye Valley came just after he had returned from a voyage to Newfoundland. This was Banks's first voyage, on the frigate HMS *Niger* in 1766, when he joined the Royal Society, aged just twenty-three.

32. Joseph Banks, 'Journal of an Excursion to Eastbury and Bristol etc May, June 1767', in *Proceedings of the Bristol Naturalists Society*, vol. IX, 1899, New Series, pp. 8–25. Also see manuscript facsimile: Sarah Banks, *Copy of Journal of an Excursion to Eastbury Bristol, etc. in May and June 1767*, https://nla.gov.au/nla.obj-223003140/view [accessed November 2021]

33. Joseph Banks, 1767, op. cit., p. 25.

34. Sarah Banks, op. cit.

35. For background, see Hauser, 2015, op. cit.; Janzen, 2013, op. cit.; and 'Sir Hugh Pallisser', *Dictionary of Canadian Biography*, available online at http://www.biographi.ca/en/bio/palliser_hugh_4E.html [accessed July 2021].

36. Banks, PRO, C.O, 101/17, 30 April 1773, cited in Waters, 1964, op. cit., p. 34.

37. See Joseph Banks, *Journal of the Right Hon. Sir Joseph Banks*, (ed. by Joseph Dalton Hooker), 1896, for an account of the whole expedition and Bernard Smith, 'European Vision and the South Pacific', *Journal of the Warburg and Courtauld Institutes*, vol. 13, no. 1/2, 1950, pp. 65–100, for examples of engravings of Parkinson's and others' sketches and a discussion of the role of art in documenting Cook's voyages.

38. *The Kongouro from New Holland* by George Stubbs, 1772 is thought to be based on Parkinson's sketches, too. The name was first applied to the continent by the Dutch explorer Abel Tasman in 1644, but they never settled. The south-eastern part was renamed New South Wales by Captain Cook.

39. For an examination of the picturesque approach to making sense of the experience of touring by imaginatively, in his words, 'reorganizing a shapeless, infinitely expansive, landscape into a sequence of frameable views', see Malcolm Andrews, 'A Picturesque Template: The Tourists and their Guidebooks', in Dana Arnold (ed.), *The Picturesque in Late Georgian England: Papers Given at the Georgian Group Symposium*, London: Georgian Group, 1995.

40. In 1772, the artist William Hodges was also sent on Cook's second voyage with HMS *Resolution* to the Pacific, under the patronage of the British Admiralty. After returning in 1775, he produced grand oil paintings of the Pacific colonies and of key sublime and picturesque landscape sights, including *A View of the Cape of Good Hope, Taken on the Spot from on Board the Resolution, Capt Cook*; *A View of the Monuments of Easter Island;* and *A View of Cape Stephens in Cook's Straits with waterspout*. The picturesque tour had, evidently, become a state-sanctioned means of 'cultivating the remote'.

41. For a discussion of how the eighteenth-century fashion for landscape

tourism both highlighted and glossed over wealth differences in Britain see, for example, Anne Janowitz, 'The Chartist Picturesque', in Stephen Copley and Peter Garside (eds), *The Politics of the Picturesque*, Cambridge: Cambridge University Press, 1994, p. 62; and John Wale, 'Romantics, Explorers and Picturesque Travellers', in the same publication, p. 177.

42. Anon., *Jamaica: A Poem, in Three Parts. Written in that island, in the year MDCCLXXVI*, London: William Nichol, 1777.

43. Victoria Finlay, *Colour*, London: Sceptre, 2002, p. 19.

44. In the late eighteenth century, prints—such as those like Thomas Gainsborough's landscape paintings depicting the English rural poor—were often manipulated to appeal to a wider market. See John Barrell, *The Dark Side of the Landscape: The Rural Poor in English Painting, 1730–1840*, Cambridge: Cambridge University Press, 1980.

45. See David Morris, *Thomas Hearne and his Landscapes*, London: Reaktion, 1989, particularly Chapter 2, 'A colonial Commission: Antigua and the Leeward Isles', pp. 9–22.

46. See https://www.ucl.ac.uk/lbs/person/view/284 for details of the compensation later paid to the Tudways for their Antiguan estates.

47. See also the discussion in Seymour, Daniels and Watkins, 1998, op. cit., pp. 316–17.

48. See O'Shaughnessy, 2000, op. cit.

49. Some intrepid travellers, such as Richard Payne Knight and William Beckford of Fonthill (both from families with interests in the Americas), took the northern Alpine route to Italy. Their trips followed the route of an earlier tourist, the poet Thomas Gray. However, Payne, Knight and Beckford took with them the artist John Robert Cuzons, who produced his extraordinary sublime watercolours of the Alps.

50. See Heath, 1793, op. cit.

51. Gilpin, *Observations…. particularly the High-Lands of Scotland*, 1792, op. cit.

52. William Beckford, *A Descriptive Account of The Island of Jamaica, With Remarks upon the Cultivation of the Sugar-Cane throughout the different Seasons of the Year, and chiefly considered in a Picturesque Point of View*, London: T. & J. Egerton, 1790, p. 42.

53. Ibid., p. 7.

54. Ibid.

55. Ibid., p. 11.

56. Ibid., p. 22.

57. The copy of Beckford's *Description* held in the British Library is from Banks's collection. In the early 1790s, Parliament was in the midst of debating a bill to abolish the slave trade and absentee proprietors had

perhaps more pressing concerns than the aesthetics of picturesque landscapes.

58. British Library, Maps K. Top CXXIII 55 a-f (they have been misattributed to the French artist Louis Belanger).

59. Maria Nugent, *Lady Nugent's Journal of Her Residence in Jamaica from 1801 to 1805*, (ed. by Philip Wright), Mona, Jamaica: University of the West Indies Press, 2002, journal entry from 24 February 1802, p. 60.

60. Beckford, 1790, op. cit., p. 60.

61. McKinnen, 1804, op. cit., p. 108

62. In 1820, artist James Hakewill also embarked on a painting tour of the Caribbean where he produced seven folios of aquatints illustrating his *Picturesque tour of the island of Jamaica*.

63. Included in the eleven copper-plate etchings, mostly maps and prospects of harbours, were four 'scenic' images: *View of the Cascade at Roaring River; View of the White-river Cascade*; *A view of the Bath Hot Spring*; and *Cascade at YS River*. Edward Long, *A History of Jamaica: Or, General Survey of the Antient and Modern State of the Island*, London: T. Lowdes, 1774, book II.

64. See Thomas Jefferson, *Notes on the State of Virginia*, (ed. by William Peden), Chapel Hill, NC: University of North Carolina Press, 1955.

65. Ibid., p. 17

66. Ibid.

67. Ibid.

68. See Frank Shuffleton, 'Binding Ties: Thomas Jefferson, Francis Hopkinson and the Representation of the Notes on the State of Virginia', in Mark Kamrath and Sharon Harris (eds), *Periodical Literature in Eighteenth-Century America*, Knoxville, TN: University of Tennessee Press, 2005, pp. 255–72.

69. Ibid.

70. See Richard Gassan, 'The First American Tourist Guidebooks: Authorship and the Print Culture of the 1820s', *Book History*, vol. 8, 2005, pp. 51–74.

71. Ibid., p. 54. South Carolinian planter Isaac Ball and his family were an example. Also see Thomas Chambers, *Drinking the Waters: Creating an American Leisure Class at Nineteenth-Century Mineral Springs*, Washington: Smithsonian Institute Press, 2002.

72. Henry's father, Joshua Gilpin, established cotton and paper mills on the Brandywine River, near Philadelphia. He made several tours of Britain and Europe during the 1790s, visiting scenic sites as well as paper factories. His extensive travel diaries are held in the Pennsylvania archives.

73. Henry Gilpin, *A Northern Tour*, s.l: s.n., 1825, p. 1.

74. Ralph Gray (ed.), 'A tour of Virginia in 1827: Letters of Henry

D. Gilpin to his Father', *The Virginia Magazine of History and Biography*, vol. 76, no. 4, October 1968, pp. 444–71.

75. Ibid., p. 448.

76. One of America's most renowned landscape artists, Lancashire-born Thomas Cole, visited the Caribbean before his arrival in New York in 1825. Thomas Cole, *Saturday Evening Post*, 14 May 1825, cited in Ron Wetterworth, 'Thomas Cole, American Landscape Painter visited Statia in 1819', *Newsletter of the St Eustatius Historical Foundation*, Winter 2009.

77. Henry Gilpin, 1825, op. cit., p. 1.

8. THE MOCK TURTLE'S STORY

1. William Thomas Beckford, cited in Jon Millington, *Beckford's Tower: An Illustrated Guide*, Bath: Bath Preservation Trust, 1994.

2. See Blackburn, 1997, op. cit., pp. 545–7 for a discussion of West Indian investment in the construction of British canals during the eighteenth century.

3. Quoted in Millington, 1994, op. cit., p. 2.

4. See the Bibliography in Millington, 1994, op. cit.

5. See www.bath-preservation-trust.org.uk/BeckfordsTower [accessed November 2021]. The interpretation of the tower has changed dramatically since my first visit in 2005, and Beckford's connection to slavery is now fully acknowledged.

6. For more information, see C. L. R. James's pioneering history of the Haitian Revolution: *The Black Jacobins: Toussaint L'Ouverture and the San Domingo Revolution*, London: Allison and Busby, 1989, (first published in New York in 1938), and many other editions.

7. See Blackburn, 1997, op. cit., p. 543.

8. Anon., *A New Guide to Fonthill Abbey, Wiltshire*, London: s.n., 1822, p. 11.

9. The revolution in St Domingue, previously France's largest sugar colony, coupled with British blockades of Caribbean shipping routes, had stopped the import of cane sugar into Continental Europe, leading Napoleon to encourage research into sugar beet production.

10. Anon., *A New Guide to Fonthill Abbey, Wiltshire*, London: s.n., 1822, preface.

11. Ibid.

12. Ibid., p. iii.

13. Beckford himself was known to have called the project his 'abbatial folly'. See Gwyn Headley, *Follies of London*, London: Headley & Meulenkamp, 2011, p. 2.

14. Richard Cobham (Barbados) to John Wood Nelson (London) *1ˢᵗ & twen-*

tieth Sept 1816, West Yorkshire Records Office, HAR/WI/Bundle 2, Accounts and miscellaneous papers,1790–1848.

15. See Mike Kaye, 'The Development of the Anti-Slavery Movement after 1807', in Stephen Farrell, Melanie Unwin and James Walvin (eds), *The British Slave Trade: Abolition, Parliament and People*, Edinburgh: Edinburgh University Press, 2007, pp. 238–40.

16. Demerara, Essequibo and Berbice were three colonies on the South American mainland originally founded by the Dutch. See also Peter Hinks, John McKivigan, Owen Williams (eds), *Encyclopedia of Antislavery and Abolition*, Santa Barbara, CA: Greenwood Press, 2006, p. 123.

17. British women did not then have the vote; however, married women would be responsible for daily household expenditure.

18. Amelia Alderson Opie, *The Black Man's Lament; Or, How To Make Sugar*, London: Harvey and Darton, 1826. Italics in the original.

19. See Robin Blackburn, 1988, op. cit., and Adam Hochschild, *Bury the Chains: Prophets and Rebels in the Fight to Free an Empire's Slaves*, Boston and New York: Houghton Mifflin, 2005, for an outline of the eighteenth-century British anti-slavery movement.

20. For the Youngs' views see *Report of Committees of Legislature appointed by both Houses in November 1796*, Rhodes House, Young Manuscripts, MS W. Ind. t.1, vol. 5.

21. In the painting, the eldest son, later to become Sir William and second Baronet of North Dean in Buckinghamshire, is on the far right. He was an MP from 1784 to 1807 and Governor of Tobago from 1807 to 15. He inherited four plantations and nearly 900 enslaved Africans from his father.

22. Gretchen Gerzina, *Black England: Life before Emancipation*, London: Allison and Busby, 1995, pp. 33–6.

23. Christine Eickelmann and David Small, *Pero: The Life of a Slave in Eighteenth-Century Bristol*, Bristol: Redcliffe Press, 2004.

24. See Blackburn, 1988, op. cit., pp. 98–100. The case was pursued by reformer Granville Sharp on behalf of James Somerset, an enslaved African bought by former Boston, Massachusetts customs collector Charles Stewart. Mansfield himself had brought up a mixed-race child, Dido Elizabeth Belle, a second cousin of his great-niece Lady Elizabeth Murray, at his grand home at Kenwood, next to Hampstead Heath in north London. The two women are depicted at the estate in a striking 1779 portrait, once attributed to Zoffany, but now to Scottish artist David Martin, which is now at the home of the present Earl of Mansfield at Scone Palace, Perth, Scotland.

25. William Young's son William, the Governor of Tobago, was among the

several members of the West Indian Interest in the British Parliament who argued against slavery's abolition.

26. See Blackburn, 1988, op. cit., pp. 419–68 and Kaye, 2007, op. cit.

27. See Historic England, 'ARCHWAY, FORMERLY TO FARM HILL PARK', https://historicengland.org.uk/listing/the-list/list-entry/1274282 [accessed April 2021]; and also A. P. Baggs, A. R. J. Jurica and W. J. Sheils, 'Stroud: Manors and other estates', in N. M. Herbert and R. B. Pugh (eds), *A History of the County of Gloucester*, London: Bisley and Longtree Hundreds, 1976, vol. 11, pp. 111–19. And British History Online, http://www.british-history.ac.uk/vch/glos/vol11/pp111–119 [accessed 7 May 2021].

28. Elizabeth Moulton-Barrett to Lady Margaret Cocks, 14 September 1834, quoted in R. A. Barrett, *The Barretts of Jamaica*, Winfield, KS: Wedgestone Press, 1999, p. 90.

29. See Colley, 1994, op. cit.

30. See UCL's searchable 'Legacies of British Slave-ownership' database, https://www.ucl.ac.uk/lbs/search/. Her father Edward Barrett Moulton-Barrett received compensation in respect of three Jamaican plantations.

31. F. Clarke to Henry Gicklow and Samuel Hinkson, Barbados, September 1836, West Yorkshire Records Office, HAR/ACC/Box1/37.

32. West Yorkshire Records Office, HAR/ACC/Box1/37:*1836 Accounts*, 'Account for compensation for Negros'.

33. See Kaye, 2007, op. cit. HM Treasury announced on 9 February 2018 that the loan, raised through government bonds, had finally been paid off in 2015.

34. See Blackburn, 1997, op. cit., pp. 522–3, for further discussion.

35. Again, see UCL's 'Legacies of British Slave-ownership' website.

36. Claypole and Robottom, 1990, op. cit., vol. II, 'The Changing Sugar Plantation'.

37. Claypole and Robottom, 1990, op. cit., p. 15.

38. Anon., *Jamaica: A Poem, in Three Parts. Written in that island, in the year MDCCLXXVI*, London: William Nichol, 1777.

39. Dasent, 1870, op. cit., p. 10.

40. Catherine Hall, 'Reconfiguring Race; the stories the slave-owners told,' in Hall, Draper and McCelland, 2014, op. cit., p. 173.

41. Dasent, 1870, op. cit., p. 36.

42. Lewis Carroll, *Alice's Adventures in Wonderland*, London, Bell & Hyman, 1985, (originally published in 1965), p. 107.

43. See Nigel Tattersfield, *The Forgotten Trade: Comprising the Log of the Daniel and Henry of 1700 and Accounts of the Slave Trade from the Minor Ports of*

England, 1698–1725, London: Pimlico, 1991. Carroll's mother, Frances Jane Lutwidge, was Thomas's great-granddaughter.

44. Carroll, 1985, op. cit.
45. Construction began in 1831, but was abandoned following riots and a general collapse in Bristol's economy after the 1831 Jamaican rebellion, and the bridge was not completed until 1864.
46. The extensive records of Bristol's Society of Merchant Venturers are held in Bristol Archives. See Minutes relating to Clifton Suspension Bridge 1755–1896. SMV/10/6/1.
47. See Alan Baxter, *History and Significance of the Great Western Main Line*, report published by Alan Baxter & Associates LLP for Network Rail, 2012, pp. 36–7, available at https://historicengland.org.uk/images-books/publications/history-significance-gwml/ [accessed April 2021] and J. C. Bourne, *The History and Description of the Great Western Railway*, London: David Bogue, 1846.
48. The shift in attitudes to Caribbean buildings constructed during the era of slavery is examined in David Buckley, *The Right to Be Proud: Selected Jamaican Heritage Sites*, Jamaica and London: Lewis Hanson, 2007.
49. See Sally-Anne Huxtable, Corinne Fowler, Christo Kefalas and Emma Slocombe (eds), 'Interim Report on the Connections between Colonialism and Properties now in the Care of the National Trust, Including Links with Historic Slavery', *National Trust*, September 2020, available at https://nt.global.ssl.fastly.net/documents/colionialism-and-historic-slavery-report.pdf and, for the Trust's reaction, see https://www.nationaltrust.org.uk/blogs/directors-blog/responding-to-the-charity-commissions-statement [accessed October 2021]. Scotland possesses its own separate body, the National Trust for Scotland, to similarly manage historic properties left in trust for the nation.
50. In October 2021, a rebel faction had tried (unsuccessfully) to take over the National Trust's governing Council at its annual general meeting, but rebel-backed candidates secured only three of the thirty-six seats. The body's membership rose to a record 5.7 million ahead of the annual gathering.
51. See J. A. H. Evans, 'Nathaniel Wells of Piercefield and St Kitts: From Slave to Sheriff', *The Monmouthshire Antiquary*, 2002, pp. 92–106.
52. See entry for Nathaniel Wells in the 'Legacies of British Slave-ownership' database, https://www.ucl.ac.uk/lbs/person/view/25474 and also https://www.facebook.com/GwentArchives/photos/nathaniel-wells-of-piercefield-monmouthshire-and-the-slaves-of-vambells-stkitts-/785984668213889/ [accessed November 2021].

BIBLIOGRAPHY

Unpublished sources

Manuscripts

Bexley Local Studies Centre, Bexley
Danson Deeds

The British Library, London

Long family papers (Additional Manuscripts, 27, 968).
Pollard family papers (Additional Manuscripts, Hardwicke Papers, vol. CCCV11, 35, 655).
Letters of James Knight, C. Long and planters and merchants of Jamaica 1725–1789 (Additional Manuscripts, 12, 402–12, 421).
Peter Oliver, *Journal of a Voyage to England*, summer 1777 (Egerton Manuscripts, 2,673, vol. I).
Letters from the Boyds of Danson to Sir Robert Murray Keith, British Ambassador in Vienna (Additional Manuscripts, 35, 516).

The Huntingdon Library, Pasadena, California.

Pulteney Papers, Box 8, Bath Spa

The Institute of Commonwealth Studies, University of London

18/19th century maps and watercolour images of Tobago, WIC103

The National Archives, Public Record Office, Kew

Correspondence of William Young, E219/105

The National Library of Wales, Aberystwyth

West Indies Collections: Ottley (West Indies) (Additional papers, GB 0210 OTWINDIES)
H.J. Lloyd-Johnes collection (1976 deposit)

BIBLIOGRAPHY

Monmouthshire Record Office, Newport

Piercefield Estate Archives

Royal Bank of Scotland Archives, London

Boyd family accounts (formerly Drummonds Bank), GM1018, DR/382, DR/284/9/S, DR427 (nos 88–255)

The Society of Genealogists Archives, London

Papers of Morris family of Antigua (Ac. no. 22138)

University of Oxford, Bodleian Library of Commonwealth and African Studies at Rhodes House

Willam Pulteney, *Copy of resolutions on complaint of merchants trading in the West Indies 1738*, B MS DD, Dashwood Bucks D.1/3
Young Family Papers and Correspondence 1768–1835
William Young, 1st Baronet, Governor of Dominica
William Young, 2nd Baronet, Governor of Tobago
West Indies Collections MSS W Ind t 1

West Yorkshire Record Office, Leeds

Harewood Archives
Harewood West Indies papers
Letterbook of Lascelles and Maxwell, 1743–5 (CD Rom format of original in the archives of Wilkinson and Gavillier)

Theses and reports

Bowett, Adam, *The English Mahogany Trade, 1700–1793: A Commercial History*, PhD thesis, Department of Furniture, Faculty of Design, Buckinghamshire College, Brunel University, November 1996, available at https://core.ac.uk/download/pdf/288218482.pdf [accessed November 2020].
Gregory, Ian and Sally Bushell, 'Analysing 18-Century Tourism in the English Lake District', *Spatial Humanities: Texts, GIS and Places*, Research Project 2012–16, University of Lancaster, available at https://www.lancaster.ac.uk/fass/projects/spatialhum.wordpress [accessed August 2021].
Lea, Richard, 'Danson: the "Blue Silk Damask", is this an accurate description of the saloon's original wall covering?', *English Heritage Historical Analysis and Research Team, Reports and Papers*, 2002.

McCreery, Alexander, *Turnpike Roads and the Spatial Culture of London, 1756–1830*, PhD thesis, University College London, 2004.

Miele, Chris and Richard Lea, 'The House and Park at Danson, London Borough of Bexley: The anatomy of a Georgian Suburban Estate', *English Heritage Historical Analysis and Research Team, Reports and Papers*, 2000.

Trafford-Roberts, Roland, *An Assessment of the Historic and Picturesque Viewpoints in the Wye Valley*, report commissioned for the Wye Valley Area of Outstanding Natural Beauty, February 2001.

Published primary sources

Anon., *A Short Journey in the West Indies, in which are interspersed Curious Anecdotes and Characters*, London: J. Murray, 1790.

Anon., *Britannia: A Poem*, London: *s.n.*, 1767.

Anon., *Jamaica: A Poem, in Three Parts. Written in that island, in the year MDCCLXXVI*, London: William Nichol, 1777.

Anon., *A Description of Fonthill Abbey, Wiltshire*, London: *s.n.*, 1812.

Anon., *A New Guide to Fonthill Abbey, Wiltshire*, London: *s.n.*, 1822.

Anon., *City Biography: Memoirs of the Aldermen of London*, London: *s.n.*, 1800.

Anstey, Christopher, *The new Bath guide: or, memoirs of the B-r-d family. In a series of poetical epistles*, Dublin: *s.n.*, 1766, (reprint in 1978 of 1820 edition).

Aspinall, Algernon E., *West Indian Tales of Old*, London: Duckworth & Co, 1912.

Austen, Jane, *Northanger Abbey*, London: *s.n.*, 1906 (originally published in 1817).

Baker, John, *The Diary of John Baker, 1751–1778*, (ed. by Philip Yorke), London: Hutchinson, 1931.

Banks, Joseph, 'Journal of an Excursion to Eastbury and Bristol etc May, June 1767', 25 May 1767, *Proceedings of the Bristol Naturalists Society*, vol. IX, 1899, (New Series).

Beckford, William, *A Descriptive Account of The Island of Jamaica, With Remarks upon the Cultivation of the Sugar-Cane throughout the different Seasons of the Year, and chiefly considered in a Picturesque Point of View*, London: T. & J. Egerton, 1790.

Boswell, James, *A Journal of a Tour to the Hebrides with Samuel Johnson*, London: T. Cadell and W. Davies, 1812, (originally published in 1785).

Bradley, Richard, *The Country Housewife and Lady's Director, in the Management of a House and the Delights and Profits of a Farm*, London: Woodman and Lyon, 1732.

Burke, Edmund, *A Philosophical Enquiry into the Origin of our Ideas of the Sublime and the Beautiful*, London: R. & J. Dodesly, 1764, (fourth edition).

Burke, Edmund and William Burke, *An Account of the European Settlements in America*, London: R. & J. Dodesly, 1757.

Byng, John, *The Torrington Diaries, containing the tours through England and Wales of the Hon. John Byng between the years 1781 and 1794*, (ed. by C. Bruyn Andrews), London: Eyre & Spottiswoode, 1936.

Caines, Clement, *Letters on the Cultivation of The Otaheite Cane*, London: Messrs. Robinson, 1801.

Cargill, Morris (ed.), *Ian Fleming Introduces Jamaica*, London: André Deutsch, 1965.

Carroll, Lewis, *Alice's Adventures in Wonderland*, London: Bell & Hyman, 1985, (originally published in 1865).

Chambers, William, *A Dissertation on Oriental Gardening*, London: W. Griffin, 1772.

Cooper, Anthony Ashley, *The Moralists: A Philosophical Rhapsody*, London: John Wyat, 1709.

Coxe, William, *An Historical Tour in Monmouthshire illustrated with views by Sir R.C. Hoare, Bart*, London: T. Cadell & W. Davies, 1801.

Cumberland, Richard, *The West Indian: A Comedy*, Dublin: P. & W. Wilson, 1771.

Dasent, George Webbe, *Annals of an Eventful Life*, London: Hurst and Blackett, 1870, (fifth edition).

Dasent, John Roche, *A West Indian Planter's Family: Its Rise and Fall*, Edinburgh: David Douglas, 1914.

Davies, Edward, 'Blaise Castle: A prospective poem', Bristol: William Pine, 1783.

Defoe, Daniel, *A Tour thro' the Whole Island of Great Britain*, London: S. Birt and T. Osborne, 1748, vol. III, (fourth edition).

———, *A Tour thro' the Whole Island of Great Britain*, London: J. Rivington, 1769, vol. II, (seventh edition).

———, *The Compleat Gentleman: Edited for the First Time from the Author's Autograph Manuscript in the British Museum, with Introduction, Notes, and Index*, (ed. by Karl D. Bülbring), London: David Nutt, 1890.

Edwards, Bryan, *The History, Civil And Commercial, Of The British Colonies In The West Indies, 1793–4*, London: John Stockdale, 1807, (fourth edition).

Egan, Pierce, *Walks through Bath, describing every thing worthy of interest, including Walcot and Widcombe, and the surrounding vicinity, also an excursion to Clifton and Bristol hot-wells*, Bath: Meyler and Son, 1819.

Equiano, Olaudah, *The Interesting Narrative and Other Writings*, (ed. by Vincent Carretta), London: Penguin, 1995, (originally published 1789).

Foote, Samuel, *The Patron: A Comedy in Three Acts*, Dublin: P. Wilson, 1764.

Fosbrooke, T. D., *The Wye Tour: Or, Gilpin On The Wye, With Historical And Archeological Additions, Especially Illustrations Of Pope's Man of Ross*, Ross: W. Farrer, 1818.

Gibbon, Edward, *The Decline and Fall of the Roman Empire, London: Penguin, 1985*, (originally published in 1776).

Gilpin, William, *Observations on the River Wye and several parts of South Wales, &c: Relative Chiefly to Picturesque Beauty: Made in the Summer of the Year 1770*, London: T. Cadell and W. Davies, 1800, (fifth edition, originally published in 1782).

———, *Observations, Relative Chiefly to Picturesque Beauty, Made in the Year 1772, On several Parts of England; Particularly the Mountains, and Lakes of Cumberland, and Westmoreland*, London: R. Blamire, 1792, (third edition, originally published in 1786).

———, *Observations, Relative Chiefly to Picturesque Beauty, Made in the Year 1776, on Several Parts of Great Britain; Particularly the High-lands of Scotland*, London: R. Blamire, 1792, (second edition, originally published in 1789).

Goldsmith, Oliver, *The Deserted Village*, (ed. by Desmond Egan), The Curragh, Ireland: Goldsmith Press, 1978, (facsimile edition, originally published in 1770).

Heath, Charles, *Descriptive Accounts of Persfield and Chepstow, including Caerwent, and the Passages; also, the Road to Bristol and Gloucester; Interspersed with Local and Interesting Particulars*, Monmouth: *s.n.*, 1793.

Heath, George, *The New History, Survey and Description of the City and Suburbs of Bristol, or complete Guide*, Bristol: W. Mathews, 1794.

———, *The Bristol Guide; Being A Complete and Ancient and Modern History of this City of Bristol: Including a Description of the Interesting Curiosities of its Vicinity*, Bristol: J. Mathews, 1815, (third edition, revised and considerably enlarged by Bristoliensis.

Hotten, John (ed.), *The Original Lists of Persons of Quality: Emigrants; Religious Exiles; Political Rebels; Serving Men Sold for a Term of Years; Apprentices; Children Stolen; Maidens Pressed; and Others Who Went From Great Britain to the American Plantations, 1600–1700*, New York: Empire State Book Co., 1931.

Hull, Thomas, *Select Letters between the late Duchess of Somerset*, *Lady Luxborough and others*, London: *s.n.*, 1778.

Ireland, Samuel, *Picturesque Views on the River Wye, From Its source at Plinlimmon Hill, to its Junction with the Severn below Chepstow*, London, R. Faulder, 1797.

Jewell, John, *The Tourist's Companion and Guide to the Antiquities of Harewood*, Leeds: B. Dewhirst, 1819.

Johnson, Samuel, *A Journey to the Western Islands of Scotland*, London: T. Cadell and W. Davies, 1816, (new edition, originally published in 1775).

Langley, Batty, *A sure method of improving estates*, *By plantations of oak, elm, ash, beech, and other timber-trees, coppice-woods. &c.*, London: Francis Clay, 1728, (re-published as *The Landed Gentleman's useful companion* in 1741).

Long, Edward, *A History of Jamaica: Or, General Survey of the Antient and Modern State of the Island*, London: T. Lowdes, 1774.

Loudon, John C., *The Differing Modes of Cultivating the Pine-Apple, From Its First Introduction to Europe to the Late Improvements of T. A. Knight Esq.*, London: Longman, Hurst, Rees, Orme, and Brown, 1822.

Lynch, Theodora, *The Wonders of the West Indies*, London: Seeley, Jackson, and Halliday, 1861.

McKinnen, Daniel, *A Tour through the British West Indies, In the Years 1802 and 1803*, London: J. White, 1804.

Manby, George, *An Historic and Picturesque Guide from Clifton through the Counties of Monmouth, Glamorgan and Brecknock, etc.*, Bristol: *s.n.*, 1802.

Newbery, John, *The Twelfth Day Gift*, London: *s.n.*, 1774, (third edition).

Nugent, Maria, *Lady Nugent's Journal of Her Residence in Jamaica from 1801 to 1805*, (ed. by Philip Wright), Mona, Jamaica: University of the West Indies Press, 2002.

Nugent, Thomas, *The Grand Tour, Containing an Exact Description of The Cities, Towns and Remarkable Places of Europe*, London: S. Birt, 1749.

Oliver, Vere, *The History of the Island of Antigua, One of the Leeward Caribbees in the West Indies, From the First Settlement in 1635 to the Present Time*, London: Mitchell and Hughers, 1896, vol. II.

————(ed.), *Caribbeana: Being Miscellaneous Papers Relating to the History, Genealogy, Topography and Antiquities of the British West Indies*, London: *s.n.*, 1900–19, (six volumes).

Opie, Amelia Alderson, *The Black Man's Lament; Or, How To Make Sugar*, London: Harvey and Darton, 1826.

Pennant, Thomas, *A Tour in Scotland*, London: Benjamin White, 1772.

————, *A Tour in Wales*, London: Benjamin White, 1784.

Penrose, John, *Letters from Bath, 1766–1767*, (ed. by Bridgette Mitchell and Hubert Penrose), Bath: A. Sutton, 1983.

Pope, Alexander, *Of the Use of Riches: Epistle to the Right Honorable Allen Lord Bathurst*, London: George Faulkner, 1733.

Postlethwayt, Malachy, *The African Trade, the Great Pillar and Support of the British Plantation trade in America*, London: *s.n.*, 1745.

————, *The National and Private Advantages of the African Trade*, London: John and Paul Knapton, 1746.

————, *The Merchant's Public Counting House: Or, New Mercantile Institution*, London: John and Paul Knapton, 1750.

————, *Britain's commercial interest explained and improved*, London: D. Browne, 1757.

Schaw, Janet, *Journal of a Lady of Quality: Being the Narrative of a Journey from Scotland to the West Indies, North Carolina and Portugal in the years 1774–1776*, (ed. by Evangeline Walker Andrews), New Haven, CT and London: Yale University Press, 1921.

Smith, Adam, *An Inquiry into the Nature and Causes of The Wealth of Nations*, London: Strahan and Cadell, 1776, vol. II, (first edition).

Smollett, Tobias, *The Expedition of Humphrey Clinker*, (ed. by Thomas R. Preston), Athens, GA: University of Georgia Press, 1900, (originally published in 1771).

Stuart, John, *A Tour in the United States of America*, London: G. Robinson, 1784.

Thicknesse, Phillip, *The Valetudinarians Bath Guide. Or, The Means of Obtaining Long Life and Health*, London: Dodsley and Brown, 1780.

————, *Memoirs and Anecdotes of Phillip Thicknesse*, London: *s.n.*, 1788, vol. II.

Ward, J. R., *British West Indian Slavery, 1750–1834: The Process of Amelioration*, Oxford: Clarendon Press, 1988.

Ware, Isaac, *A Complete Body of Architecture*, London: T. Osborne and J. Shipton, 1756.

Watts, William, *The Seats of the Nobility and Gentry In a collection of the most Interesting and Picturesque Views*, London: *s.n.*, 1779.

West, Thomas, *Guide to the Lakes in Cumberland, Westmorland, and Lancashire*, London: W. Pennington, 1812, (tenth edition).

Whateley, Thomas, *Observations on Modern Gardening*, Dublin: James Williams, 1770.

Williams, David, *The History of Monmouthshire ... illustrated and ornamented by views of its principal landscapes, ruins and residences*, London: H. Baldwin, 1796.

Wood, John, *An Essay towards a Description of Bath ... the second edition corrected and enlarged*, London: C. Hitch, 1749.

Wordsworth, William, *Lines Composed a Few Miles above Tintern Abbey, On Revisiting the Banks of the Wye during a Tour. July 13, 1798*, available at https://www.poetryfoundation.org/poems/45527/lines-composed-a-few-miles-above-tintern-abbey-on-revisiting-the-banks-of-the-wye-during-a-tour-july-13–1798 [accessed January 2022].

———, 'The Banished Negroes', *The Morning Post*, 11 February 1803.

Wray, Leonard, *The Practical Sugar Planter: A complete account of the cultivation and manufacture of the sugar cane according to the latest and most improved process*, London: Smith, Elder & Co, 1848.

Young, Arthur, *A Six Weeks Tour though the Southern Counties of England and Wales*, London: W. Nicholl, 1769, (second edition).

———, *A Six Months Tour through the North of England*, London: W. Strahan, 1770.

Select Secondary Sources

Ackerman, James, *Palladio*, London: Penguin, 1977, (second edition).

———, *The Villa: Form and Ideology of Country Houses*, London: Thames & Hudson, 1990.

Alexander, Boyd, *England's Wealthiest Son: A Study of William Beckford*, London: Centaur, 1962.

Anderson, Jennifer, *Mahogany: The Costs of Luxury in Early America*, Cambridge, MA: Harvard University Press, 2012.

Andrews, Malcolm, *The Search for the Picturesque: Landscape Aesthetics and Tourism in Britain, 1760–1880*, Aldershot: Scholar, 1989.

Anstey, R. and P. Hair (eds), *Liverpool, the African Slave Trade, and*

Abolition, Liverpool: Historical Society of Lancashire and Cheshire, 1989.

Armitage, David and Michael J. Braddick (eds), *The British Atlantic World, 1500–1800*, Basingstoke: Palgrave Macmillan, 2002.

Arnold, Dana (ed.), *The Georgian Country House: Architecture, Landscape and Society*, Stroud: Sutton, 2003.

Ayres, Philip, *Classical Culture and the Idea of Rome in Eighteenth-Century England*, Cambridge: Cambridge University Press, 1997.

Baetjer, Katherine (ed.), *Glorious Nature: British Landscape Painting, 1750–1850*, London: Zwemmer, 1993.

Bailey, Anne, *African Voices of the Atlantic Slave Trade: Beyond the Silence and the Shame*, Boston, MA: Beacon Press, 2005.

Barrell, John, T*he Idea of the Landscape and the Sense of Place, 1730–1840*, Cambridge: Cambridge University Press, 1972.

———, *The Dark Side of the Landscape: The Rural Poor in English Painting, 1730–1840*, Cambridge: Cambridge University Press, 1980.

Barringer, Tim, Gillian Forrester and Barbaro Martinez-Ruiz (eds), *Art and Emancipation in Jamaica: Isaac Belisario and His Worlds*, New Haven, CT and London: Yale University Press, 2007.

Beard, Geoffrey, *Stucco and Decorative Plasterwork in Europe*, London: Thames and Hudson, 1983.

Beauman, Fran, *The Pineapple: King of Fruits*, London: Chatto & Windus, 2005.

Beckett, J. V., *Coal and Tobacco: The Lowthers and the Economic Development of West Cumberland, 1660–1760*, Cambridge: Cambridge University Press, 1981.

———, 'Inheritance and Fortune in the eighteenth century: the rise of Sir James Lowther, Earl of Lonsdale', *Transactions of the Cumberland and Westmoreland Antiquarian Society*, vol. 87, series 2, 1987, pp. 171–8.

Bentmann, Reinhard and Michael Muller, *The Villa as Hegemonic Architecture*, New Haven, CT and London: Yale University Press, 1992, (English translation of *Die Villa als Herrschaftsarchitekur*).

Binney, Marcus, *Sir Robert Taylor: From Rococo to Neoclassicism*, London: Allen & Unwin, 1984.

Black, Jeremy, *The British Abroad: The Grand Tour in the Eighteenth Century*, Stroud: Sutton, 1992.

Blackburn, Robin, *The Overthrow of Colonial Slavery*, London and New York: Verso, 1988.

————, *The Making of New World Slavery: From the Baroque to the Modern, 1492–1800*, London and New York: Verso, 1997.

Blunt, Alison and Gillian Rose (eds), *Writing, Women and Space: Colonial and Postcolonial Geographies*, New York and London: Guildford Press, 1994.

Bonfield, Lloyd, 'Affective Families, Open Elites and Strict Family Settlements in Early Modern England', *Economic History Review*, vol. 39, no. 3, 1986, pp. 341–54.

Brewer, John and John Porter (eds), *Consumption and the World of Goods*, New York: Routledge, 1993.

Bristow, Ian, *Architectural Colours in British Interiors, 1615–1840*, London and New Haven: Yale University Press, 1996.

Brown, John, 'Lancelot Brown and his Associates', *Garden History: Journal of the Garden History Society*, vol. 29, no. 1, summer 2001, pp. 2–11.

Buckley, David, *The Right to be Proud: Selected Jamaican Heritage Sites*, Jamaica and London: Lewis Hanson, 2007.

Buisseret, David, *Historic Architecture of the Caribbean*, London: Heinemann, 1980.

Burnard, Trevor, *Mastery, Tyranny and Desire: Thomas Thistlewood and his Slaves in the Anglo-Jamaican World*, Chapel Hill, NC: University of North Carolina Press, 2004.

Carretta, Vincent, *Equiano, the African: The Biography of a Self-Made Man*, Athens, GA: University of Georgia Press, 2005.

Carter, Paul, *The Road to Botany Bay: An Essay in Spatial History*, London and Boston, MA: Faber and Faber, 1987.

Chambers, Thomas, *Drinking the Waters: Creating an American Leisure Class at Nineteenth-Century Mineral Springs*, Washington: Smithsonian Institute Press, 2002.

Clarkson, Janet, *Soup: A Global History*, London: Reaktion, 2010.

Claypole, William and John Robottom, *Caribbean Story, Book One: Foundations*, Jamaica, Trinidad and Harlow: Longman Caribbean, 1990.

Clayton, Timothy, *The English Print, 1688–1802*, New Haven, CT and London: Yale University Press, 1997.

Colley, Linda, *Britons: Forging the Nation, 1707–1837*, London: Pimlico, 1994.

————, *Captives: Britain, Empire and the World, 1600–1850*, London: Jonathan Cape, 2002.

Copley, Stephen and Peter Garside (eds), *The Politics of the Picturesque:*

Literature, Landscape and Aesthetics Since 1770, Cambridge: Cambridge University Press, 1994.

Cosgrove, Dennis, *Social Formation and Symbolic Landscape*, Wisconsin: Madison, 1998.

Crain, Edward, *Historic Architecture of the Caribbean Islands*, Gainesville, FL: University Press of Florida, 1994.

Craton, Michael, *Sinews of Empire: A Short History of British Slavery*, London: Temple Smith, 1974.

——————, *Testing the Chains: Resistance to Slavery in the British West Indies*, Icatha, NY and London: Cornell University Press, 1982.

Dabydeen, David, *Hogarth's Blacks: Images of Blacks in Eighteenth Century English Art*, Manchester: Manchester University Press, 1987.

——————, John Gilmore and Cecily Jones (eds), *The Oxford Companion to Black British History*, Oxford: Oxford University Press, 2007.

Daniels, Stephen, 'Goodly Prospects: English Estate Portraiture, 1630–1730', in Nicholas Alfey and Stephen Daniels (eds.), *Mapping the Landscape: Essays on Art and Cartography*, Nottingham: University Art Gallery, 1990.

——————, *Fields of Vision: Landscape Imagery and National Identity in England and the United States*, Cambridge: Polity, 1993.

—————— and Charles Watkins (eds), *The Picturesque Landscape: Visions of Georgian Herefordshire*, Nottingham: Department of Geography University of Nottingham in association with Hereford City Art Gallery, 1994.

Davidson, Alan, *Oxford Companion to Food*, Oxford and New York: Oxford University Press, 2006, (second edition).

Davis, Ralph M., *The Rise of the English Shipping Industry in the Seventeenth and Eighteenth Centuries*, London and New York: Macmillan, 1962.

Day, Ivan P., *Royal Sugar Sculpture: 600 years of Splendour*, Barnard Castle: The Bowes Museum, 2002.

De Thierry, C., 'Colonials at Westminster', *United Empire Magazine*, vol. III, January 1912.

Devine, Tom M., 'Glasgow Colonial Merchants and Land, 1770–1815', in J. T. Ward and R. G. Wilson (eds.), *Land and Industry: The Landed Estate and the Industrial Revolution*, Newton Abbot: David & Charles, 1971.

——————, *Scotland's Empire, 1600–1815*, London: Allen Lane, 2003.

——————(ed.), *Recovering Scotland's Slavery Past: The Caribbean Connection*, Edinburgh: Edinburgh University Press, 2015.

Dingwall, Christopher, 'Gardens in the wild', *Garden History: Journal of the Garden History Society*, vol. 22, no. 2, 1994, pp. 133–56.

Draper, Nicholas, *The Price of Emancipation: Slave-Ownership, Compensation and British Society at the End of Slavery*, Cambridge: Cambridge University Press, 2014.

Drayton, Richard, *Nature's Government: Science, Imperial Britain and the 'Improvement' of the World*, New Haven, CT and London: Yale University Press, 2000.

Dresser, Madge, *Slavery Obscured: The Social History of the Slave Trade in an English Provincial Port*, London: Continuum, 2001.

————, and Andrew Hann (eds), *Slavery and the British Country House*, Swindon: English Heritage, 2013.

————, and Mary Wills, 'The Transatlantic Slave Economy and England's Built Environment: A Research Audit', *Historic England*, no. 247, 2020, available at https://historicengland.org.uk/research/results/reports/247–2020

Dunn, Richard, *Sugar and Slaves: The rise of the Planter Class in the English West Indies, 1624–1713*, Chapel Hill, NC and London: University of North Carolina Press, 1972.

Eickelmann, Christine and David Small, *Pero: The Life of a Slave in Eighteenth-Century Bristol*, Bristol: Redcliffe Press, 2004.

Elder, Melinda, *The Slave Trade and the Economic Development of 18th-century Lancaster*, Halifax: Ryburn, 1992.

Evans, Chris, *Slave Wales: The Welsh and Atlantic Slavery, 1660–1850*, University of Wales Press, 2010.

Evans, J. A. H., 'Nathaniel Wells of Piercefield and St Kitts: From Slave to Sheriff', *The Monmouthshire Antiquary*, 2002, pp. 92–106.

Everett, Nigel, *The Tory View of Landscape*, New Haven, CT and London: Yale University Press, 1994.

Fabian, Steven, 'East Africa's Gorée: Slave Trade and Slave Tourism in Bagamoyo, Tanzania', *Canadian Journal of African Studies*, vol. 47, no. 1, 2013, pp. 95–114.

Farrell, Stephen, Melanie Unwin and James Walvin (eds), *The British Slave Trade: Abolition, Parliament and People*, Edinburgh: Edinburgh University Press, 2007.

Ferguson, Moira, 'Mansfield Park: Slavery, Colonialism, and Gender', *Oxford Literary Review*, vol. 13, no. 1/2, 1991, pp. 118–39.

Fishman, Robert, *Bourgeois Utopia: The Rise and Fall of Suburbia*, New York: Basic Books Inc., 1997.

Fladeland, Betty, '"Our Cause being One and the Same": Abolitionists and Chartism', in James Walvin (ed.), *Slavery and British Society, 1776–1846*, London: Palgrave Macmillan, 1982.

Forster, Robert, 'Three Slave Holders in the Antilles: Saint-Domingue, Martinique and Jamaica', *Journal of Caribbean History*, vol. 36, no. 1, 2002.

Forsyth, Michael, *Bath: Pevsner Architectural Guides*, New Haven, CT and London: Yale University Press, 2003.

Freeman, Michael, Early Tourists in Wales: 18th and 19th century tourists' comments about Wales, available at https://sublimewales.wordpress.com

Gassan, Richard, 'The First American Tourist Guidebooks: Authorship and the Print Culture of the 1820s', *Book History*, vol. 8, 2005, pp. 51–74.

Gauci, Perry, *William Beckford: First Prime Minister of the London Empire*, New Haven, CT and London: Yale University Press, 2013.

Geggus, David (ed.), *The Impact of the Haitian Revolution in the Atlantic World*, Columbia; University of South Carolina Press, 2002.

Gerzina, Gretchen, *Black England: Life before Emancipation*, London: Allison and Busby, 1995.

Gibbons, Luke, *Edmund Burke and Ireland: Aesthetics, Politics and the Colonial Sublime*, Cambridge: Cambridge University Press, 2003.

Gikandi, Simon, *Slavery and the Culture of Taste*, Princeton, NJ and Oxford, UK: Princeton University Press, 2011.

Gilmore, John, *The Poetics of Empire: A Study of James Grainger's The Sugar Cane*, London: Athlone Press, 2000.

Girouard, Mark, *Life in the English Country House: A Social and Architectural History*, Harmondsworth: Penguin, 1980.

Gosner, Pamela, *Caribbean Georgian: The Great and Small Houses of the West Indies*, Washington: Three Continents, 1982.

Goveia, Elsa, *Slave Society in the British Leeward Islands at the End of the Eighteenth Century*, New Haven, CT and London: Yale University Press, 1965.

Grove, Richard, *Green Imperialism: Colonial Expansion, Tropical Island Edens and the Origins of Environmentalism, 1600–1860*, Cambridge: Cambridge University Press, 1995.

Habakkuk, John, *Marriage, Debt and the Estates System: English Landownership, 1650–1950*, Oxford: Clarendon, 1994.

Hackforth-Jones, Jocelyn, '"A Landed Gentleman's Paradise"? Literature and the Representation of Landscape in Wales during the Eighteenth Century', *Georgian Group Journal*, vol. V, 1985, pp. 9–24.

Hague, Stephen, *The Gentleman's House in the British Atlantic World*, *1680–1780*, London: Palgrave Macmillan, 2015.

Hall, Catherine, *Civilising Subjects: Metropole and Colony in the English Imagination, 1830—1867*, Cambridge: Polity, 2002.

————, Nicholas Draper and Keith McCelland (eds), *Legacies of British Slave-ownership: Colonial Slavery and the Formation of Victorian Britain*, Cambridge: Cambridge University Press, 2014.

Hall, Douglas, *In Miserable Slavery: Thomas Thistlewood in Jamaica*, *1750–86*, Mona, Jamaica: University of the West Indies Press, 1989.

Hamilton, Douglas, *Scotland, the Caribbean and the Atlantic World, 1750–1820*, Manchester: Manchester University Press, 2005.

Hancock, David, *Citizens of the World: London Merchants and the Integration of the British Atlantic Community*, Cambridge: Cambridge University Press, 1995.

————, 'Oswald, Richard', *Oxford Dictionary of National Biography*, Oxford and New York: Oxford University Press, (online edition).

Harris, Eileen, *The Genius of Robert Adam: His Interiors*, New Haven, CT and London: Yale University Press, 2001.

Harris, John, 'English Country House Guides, 1740–1840', in John Summerson (ed.), *Concerning Architecture. Essays on architectural writers and writing, presented to Nicholas Pevsner*, London: Allen Lane, 1968, pp. 58–74.

Harvie, Christopher, *A Floating Commonwealth: Politics, Culture and Technology on Britain's Atlantic Coast, 1860–1930*, Oxford and New York: Oxford University Press, 2008.

Hay, Douglas and Nicholas Rogers, *Eighteenth-Century English Society: Shuttles and Swords*, Oxford and New York: Oxford University Press, 1997.

Henisch, Bridget, *Cake and Characters: An English Christmas Tradition*, London: Prospect, 1984.

Herman, Bernard and Daniel Maudlin (eds), *Architecture of the British Atlantic World*, Chapel Hill, NC and London: University of North Carolina Press, 2016

Higman, Barry, *Montpelier Jamaica: A Plantation Community in Slavery and Freedom, 1739–1912*, Mona, Jamaica: University of the West Indies Press, 1998.

————, *Writing West Indian Histories*, London: Macmillan, 1999.

————, *Jamaica Surveyed: Plantation Maps and Plans of the Eighteenth and Nineteenth Centuries*, Mona, Jamaica: University of the West Indies Press, 2001.

Hindle, Paul, *Roads and Tracks of the Lake District*, Milnthorpe: Cicerone Press, 1998.

————, *Roads and Tracks for Historians*, Bognor Regis: Phillimore, 2001.

Hussey, Christopher, *The Picturesque: Studies in a Point of View*, London: Frank Cass, 1967, (new impression with preface by the author, originally published in 1927).

Jacques, David, *Georgian Gardens: The Reign of Nature*, London: Batsford, 1983.

James, C. L. R., *The Black Jacobins: Toussaint L'Ouverture and the San Domingo Revolution*, London: Allison and Busby, 1989 (first published in New York in 1938).

Knight, Derrick, *Gentlemen of Fortune: The Men who Made their Fortunes in Britain's Slave Colonies*, London: Frederick Muller, 1978.

Kriz, Kay Dian, *The Ideas of the English Landscape Painter; Genius as Alibi in the Early Nineteenth Century*, New Haven, CT and London: Yale University Press, 1997.

————, *Slavery, Sugar and the Culture of Refinement: Picturing the British West Indies, 1700–1840*, New Haven, CT and London: Yale University Press, 2008.

Langford, Paul, *A Polite and Commercial People: England, 1727–83*, Oxford and New York: Oxford University Press, 1992.

Lefrancois, Thierry, *L'esclavage dans les collections du Musée du Nouveau Monde*, La Rochelle: Editions du Musée d'art et d'histoire, 1998.

Levinson, Marjorie, *Wordsworth's great period poems: Four essays*, Cambridge: Cambridge University Press, 1996.

Lewis, Lesley, 'Elizabeth, Countess of Home, and her house in Portman Square', *Burlington Magazine*, CIX August 1967, pp. 443–53.

Lindsay, Jean, 'The Pennants and Jamaica, 1665–1808: The Growth and Organisation of the Pennant Estates', *Transactions of the Caernarvonshire Historical Society*, no. 43, 1982.

Livesay, Daniel, *Children of Uncertain Fortune: Mixed Race Jamaicans in Britain and the Atlantic Family, 1733–1833*, Chapel Hill, NC: University of North Carolina Press, 2018.

Lubbock, Jules, *The Tyranny of Taste: The Politics of Architecture and Design in Britain, 1550–1960*, New Haven, CT and London: Yale University Press, 1995.

Karras, Alan, *Sojourners in the Sun: Scottish Migrants in Jamaica and the Chesapeake, 1740–1800*, Icatha, NY and London: Cornell University Press, 1993.

Knapp, Lewis Mansfield, *Tobias Smollett: Doctor of Men and Manners*, Princeton, NJ: Princeton University Press, 1949.

Mackay, David, *In the Wake of Cook: Exploration, Science and Empire, 1780–1801*, London: Croom Helm, 1985.

MacKinnon, Iain and Andrew Mackillop, 'Plantation slavery and land-ownership in the west Highlands and Islands: legacies and lessons', *Community Land Scotland*, November 2020, available at https://www.communitylandscotland.org.uk/wp-content/uploads/2020/11/ANNEX-report-data-references.pdf

Martin, Luciana, 'The Art of Tropical Travel, 1768–1830', in Miles Ogborn and Charles Withers (eds), *Georgian Geographies: Essays on Space, Place and Landscape in the Eighteenth Century*, Manchester: Manchester University Press, 2004.

Mauchline, Mary, *Harewood House*, London: David & Charles, 1974.

Menard, Russell, *Sweet Negotiations: Sugar, Slavery and Plantation Agriculture in Early Barbados*, Charlottesville, VA: University of Virginia Press, 2006.

Mentz, Søren, *The English Gentleman Merchant at Work: Madras and the City of London, 1660–1740*, Copenhagen: Museum Tusculanum, 2006.

Miller, David and Peter Reill (eds), *Visions of Empire: Voyages, Botany and representations of Nature*, Cambridge: Cambridge University Press, 1996.

Mingay, Gordon, *English Landed Society in the Eighteenth Century*, London: Routledge & Kegan Paul, 1963.

Monteith, Kathleen E. A. and Glen Richards (eds), *Jamaica in Slavery and Freedom: History, Heritage and Culture*, Mona, Jamaica: University of the West Indies Press, 2002,

Moore-Colyer, Richard, *Roads and Trackways of Wales*, Ashbourne: Landmark Publishing, 2001.

Morgan, Kenneth, *Slavery, Atlantic Trade and the British Economy, 1660–1800*, Cambridge: Cambridge University Press, 2000.

Moritz, Albert, *America: The Picturesque in Nineteenth Century Engraving*, New York: New Trend, 1983.

Morris, David, *Thomas Hearne and his Landscape*, London: Reaktion, 1989.

Mowl, Tim, *William Beckford: Composing for Mozart*, London: John Murray, 1998.

Mulvey, Christopher, *Transatlantic Manners: Social patterns in nineteenth-century Anglo-American travel literature*, Cambridge: Cambridge University Press, 1990.

Murdoch, D. H., 'Land Policy in the Eighteenth-Century British Empire: The Sale of Crown lands in the Ceded Islands, 1763–1783', *Historical Journal*, vol. 27, no. 3, September 1984, pp. 549–74.

Neale, R. S., *Bath: A Social History, 1680–1850 or A Valley of Pleasure, yet a Sink of Iniquity*, London: Routledge, 1981.

Nelson, Louis, *Architecture and Empire in Jamaica*, New Haven, CT and London: Yale University Press, 2016.

Newman, John, *The Buildings of Wales: Gwent/Monmouthshire*, London: Penguin, 2000.

Ogborn, Miles, *Spaces of Modernity: London's Geographies, 1680–1780*, New York and London: Guildford Press, 1998.

————, *Global Lives: Britain and the World, 1550–1800*, Cambridge: Cambridge University Press, Cambridge, 2008.

O'Shaughnessy, Andrew Jackson, *An Empire Divided: The American Revolution and the British Caribbean*, Philadelphia: University of Pennsylvania Press, 2000.

Ostergard, Derek (ed.), *William Beckford, 1760–1844: An Eye for the Magnificent*, New Haven, CT and London: Yale University Press, 2001.

Pares, Richard, *A West India Fortune*, London: Longmans, Green & Co, 1950.

————, 'A London West India Merchant's House', in R. A. and E. Humphreys (eds), *The Historian's Business and Other Essays*, Oxford: Clarendon Press, 1961.

Pearsall, Sarah, *Atlantic Families: Lives and Letters in the Later Eighteenth Century*, Oxford and New York: Oxford University Press, 2008.

Pointon, Marcia, *Hanging the Head: Portraiture and Social Formation in Eighteenth-Century England*, New Haven, CT and London: Yale University Press, 1993.

Pugh, Simon (ed.) *Reading Landscape, Country, City, Capital*, Manchester: Manchester University Press, 1990.

Quilley, Geoff and Kay Dian Kriz (eds), *An Economy of Colour: Visual Culture and the Atlantic World*, Manchester: Manchester University Press, 2003.

Rainey, Sue, *Creating Picturesque America: Monument to the Natural and Cultural Landscape*, Nashville, TN: Vanderbilt University Press, 1994.

Ragatz, Lowell J., *The Fall of the Planter Class in the British Caribbean, 1763–1833*, New York and London: Century Co., 1929.

Raven, James, *Judging New Wealth: Popular Publishing and Responses to Commerce in England, 1750–1800*, Oxford and New York: Oxford University Press, 1992.

Rhys, Jean, *Wide Sargasso Sea*, London: Penguin, 2000, (originally published in1966).

Rice, Alan, *Radical Narratives of the Black Atlantic*, London and New York: Continuum, 2003.

Richards, Eric, *The Highland Clearances*, Edinburgh: Birlinn, 2013.

Rogers, Nicholas, 'Money, Land and Lineage: The Big Bourgeoisie of Hanoverian London', *Social History*,vol. 4, no. 3, October 1979, pp. 437–93.

Rowan, Alistair, *Bob the Roman: Heroic Antiquity & the Architecture of Robert Adam*, London: Soane Gallery, 2003.

Said, Edward, *Culture and Imperialism*, London: Chatto and Windus, 1993.

Sandiford, Keith, *The Cultural Politics of Sugar: Caribbean Slavery and Narratives of Colonialism*, Cambridge: Cambridge University Press, 2000.

Satchell, Veront, *Sugar, Slavery and Technological Change: Jamaica, 1760–1830*, Saarbrucken: VDM Verlag, 2010.

Schama, Simon, *Landscape and Memory*, London: Harper Collins, 1995.

————, *Rough Crossings: Britain, the slaves and the American Revolution*, London: BBC Books, 2005.

Seymour, Susanne, Stephen Daniels and Charles Watkins, 'Picturesque Views of the British West Indies', *The Picturesque: Journal of the Picturesque Society*, no. 10, Spring 1995, pp. 23–8.

————, 'Estate and empire: Sir George Cornewall's management of Moccas, Herefordshire and La Taste, Grenada, 1771–1819', *Journal of Historical Geography*, vol. 24, issue 3, 1998, pp. 313–51.

Sheridan, Richard, *Sugar and Slavery: An Economic History of the British West Indies from 1623–1775*, Barbados: Canoe Press, 1994.

————, *Doctors and Slaves: A Medical and Demographic History of Slavery in the British West Indies, 1680–1834*, Cambridge: Cambridge University Press, 2009.

Shuffleton, Frank, 'Binding Ties: Thomas Jefferson, Francis Hopkinson and the Representation of the Notes on the State of Virginia', in Mark Kamrath and Sharon Harris (eds), *Periodical Literature in Eighteenth-Century America*, Knoxville, TN: University of Tennessee Press, pp. 255–72.

Sloan, Kim, *Alexander and John Robert Cozens: The Poetry of Landscape*, New Haven, CT and London: Yale University Press, 1986.

Sloman, Susan, *Gainsborough in Bath*, New Haven, CT and London: Yale University Press, 2002.

Smith, Bernard, *European Vision and the South Pacific*, New Haven, CT and London: Yale University Press, 1985.

Smith, Simon D., *Slavery, Family and Gentry Capitalism in the British Atlantic: The World of the Lascelles, 1648–1834*, Cambridge: Cambridge University Press, 2006.

————, (ed.), *The Lascelles and Maxwell Letter Book (1739–1769)*, Wakefield: Microform Academic Publishers, 2002.

Solkin, David, *Richard Wilson: The Landscape of Reaction*, London: Tate Gallery, 1982.

Spending, Stephen, 'One Among the Many: Popular Aesthetics, Polite Culture and the Country House Landscape', in Dana Arnold (ed.), *The Georgian Country House: Architecture, Landscape and Society*, Stroud: Sutton, 1998, pp. 61–78.

Staff, Frank, *The Transatlantic Mail*, Lawrence Mass: Quarterman, 1980.

Stafford, Barbara, *Voyage into Substance: Art, Science, Nature and the Illustrated Travel Account, 1760–1840*, Cambridge, MA: MIT Press, 1984.

Starkey, Pat (ed.) *Riches into Art: Liverpool Collectors, 1770–1880*, Liverpool: Liverpool University Press, 1993.

Stembridge, P. K., *Goldney: A House and a Family*, Bristol: P. K. Stembridge, 1991.

Stone, Lawrence and Jeanne Fawtier Stone, *An Open Elite? England, 1540–1880*, Oxford: Clarendon Press, 1984

Stroud, Dorothy, *Capability Brown*, London: Faber and Faber, 1950.

Summerson, John, *The Classical Language of Architecture*, London: Thames and Hudson, 1980.

————, *Georgian London*, London: Pimlico, 1991 (originally published in 1945).

Thomas, Sarah, *Witnessing Slavery: Art and Travel in the Age of Abolition*, New Haven, CT and London: Yale University Press, 2019.

Thompson, Krista, *An Eye for the Tropics: Tourism, Photography and the Framing of the Caribbean Picturesque*, Durham, NC: Duke University Press, 2006.

Thorn, Colin (ed.), *Robert Adam and His Brothers: New Light on Britain's Leading Architectural Family*, Swindon: Historic England, 2019.

Turner, Michael, *Enclosures in Britain, 1750–1830*, London: Palgrave Macmillan, 1984.

University College London, 'Legacies of British Slave-ownership' project, 2009–12, available at https://www.ucl.ac.uk/lbs/

Vickery, Amanda, *The Gentleman's Daughter: Women's Lives in Georgian England*, New Haven, CT and London: Yale University Press, 1998.

Walvin, James, *Black Ivory: A History of British Slavery*, London: Harper Collins, 1992.

————, *Fruits of Empire: Exotic Produce and British Taste*, London: Macmillan, 1997.

Waters, Ivor, *Piercefield on the Banks of the Wye*, Chepstow: Chepstow Society, 1975.

————, *The Unfortunate Valentine Morris*, Chepstow: Chepstow Society, 1964.

————, *Turnpike Roads the Chepstow and New Passage Turnpike Districts*, Chepstow: Moss Rose Press, 1985.

Watkin, David, *The English Vision: The Picturesque in Architecture, Landscape and Garden Design*, London: John Murray, 1982.

Whittle, Elisabeth, *The Historic Gardens of Wales*, London: HMSO, 1992.

Whyte, Ian, *Transforming Fell and Valley: Landscape and Parliamentary Enclosure in North West England*, Lancaster: Centre for North-West Regional Studies, 2003.

Williams, Eric, *Capitalism and Slavery*, Chapel Hill, NC and London: University of North Carolina Press, 1944.

Williams, Raymond, *The Country and the City*, London: Chatto and Windus, 1973.

Williamson, Tom, 'The Landscape Park: Economics, Art and Ideology,' *Garden History: Journal of the Garden History Society*, vol. 13, 1993, pp. 49–55.

————, *Polite Landscapes: Gardens and Society in Eighteenth-Century England*, Stroud: Sutton, 1995.

Wilson, Kathleen, 'The good, the bad and the impotent: Imperialism and the Politics of Identity in Georgian England', in Ann Bermingham and

John Brewer (eds), *The Consumption of Culture, 1600–1800: Image, Object, Text*, London: Routledge, 1995.

————, *The Sense of the People: Politics, Culture and Imperialism in England, 1715–1785*, Cambridge: Cambridge University Press, 1995.

Wittkover, Rudolph, *Palladio and English Palladianism*, London: Thames and Hudson, 1974.

Worden, Sarah (ed.), *David Livingstone: Man, Myth and Legacy*, Edinburgh: NMS Enterprises, 2012.

Worsley, Giles (ed.), *Adam in Context: Papers Given at the Georgian Group symposium 1992*, London: Georgian Group, 1993.

Zahedieh, Nuala, 'Trade, Plunder and Economic Development in Early English Jamaica', *Economic History Review*, vol. 39, no. 2, 1986, pp. 205–22.

INDEX